A Response to the Video:

Seventh-day Adventism
The Spirit Behind the Church

Bob Pickle

Answers to Questions Raised by:
Mark Martin • Sydney Cleveland
Dale Ratzlaff • *The White Lie*
. . . and Others

Discern Fact from Fiction

Decisions • Halstad, Minnesota

Published and distributed by:

Pickle Publishing Company
www.pickle-publishing.com

Library of Congress Control Number: 2002101943

ISBN 0-9627645-1-5

"You really just have to search for it yourself,
and if you, if you love the Lord, if you really do, then
you really want to know the truth."

—Kim Marshall near the end of
Seventh-day Adventism:
The Spirit Behind the Church.

To all who "really want to know the truth,"
this work is dedicated.

Introduction

It all began one pleasant Saturday afternoon in the foothills of the Colorado Rockies. This writer and his family were driving up the Big Thompson River Canyon in October 1999, inviting residents to a lecture series on Bible prophecy. Pulling up to a gentleman working outside his home, we handed an invitation to him. He handed it back saying, "Not interested."

"How do you know? You don't know what it's about, do you?"

He then enquired what church was conducting the lecture series, and after finding out, repeated his first reply.

"What church do you fellowship at?" we then asked. That question began a lovely, hour-long conversation. Turned out that he had sent his kids to an Adventist school, and had appreciated the experience.

But something was bothering him, and he was having a hard time saying what it was. Finally he opened up. His church's Bible study group that very week was going to show a video critical of the Adventist Church. This prompted the question, "May I come?"

Before we left his house he declared that it was no accident that we had come by that day. Providence was at work.

So this writer went to see *Seventh-day Adventism: The Spirit Behind the Church*, copyright 1999 by Jeremiah Films. What an incredible production it was! Fifty minutes of video tape packed with information about Mrs. White and the Adventist Church, facts about their history and teachings. It was all the more convincing since the facts were being propounded by six former Adventist pastors, and five other former Adventists. If anyone should know the real scoop, they should, shouldn't they?

Yet as this writer heard the charges and accusations being leveled by Dale Ratzlaff, Sydney Cleveland, Mark Martin, and the others, something didn't quite ring true. It cannot be denied that this writer's bias is quite different from theirs, yet some of the "facts" presented were indisputably proven false decades ago. Why then was this video still making an issue of such things in 1999?

Then commenced three months of dialoguing with some of the principal folk behind the video, which didn't really accomplish much (see Appendix). At the end of that period, this writer promised Jeremiah Films that he would not rest until every error in their video was exposed. That promise resulted in the work you now hold in your hands. It first appeared on the internet in March 2000, and now resides at pickle-publishing.com. After undergoing a bit of revision, it now appears in this printed form.

The video, *Seventh-day Adventism: The Spirit Behind the Church*, endeavors to prove that the Adventist Church is a cult, or nearly so. But it only presents one side, and unless a person has both sides to consider, an objective evaluation is impossible. Yet the average viewer cannot conduct the horrendous amount of research required to determine the accuracy of the video's claims. How then can someone decide for himself whether Adventism really is a cult? This book solves that dilemma. It puts within everyone's grasp the other side of the question.

The following factors should be considered when objectively evaluating each of the video's accusations:

1. Is the charge being made really factual?
2. If so, is it relevant to the question of whether Adventism is a cult?
3. Are the quotations and pictures used by the video to make its case accurate?
4. Is the charge biblical, or does it undermine the authority of Scripture?
5. Does the charge attack prominent Christian leaders as well as Adventists?
6. Has the charge been oversimplified? Would greater detail change the conclusion?
7. Does the logic or support used in one charge contradict that of another charge?

8. Do some statements beg the question, assume to be true what must first be proven?

This book examines, in the light of these eight questions, each claim made by each speaker on the video. Each speaker one by one is quoted, and then his or her comments are analyzed.

Rather than topically, this book is arranged in the order that the statements appear in the video. While this format reproduces to some extent the video's repetitiveness, it makes it as easy as possible to compare the two sides.

Such a format also necessitates frequent cross-referencing, that the entire case for a topic might not be made multiple times throughout the book. Thus under #1 can be seen the note, "see #10."

Another consequence of this type of format is that a large portion of this book ends up vindicating a single individual, the "spirit" or ghost the video claims is behind Adventism. Yet in writing such a response, what else can one do when so much of the video represents attacks on that single individual?

All Scriptures quoted by this writer are from the *King James Version*. Feel free to compare the wording to that of other translations, if you wish.

At the very end of the video is advertised "a documentation package substantiating the information contained in this program." Since it is supposed to prove the video's case, this response frequently refers to it, critiquing it along with the video.

If you've never seen the video before, that's no problem. Since it covers most of the same old criticisms that have been leveled at Adventism over the last 150 years or so, you'll probably find answers here to questions you've seen raised elsewhere. For as Walter Martin wrote, who thought Adventism was not a cult, practically no critic since the days of D. M. Canright has been able to come up with anything new:

> . . . careful research has confirmed the impression that nearly all subsequent similar publications are little more than repetitions of the destructive areas of Canright's writings . . . .—*Kingdom of the Cults*, p. 443; cf. p. 409.

Even so, the recycling of old criticisms has reached incredible proportions today. Books and web sites seem on the rise. And if Mrs. White was right at all, such things will increase in the days ahead.

Dear reader, you have the opportunity to sort through some of the claims being made. While this book can't cover all the criticisms out there, it can provide you with some tools for investigating further. You'll learn some of the counter-questions to ask, and some of the primary sources to read.

Then you can decide for yourself the answer to the following questions, instead of having someone else do your deciding for you: Is Adventism a Christian religion? Or is it a cult?

Table of Contents

Table of Accusations Covered
Whether Fact or Fiction, Implied or Stated

Initial Points

1. All quotes of Mrs. White in the video are from official sources.
2. Adventism is based around her teachings and philosophies.
3. She was the founder of the Adventist Church.

The Millerite Movement

4. William Miller was a powerful preacher.
5. He taught that Christ would return in 1843.
6. He taught that Christ would return on October 22, 1844.
7. That date was not the Day of Atonement in 1844.
8. Miller's meetings were marked by emotionalism and hysteria.
9. This picture depicts the radical fanaticism of his meetings.
10. When Christ did not return, Mrs. White said she was in a "hopeless condition for months."
11. She was depressed when Christ did not return.
12. She could not admit her mistake of expecting Christ to return.
13. Miller did admit his mistake.
14. Mrs. White's first vision said that the 1843 chart should not be altered.
15. She claimed God hid the mistake.
16. She claimed God made the mistake.
17. Her first vision was controversial.
18. It forced the readjustment of many Adventist dates and doctrines.
19. It adjusted the 1843 date to 1844.
20. The 1844 date was still an error.

The Role of Mrs. White and Her Writings

21. Mrs. White became the absolute authority figure.
22. Her writings grew to be seventeen times larger than the Bible.
23. Adventists view her writings as inspired as the Bible.
24. Church publications use her writings as the last word on doctrine.
25. Adventism's twenty-seven fundamental beliefs say that the Bible is a source of authority.
26. They also say Mrs. White's writings are an authoritative source of truth.
27. Some of her writings are unavailable, locked in a vault.
28. These writings are her more embarrassing ones.
29. She claimed an angel came and talked to her.

Her Predictions and Views

30. History shows that her prophecies did not come true.
31. She said Jerusalem would never be built up and grow.
32. She said she would be alive when Jesus came.
33. She said the second coming was only months away.
34. She said that some present at an 1856 conference would be alive when Jesus came.
35. She would have been stoned in Bible times for being a false prophet.
36. She predicted the downfall of the United States during the Civil War.
37. She predicted England would declare war on the United States.

38. These prophecies were utterly erroneous.

39. She predicted world war during the Civil War.

40. She predicted the humbling of the United States in defeat.

41. She claimed to travel to other planets in vision.

42. She said animals and people crossed sexually.

43. She believed that this produced the black race.

44. Her visions are unbiblical.

45. Adventists say her writings are as inspired as the Bible.

The Investigative Judgment and Shut Door, and Their Ramifications

46. The investigative judgment doctrine was a reinterpretation.

47. Miller's prediction of October 22, 1844, failed.

48. Adventists believed that the door of mercy was shut on October 22.

49. They've got to be wrong if they believed that.

50. With prophetic authority Mrs. White supported the shut-door-of-mercy doctrine.

51. Her first vision taught this doctrine.

52. When reprinted, that part was left out, though the preface said there were no changes.

53. The other shut-door-of-mercy passages were dropped after 1851.

54. Or else they were reinterpreted.

55. Adventists never admitted their error regarding expecting Jesus to come in 1844.

56. Mrs. White immediately put God's endorsement on Edson and Crosier's explanation of why Christ had not come.

57. Certain doctrines were soon adjusted to fit their cleansing of the sanctuary and investigative judgment doctrines.

58. The shut door was then opened.

59. Soul sleep was introduced because of the investigative judgment doctrine.

60. The prophecies of Daniel and Revelation were reinterpreted to fit the investigative judgment.

61. It was a time of doctrinal reversal.

62. The idea that an angel is recording everything we do, and that we will be judged by such a record, is harsh.

63. Mrs. White taught that we would be judged for trying to have some leisure time.

64. The investigative judgment doctrine is unique to Seventh-day Adventists.

65. It can't be supported by the Scriptures.

66. It states that a believer's works determines their salvation.

67. It is blatantly unbiblical.

68. Seventh-day Adventism is not a legitimate Christian denomination.

69. The investigative judgment doctrine teaches that believers will be lost if they have unconfessed sins.

70. Even forgotten sins.

71. It requires perfect obedience to the Ten Commandments.

72. Especially the Fourth Commandment.

73. It is diametrically opposed to the gospel of grace.

Bible Versions and Footnotes

74. Seventh-day Adventism is a man-made religion.

75. Adventists have their own version of the Bible.

76. It's called *The Clear Word Bible.*

77. In it, the words and ideas of Mrs. White are inserted into the biblical text.

78. It adds 300 words to Daniel 9.

79. Daniel 8:14 is a blatant example of such alteration of the biblical text.

80. It's called *The Clear Word Version.*

81. It was written to support their prophetess.

82. It manipulates and distorts Scripture.

83. And then we have their *Study Bible.*

84. It was published by the Seventh-day Adventists.

85. It contains quotes from Mrs. White.

Other Doctrines; the Jehovah's Witnesses

86. Adventists teach that Christ's atonement on the cross was incomplete.

87. They teach the heresy that Michael is Christ.

88. They teach that there is no hell.

89. They teach doctrines contrary to tradition.

90. Many of their doctrines are similar to Jehovah's Witnesses.

91. N. H. Barbour was an early Adventist.

92. Both Jehovah's Witnesses and Seventh-day Adventists teach the heresy of soul sleep.

93. Both teach the heresy that Michael is Christ.

94. Early Adventists like Uriah Smith and James White denied the deity of Christ, just like Jehovah's Witnesses.

95. Both Jehovah's Witnesses and Adventists have produced altered versions of the Bible.

96. Both have set dates for Christ's return.

97. Both claim to be the only remnant church.

Jehovah's Witnesses, Cont.; Plagiarism

98. Both plagiarized.

99. Both really were guilty of this crime.

100. Walter Rea's *The White Lie* was dedicated to those who would rather believe a bitter truth than a sweet lie.

101. Mrs. White's inspiration was borrowed from others without credit.

102. Her major books contain "stolen" material.

103. *Sketches from the Life of Paul* was plagiarized in its entirety.

104. This resulted in a lawsuit.

105. The book was then quickly taken out of print.

106. The evidence is irrefutable that she "stole" her inspiration from others.

107. The main line of defense in *The White Truth* was regarding copyright laws back then.

108. It says that there were no copyright laws back then, so Mrs. White didn't break the law.

109. This sidestepped the issue.

110. The Adventist hierarchy has never responded to Rea's challenge:

111. "Prove that 20% of Mrs. White's writings are original."

112. Her visions which she claimed came from God were shaky.

Health Counsel, Wigs, and the Reform Dress

113. The Seventh-day Adventist ministry is not a Christian ministry.

114. Mrs. White's early health documents produce a rude awakening because of their fixation on moral purity.

115. Most of her health advice dealt with suppressing the male sexual urge.

116. She thought this urge was excessive.

117. [Not in all editions of the video.] She felt she had been given special light on the subject of masturbation.

118. [Not in all editions of the video.] Here is a list she gave of diseases caused by this practice.

119. [Not in all editions of the video.] She said kids who do this get green skin.

120. She said that meat inflames the passions.

121. She said rich and highly seasoned foods act as aphrodisiacs.

122. She said, "Sip no more the beverage of China, no more the drinks of Java."

123. She advised skipping all suppers in order to bring the male sexual appetites under control.

124. [Not in all editions of the video.] She said not to sleep on feather beds.

125. [Not in all editions of the video.] She hypocritically used a feather bed.

126. [Not in all editions of the video.] The Battle Creek Sanitarium used hydrotherapy to treat "secret vice."

127. [Not in all editions of the video.] This picture shows how that treatment was done.

128. Mrs. White controlled her female followers through directives on dress.

129. She was against wearing any kind of wig.

130. This picture of a skeleton looking through a window illustrates the kind of wig she didn't like.

131. After she dealt with wigs, she introduced the reform dress.

132. She tried to force it on people.

133. This dress was hot.

134. It was uncomfortable.

135. It was bulky.

136. It was long.

137. Faithful sisters struggled with it.

138. It was cumbersome.

139. Mrs. White gave no explanation for why she quit wearing hers.

140. She said those who aren't vegetarians when Jesus comes can't go to heaven.

Salvation, Grace, and Obedience

141. She taught that you have to keep the law to put yourself on the road to salvation.

142. She wrote this quote which denounces the doctrine of justification by faith.

143. She had no patience with those who believe in Jesus and say, "I am saved."

144. Adventists believe that Jesus made the down payment for our salvation.

145. But they believe that we must make the monthly installments.

146. They do not rely upon the grace of God alone.

147. They are striving to be rigidly obedient.

148. They are inflexible, guilt-ridden legalists.

149. Mrs. White said, "No one is saved who is a transgressor."

150. We don't have to worry about obeying the law, since we are under the New Covenant now, not the Old Covenant.

151. And Christ is the end of the law.

152. We are not under the tutorship of the law.

153. Christians will keep God's commandments out of love.

154. Being under the law leads to sin.

155. Being under grace leads to holiness.

Salvation, Cont.; Conditional Immortality

156. A pre-advent judgment of works is incompatible with the gospel of grace.

157. Soul sleep was introduced because of the investigative judgment doctrine.

158. The doctrine of soul sleep is unbiblical.

159. Conditional immortality flies in the face of two Scriptures.

160. Adventists do not teach the biblical doctrine of hell.

The Fourth Commandment

161. The Adventist view that Sabbath keeping is a mark of true loyalty to God is wrong.

162. After hearing about the Sabbath, Mrs. White obliged by conveniently having a vision.

163. This vision introduced the Sabbath to her followers.

164. Adventists weren't following what the Bible says about beginning the Sabbath at sunset.

165. Mrs. White decided to have another vision.

166. This vision was intended to settle the matter with the dissenters.

167. A delegate reported that "After the conference, . . . the vision was given, establishing those undecided on the sunset time."

168. But Adventists continued to ask questions.

169. Why did Mrs. White have visions saying that the Sabbath should be kept from 6 pm to 6 pm?

170. It required another vision to stop the questions.

171. In this vision she promised to question the angel.

172. The angel said, "Not yet, not yet."

173. She died without ever giving the promised explanation.

174. The promised explanation was never given.

The Seal of God and the Mark of the Beast

175. After the change of time for keeping the Sabbath, the Sabbath came to be understood as the seal.

176. It was seen to be of prime importance in determining who would and who wouldn't be saved.

177. *The Great Controversy* supports the idea that people already have the mark of the beast by keeping Sunday.

178. Adventists believe that failing to keep the Sabbath resulted in receiving the mark of the beast and losing eternal life.

179. Their view today on the subject is severe.

180. They teach that Sunday keeping is a mark of rebellion.

181. Even today, they make salvation ultimately dependent on which particular day . . .

182. . . . one worships.

183. The New Testament says that the seal of God is the work of the Holy Spirit, not the keeping of the Sabbath.

184. Mrs. White has no support at all for identifying the Sabbath as the seal of God.

Sunday vs. the Lord's Day, and the Scapegoat

185. The day Christ rose from the dead is the Lord's Day.

186. His early followers met regularly on the resurrection day for worship.

187. They did not meet regularly on the Sabbath.

188. The resurrection day was when the disciples usually broke bread.

189. They did not break bread on the Sabbath.

190. The Sabbath is Jewish.

191. Adventists teach that Satan becomes the sin-bearer.

192. Thus, they differ from the teaching of Scripture that Christ bore our sins on the cross.

Wrapping Up the Case

193. Adventists strive to be included as mainline, evangelical, Protestant Christians.

194. An Adventist pastor supplied the following five marks of a cult.

195. There is a "total reliance" by Seventh-day Adventists on Mrs. White.

196. She is revered by all Seventh-day Adventists.

197. Her comments overshadow the teachings of the Bible.

198. Adventists view her comments on the Scriptures to be more authoritative than tradition.

199. She pressured people into submission.

200. She publicly aired reproofs sent to people.

201. Usually the person conformed . . .

202. . . . under the pressure.

203. The type of pressure she used is one of the marks of a cult.

204. Acceptance and fellowship are very often withheld today from those who question the church's teachings.

205. Such treatment is a characteristic of a cult.

206. Adventists originally denied the deity of Christ.

207. They must discontinue the doctrine that "Michael" is a name for Christ.

208. This teaching contradicts Hebrews 1:13.

209. But they can't discontinue this doctrine without admitting that Mrs. White made a mistake.

210. It is impossible to accommodate both doctrines, that Christ is divine, and that Michael is Christ.

211. Adventists have added the investigative judgment to salvation by grace through faith.

212. They've also added Sabbath keeping.

213. They've added obedience to the Ten Commandments as requirements for salvation.

214. They've added obedience to other Old Testament laws as well.

215. They believe that the world's sins have been placed upon Satan . . .

216. . . . rather than upon Christ.

217. They believe that Christians must stand before God without Christ as their mediator.

218. This contradicts Hebrews 7:25.

219. Adventists believe that salvation comes by placing sin upon Satan.

220. This view of salvation is not the salvation taught in the Bible.

221. Four of the five marks of a cult apply to Seventh-day Adventists.

222. These five marks of a cult are very important.

223. Adventist leaders deceptively espoused the view of salvation by grace alone in the 1950's.

224. Many followers felt betrayed by this.

225. They began searching for themselves, and made lurid discoveries.

Testimonials, Documentation, and the Video Jacket

226. "The Adventist Church had deceived me."

227. "I was never presented with [Mrs. White's copying] in the school system."

228. ". . . when I saw that . . . . I felt like I had . . . been lied to."

229. ". . . the [Adventist] church was inconsistent theologically and politically."

230. This is a good reason for not being a member.

231. "When expedient, they . . . contradicted Ellen G. White . . . ."

232. "The last three years have been the most spiritually rewarding of my thirty-one years as a Christian."

233. "I am part of the family of God that truly upholds the Bible as the sole authority of both faith and practice."

234. "Jesus saves us not by our deeds . . . ."

235. "Because you're not going to be able to get this information from your church."

236. The *documentation package* substantiates the information contained in the video.

237. A number of former high-ranking Adventist Church leaders are featured on the video.

238. The video contains answers based on the best scholarship.

239. It contains answers based on a firm adherence to the truths of God's Word.

Initial Points

#1: "The quotes of Ellen G. White which appear in this program are taken from official Seventh-day Adventist publications. Page numbers are in reference to standard hardback editions."—Text appearing immediately before the program begins.

#1: These are official quotes of Mrs. White. The truth is that some quotes do not exist at all, some are by someone else, and some have been altered.

For example, David Snyder states that Mrs. White in her own words said that she was in "this hopeless condition for months" after Christ did not come when expected. Yet no such quotation can be found anywhere (see #10). Later, Dale Ratzlaff claims that the preface of an 1851 reprint "stated that no changes were made in idea or sentiment." Yet it said no such thing. Instead it stated, "I shall therefore leave out a portion" (see #52).

Regarding quotations really written by someone else, by folk who weren't even Adventists, it's just a simple fact that Mrs. White:

1. didn't give that list of diseases (#118);
2. didn't say kids would get green skin (#119);
3. didn't say, "Sip no more . . ." (#122); and
4. didn't say not to sleep on feather beds (#124).

The quote under #118, besides being written by someone else, was altered as well. It represents the words and thoughts of two different people fused into a single statement. There really is no way for the viewer to know this, for quotation marks and words were deleted without using an ellipsis, and words were added without the use of brackets.

But that one wasn't as serious as the one under #142. There we have a fusion into one of two different quotes from two different journals from two different continents written seven years apart. Fill in three ellipses, and the selection gives a totally different impression than the one the video gives.

Then we have the one under #37 where a sentence appearing six sentences before the rest of the quote is put at the end of the quote, and the intervening five sentences are deleted. The deleted sentences actually neutralize the point being made by the video.

Whether this video teaches one much about Adventism is debatable, but it does teach quite well a very important lesson: Don't take anyone's word for it. Read it for yourself.

#2 & #3: "Based around the teachings and philosophies of its nineteenth-century founder, prophetess Ellen G. White, Seventh-day Adventism exhibits tremendous influence world-wide." —Narrator.

#2: It's based around her teachings. To the contrary, the doctrines found in her writings did not originate with her, and generally were held and taught by Seventh-day Adventists before she wrote them out. Where then did Adventists get them from? From Bible study.

In materials prepared for the general public, Adventists quote Scripture to substantiate their beliefs, for they are based on Scripture. In material prepared for use by their own members, since her books are held in high esteem by most, they as well as the Bible are often quoted from, giving an appearance that the charge is true when it is not.

Much of what Seventh-day Adventists believe was hammered out in the Bible studies of the 1848 Sabbath Conferences. Mrs. White, to her chagrin, could not understand the topics under discussion. The only exception was when she was in vision, which occurred when the brethren could not come to agreement on their own about what the Bible said on a particular point. She wrote:

> During this whole time I could not understand the reasoning of the brethren. My mind was locked, as it were, and I could not comprehend the meaning of the scriptures we were studying. This was one of the greatest sorrows of my life. I was in this condition of mind until all the principal points of our faith were made clear to our minds, in harmony with the Word of God.—*Selected Messages*, bk. 1, p. 207.

Since much of what Adventists believe was arrived at in meetings where Mrs. White couldn't understand what was being discussed, how can it be said that Seventh-day Adventism is based around her teachings and philosophies?

#3: She's the founder. She was not the sole founder.

This distinction has more to do with psychology than with being picky. Narrowing down responsibility for an incident or teaching to a single individual makes that incident or teaching seem less credible to the average mind. Likewise, having many people say the same thing makes an incident, teaching, or allegation seem more credible. Whether intentional or not, this video utilizes this psychological principle by blaming so much on Mrs. White, and by having so many different people do the blaming.

Though a number of others played important roles in the forming of Seventh-day Adventism, there are three who are usually considered the founders: Joseph Bates, James White, and Ellen White. Without Bates's itinerant evangelism and James's publishing efforts and leadership, Seventh-day Adventism would not have gotten off the ground.

Interestingly, of these three, James White's name gets the most prominence. The *Seventh-day Adventist Encyclopedia* calls him "founder," while his wife is called "cofounder," and Bates is called "one of the founders" (pp. 1598, 1584, 132). This tendency to identify James as *the* founder is nothing new, for Uriah Smith called him "the founder" back in 1881 (*In Memoriam*, p. 11).

The Millerite Movement

#4: **"Her Methodist family [the Harmons] came under the influence of William Miller, a powerful preacher."**—David Snyder, the video's first guest speaker.

#4: Miller was a powerful preacher. No, Miller wasn't a local pastor in the Harmon's community. He was a Baptist lecturer living in New York; they lived in Maine.

The Millerite Movement was the American phase of one of the most powerful, the most widespread ecumenical revivals this world has ever seen. Its core message was spread in the U.S. and Canada by at least seven hundred ministers and lecturers from many denominations, and there were more abroad (Sylvester Bliss, *Memoirs of William Miller*, p. 327). L. D. Fleming put the count of American lecturers at 1,500 to 2,000 in March 1844 (Leroy Froom, *Prophetic Faith of Our Fathers*, vol. 4, p. 699). All this the video reduces to a single individual described only as a powerful preacher.

Such an oversimplification is quite understandable. This video is intended to attack Seventh-day Adventists, not Baptists, Congregationalists, and Presbyterians. It would therefore be counterproductive for it to acknowledge that Miller's views were shared by those of all faiths. It would likewise hurt its case to admit that most evangelicals today are more in harmony with Miller than with the views of Miller's opposition.

The core message all these ministers and lecturers were preaching was that Christ would return visibly and literally before the millennium instead of after (see #5). In connection with this, Miller and his associates called for a genuine commitment to the Lord Jesus, so that their hearers would be prepared for His return. This resulted in thousands of conversions. Miller wrote in July 1845:

> "On recalling to mind the several places of my labors, I can reckon up about six thousand instances of conversion from nature's darkness to God's marvelous light, the result of my personal labors alone; and I should judge the number to be much greater. Of this number I can recall to mind about

seven hundred, who were, previously to their attending my lectures, infidels; and their number may have been twice as great. Happy results have also followed from the labors of my brethren . . . ."—Bliss, p. 327.

At the invitation of Elder L. D. Fleming, pastor of the Christian Church in Portland, Maine, Miller gave a course of lectures in that city in March 1840. One month later, Elder Fleming described the effects of Miller's lectures:

> "At some of our meetings since Br. Miller left, as many as 250, it has been estimated, have expressed a desire for religion, by coming forward for prayers; and probably between *one* and *two hundred* have professed conversion at our meeting; and now the fire is being kindled through this whole city, and all the adjacent country. A number of rum-sellers have turned their shops into meeting-rooms, and those places that were once devoted to intemperance and revelry, are now devoted to prayer and praise. Others have abandoned the traffic entirely, and are become converted to God. One or two gambling establishments, I am informed, are entirely broken up. *Infidels, Deists, Universalists*, and the most abandoned *profligates*, have been converted; some who had not been to the house of worship for years. Prayer-meetings have been established in every part of the city by the different denominations, or by individuals, and at almost every hour. Being down in the business part of our city, I was conducted into a room over one of the banks, where I found about thirty or forty men, of different denominations, engaged with one accord in prayer, at about eleven o'clock in the day-time! In short, it would be almost impossible to give an adequate idea of the interest now felt in this city. There is nothing like extravagant excitement, but an almost universal solemnity on the minds of all the people. One of the principal booksellers informed me that he had sold more Bibles in *one month*, since Br. Miller came here, than he had in any four months

previous. A member of an orthodox church informed me that if Mr. Miller could now return, he could probably be admitted into any of the orthodox houses of worship, and he expressed a strong desire for his return to our city."—William Miller, *Miller's Works*, vol. 1, pp. 17, 18.

Sounds like we could use another William Miller today, wouldn't you say?

The movement elsewhere in the world, sometimes unconnected to Miller, was similar in its general characteristics, except for Sweden. It was against the law there to preach about Christ's soon coming and the approaching judgment. But prophecy foretold that such a message had to be given (Rev. 14:6, 7, 13-16).

To surmount this legal obstacle, the Holy Spirit moved upon children to preach, and the authorities could not get them to stop. Their sermons called upon the people to forsake drunkenness and worldly amusements, like card playing, dancing, and frivolity. It was sobering to those who heard.

The reports of that time give the ages of the large number of children involved as being six, eight, ten, twelve, sixteen, and eighteen. A brief account of this phenomenon can be found in *The Great Controversy*, pages 366, 367. For a fuller account, complete with references to Swedish sources, most of which were written by opposers to the phenomenon, see Froom, volume 3, pages 670-686.

#5 & #6: "He taught that Christ would return first in 1843, and then on October 22, 1844, supposedly the Jewish Day of Atonement for that year."—David Snyder.

#5: Miller taught Christ would return in 1843. This too is an oversimplification. The major thrust of Miller's preaching, and that which aroused so much opposition, was not that the judgment would begin and Christ would come about the year 1843. Rather, what aroused opposition was his teaching that Christ would come soon.

It sounds strange today, but at that time most churches were teaching that Christ would not come until after a thousand years of peace on earth, during which the whole world would be converted. Bible prophecies about the second coming and the resurrection they believed would not be literally fulfilled. These doctrines were popularized by Daniel Whitby, an Englishman who died in 1726 (*Ibid.*, vol. 2, pp. 651-655).

Miller and his associates taught most definitely that the whole world would not be converted, and that Christ would come personally and visibly before, not after, the thousand years. The date of 1843 only brought to a head these major points of theological difference (*Ibid.*, vol. 4, pp. 765-766).

Most churches, it seems, now believe what William Miller taught about Christ's second coming. They can thank him, in part, for this correction in their theology. Regarding this very theological correction, one British writer put it this way in an 1843 issue of *Christian Messenger and Reformer*: "We shall all, under Christ, be indebted to Mr. Miller, even if the Lord shall not come in 1843."—Froom, vol. 4, p. 716.

The *documentation package* offered at the end of the video is supposed to substantiate the video's accusations. It consists of a compilation of photocopies covering a hundred different points. "Point 4" is listed in its index as "William Miller's dates of 1843 and 1844." However, when one turns to the photocopy provided under "Point 4," the date 1843 cannot be found. Neither can Miller's views regarding either 1843 or 1844.

It is true, though, that in December 1842 Miller began to teach that Christ *would* come in 1843. This was more than eleven years after he gave his first sermon on Christ's soon return. Previous to December 1842, he had consistently said Christ would come "*about* the year 1843" "*if* there were no mistakes in my calculation" (Bliss, p. 329).

In 1842 Miller found himself falsely accused by the public press of having set the date of April 23 for Christ's return. Additionally, he was censured by some of his associates that year for constantly saying "about" and "if." Therefore, not finding any error in his calculations, Miller decided to remove the "about" and the "if" that December. From then until March 21, 1844, he taught that Christ *would* come in the Jewish year of 1843 at the end of the 2300 days of Daniel 8:14.

"And he said unto me, Unto two thousand and three hundred days; then shall the sanctuary be cleansed" (Dan. 8:14). Miller took these 2300 days to be 2300 years (Num. 14:34; Ezek. 4:6). He began them at the same time as the 70 weeks of Daniel 9 in 457 BC, and thus ended them in 1843. The cleansing of the sanctuary he identified with the day of judgment.

In many of his conclusions, Miller was in harmony with multitudes of scholars spanning centuries. For example, Reformed pastor Johann Petri in 1768 said that the 2300 days begin at the same time as the 70 weeks, and end with the second coming in 1847 (Froom, vol. 2, p. 715). His date of 1847 and Miller's of 1843 were essentially the same (see #64).

#6: Miller taught Christ would return on October 22, 1844. He never did. By claiming that the date of October 22 is based on Miller, the video can more easily attack Millerite Adventists, since views proposed by single individuals appear to have less credibility. But Miller never taught this.

He and Joshua V. Himes were preaching in the west the summer of 1844. When they returned east, they found everyone afire with the idea that Christ would come on October 22, the tenth day of the seventh Jewish month by Karaite reckoning. This fast-spreading message became known as the "seventh-month movement."

Why the tenth day of the seventh month? Because that was the Day of Atonement, called *Yom Kippur* in Hebrew, an annual feast day of ancient Israel when their sanctuary was cleansed (Lev. 16). It seemed quite natural to connect this with the cleansing of the sanctuary of Daniel 8:14.

Samuel S. Snow was the originator of the date of October 22, presenting the topic in the Boston Tabernacle on July 21, 1844. Then in August he presented his material at a camp meeting in Exeter, New Hampshire. After that the idea spread like wild fire. By October 22, fifty thousand Millerites believed Christ was coming on that day (Froom, vol. 4, pp. 799-826).

Miller, as well as the other principal Millerite leaders, resisted for awhile this pinpointing of a particular day, something they had always shunned. Miller's opposition can still be seen in his letter dated September 30 (Bliss, p. 270).

Unable to explain what was so evidently the work of the Holy Spirit reforming and converting people's lives, Miller began to capitulate on October 6. In his letter of that date, published in the October 12, 1844, issue of *Midnight Cry*, Miller said he would be disappointed if Christ did not return "within twenty or twenty-five days," which indicates he was looking toward October 26 or 31 as being the limit, not October 22.

The data from the letter follows, in the order that it appears:

When did the 2300 days end? Last spring
. . . Christ will come in the seventh month . . . .
If he does not come within 20 or 25 days, I shall feel twice the disappointment I did this spring.
. . . it must and will come this fall. . . . I see no reason why we may not expect him within twenty days. . . . just so true will redemption be completed by the fifteenth day of the seventh month . . . .
I am strong in my opinion that the next [Sunday, Oct. 13,] will be the last Lord's day sinners will ever have in probation; and within ten or fifteen days from thence, they will see Him . . . .
. . . in twenty days or less I shall see all that love Jesus.

So on October 6, Miller thought Christ would come that month, but not necessarily on the 22nd. His words most often suggest that Christ could come by the 26th, but they also suggest that Christ could return by the 23rd, 27th, 28th, and 31st, all in the same letter. And at the same time, he still maintained that the 2300 days had already ended the previous spring.

Miller's first letter to Himes after October 22 is dated November 10, and expresses his disappointment (Bliss, p. 277). This was the date of the astronomical new moon, which in Miller's mind could have marked the end of the seventh Jewish month according to the Karaite lunar calendar. The fact that Miller waited until the new moon before expressing his disappointment is further confirmation that he felt Christ would come in the seventh Jewish month, but not necessarily on the tenth day of that seventh month.

In a letter to J. O. Orr of Toronto, Canada West, on December 13, 1844, Miller wrote:

The ninth day [of the seventh month (October 21)] was very remarkable. . . . In the evening I told some of my [brethren] Christ would not come on the morrow. Why not? said they. Because he cannot come in an hour they think not, nor as a snare.

Clearly, even on October 21, Miller had not yet accepted the date of October 22, much less taught it.

#7: ". . . October 22, 1844, supposedly the Jewish Day of Atonement for that year. However, using information from the *Universal Jewish Encyclopedia* we find that in 1844, the Day of Atonement began after sundown, September 23rd, not October 22nd. So this crucial date in Adventism was flawed, incorrect, from the very beginning."—David Snyder.

#7: October 22 was not the Jewish Day of Atonement. Snow never identified October 22 as being the "Jewish" Day of Atonement per se. He knew better, as did other Millerites. And neither was September 23 the "Jewish" Day of Atonement.

There are many different sects of Judaism, and one prominent sect, the Karaites or Caraites, regularly differed from Rabbinical Judaism in how they began the year. This meant that the Karaite Jews often kept the Jewish feasts one month later than the Rabbinical

Jews. Thus, there was often more than one "Jewish" Day of Atonement per year. When this happened, no one date could be called *the* Jewish Day of Atonement.

The Rabbinical Jews accepted oral traditions in addition to the Word of God, but the Karaite Jews rejected all such traditions and relied only on the Bible. They were therefore a back-to-the-Bible movement within Judaism.

A modern-day Karaite Jewish leader in Israel, Nehemia Gordon, informs us that in 1999, the biblical Day of Atonement was on October 20, not in September like most other Jews thought ("[Karaite Korner Newsletter] #6: Biblical Holidays 1999," Aug. 31, 1999, email newsletter). That's pretty close to October 22.

The Jewish calendar is a lunar calendar. Its months are but 29 or 30 days each, with about 354 days to a year. To keep the calendar synchronized with the seasons, a thirteenth month is added about seven times every nineteen years.

When and under what circumstances should the thirteenth month be added? The Rabbinical method uses mathematical calculations to determine this. The Karaite method uses observation of the barley crop in Palestine. Biblically speaking, the Karaites are correct.

The day after the sabbath after the Passover, a sheaf of barley grain was to be waved before the Lord (Lev. 23:10-15). If the barley wasn't ripe enough, this could not be done, and so the Karaites would postpone for a month the beginning of the first month of the year.

Nisan, the first Jewish month, was originally called *Abib*. This ancient name refers to the barley being in a certain stage of ripening, a fact that lends support to the Karaite practice.

Some critics of Seventh-day Adventism cite Mr. Gordon to show that Karaites in 1844 in Palestine had long before adopted Rabbinical reckoning. However, the point is not what the Karaites were doing in 1844, but what the Bible says they should have been doing. If the barley was not ripe enough, then the year could not begin, regardless of what any Karaite or Rabbi said.

In actuality, Mr. Gordon only provides evidence indicating that the Karaites were using Rabbinical reckoning "for some time" before 1860. This does not prove what they were doing in 1844, as can readily be seen by turning to "Point 5" in the *documentation package* where some of Mr. Gordon's comments can be found. (The last ellipsis of "Point 5" represents an omission that included Mr. Gordon's signature. He is therefore the author of the "Official Karaite Documentation.")

The April 1840 issue of *American Biblical Repository* contained a letter written no earlier than 1836 by E. S. Calman, a converted Jewish rabbi and Christian missionary in Palestine. In this letter he discusses something he had discovered:

> I will begin by stating one fact of great importance, of which I was totally ignorant before I came to this country, which will prove that the *seasons of the festivals*, appointed by God for the Jewish nation, have been annulled and subverted by the oral law of the Scribes and Pharisees, which is now the ritual of the Jews.—"The Present State of the Jewish Religion," p. 411.

Then follows an explanation of the biblical requirement that the barley be ripe at Passover time, after which he states:

> But, at present, the Jews in the Holy Land have not the least regard to this season appointed and identified by Jehovah, but follow the rules prescribed in the oral law . . . . In general the proper season occurs after they have celebrated it a whole month, which is just reversing the command in the law . . . . Nothing like ears of green corn [barley] have I seen around Jerusalem at the celebration of this feast.—*Ibid.*, pp. 411, 412.

And now for the clincher:

> The Caraite Jews observe it later than the Rabbinical, for they are guided by Abib, . . . and they charge the latter with eating leavened bread during that feast. I think, myself, that the charge is well founded. If this feast of unleavened bread is not celebrated in its season, every successive festival is dislocated from its appropriate period, since the month Abib . . . is laid down in the law of God as the epoch from which every other is to follow.—*Ibid.*, p. 412.

So this letter indicates that Karaite Jews in Palestine were keeping the annual feasts generally one month later than the Rabbinical Jews around 1836. The conclusion of the critics that the Karaites had given up their special form of reckoning long before the nineteenth century is therefore unfounded. More importantly, this letter affirms the fact that usually the Rabbinical Jews kept their feasts one month too early, for the barley was not ripe enough.

The *documentation package* makes no attempt to substantiate the correctness of the Rabbinical date of September 23. Instead, it quotes Nehemia Gordon as saying, "While late September may or may not have been the correct month in which to celebrate Yom Kippur . . . ." This gives away the whole point the video is trying to prove. If late September "may not have been the correct month" for the Day of Atonement, then late October may have been the correct month after all.

S. S. Snow popularized the October 22 date during the summer of 1844, but he didn't come up with the idea of using Karaite reckoning. Karaite reckoning was the acceptable thing for a year or more prior to this.

Miller's associates, though not himself, decided that the Jewish year 1843 began on April 29 and ended on April 17, 1844. In doing so, they used the Karaite form of reckoning, as plainly stated in the June 21, 1843, issue of *The Signs of the Times*:

> The Caraite Jews on the contrary, still adhere to the letter of the Mosaic law, and commence with the new moon nearest the barley harvest in Judea; and which is one moon later than the Rabbinical year. The Jewish year of A.D. 1843, as the Caraites reckon it in accordance with the Mosaic law, therefore commenced this year with the new moon on the 29th day of April, and the Jewish year 1844, will commence with the new moon in next April, when 1843 and the 2300 days, according to their computation, will expire. But according to the Rabbinical Jews, it began with the new moon the first of last April, and will expire with the new moon in the month of March next.—Editorial, p. 123.

Between the start of the Jewish year on Nisan 1 and the Day of Atonement on Tishri 10, we have six Jewish months (averaging 29.5 days each) and nine days. Add these to the month commencing after the new moon of April 1844, and you have October 22, not September 23.

#8: "William Miller's meetings were marked by much emotionalism and a great deal of hysteria over Christ's imminent return."—David Snyder.

#8: They were marked by emotionalism and hysteria. Not at all. The fact is that Miller and his associates suppressed this kind of thing. Perhaps Mr. Snyder is confusing the Millerite Movement of the 1830's and 1840's with what happened in Kentucky during the Great Revival of 1800 (Froom, vol. 4, pp. 38-46).

In a vast ecumenical movement like the Millerite Movement, many people of many beliefs and worship styles come together. There were some in the movement who would have felt comfortable in the more emotional services of modern Pentecostal and charismatic churches, but Miller and his associates consistently sought to repress such things and even called them fanaticism.

The eyewitness account of Pastor L. D. Fleming of Portland, Maine, has already been cited where he said, "There is nothing like extravagant excitement, but an almost universal solemnity on the minds of all the people." He also testified:

> "The interest awakened by his lectures is of the most deliberate and dispassionate kind, and though it is the greatest revival I ever saw, yet there is the least passionate excitement. . . . It seems to me that this must be a little the nearest like apostolic revivals of anything modern times have witnessed." Miller, vol. 1, p. 17.

Unitarian minister A. P. Peabody of Portsmouth, New Hampshire, said pretty much the same (Bliss, p. 143).

Miller himself warned those looking for the Advent that Satan would attempt to "get us from the word of God" by "his wild-fire of fanaticism and speculation."—*Ibid.*, p. 173. In a December 1844 letter he called vocal responses from the congregation during meetings fanaticism. The one example he gives is, "Bless God," showing to what lengths he went in his opposition to "emotionalism" and "hysteria." He then went on to write, "I have often obtained more evidence of inward piety from a *kindling eye*, a *wet cheek*, and a *choked utterance*, than from all the noise in Christendom."—*Ibid.*, p. 282.

Regarding the seventh-month movement in particular, Miller testified:

> There is something in this present waking up different from anything I have ever before seen. There is no great expression of joy: that is, as it were, suppressed for a future occasion, when all heaven and earth will rejoice together with joy unspeakable and full of glory. There is no shouting; that, too, is reserved for the shout from heaven. The singers are silent: they are waiting to join the angelic hosts, the choir from heaven.—*Ibid.*, pp. 270, 271.

Joshua V. Himes, Miller's closest associate and ardent publicist, had this to say:

> Not only Mr. Miller, but all who were in his confidence, took a decided position against all fanatical extravagances. They never gave them any quarter; while those who regarded them with favor soon arrayed themselves against Mr. Miller and his adherents. Their fanaticism increased; and though opposed by Mr. Miller and his friends, the religious and secular press very generally, but unjustly, connected his name with it;—he being no more responsible for it than Luther and Wesley were for similar manifestations in their day.—*Ibid.*, p. 239.

So where exactly did this slander originate? Himes endeavors to show its origin by describing some incidents he is all too familiar with (pp. 229 ff.). In October 1842 John Starkweather, an Orthodox Congregationalist, became the assistant pastor at Himes's church, since Himes was often on the road with Miller. According to Himes,

> [Starkweather] taught that conversion, however full and thorough, did not fit one for God's favor without a second work; and that this second work was usually indicated by some bodily sensation.—*Ibid.*, p. 232.

Near the end of April 1843, things were such that Himes felt the matter had to be confronted. He addressed the congregation about the dangers of fanaticism, to which address Starkweather gave a vehement reply. So Himes gave another address, "exposing the nature of the exercises that had appeared among them, and their pernicious tendency."

> This so shocked the sensibilities of those who regarded them as the "great power of God," that they cried out and stopped their ears. Some jumped upon their feet, and some ran out of the house. "You will drive out the Holy Ghost!" cried one. "You are throwing on cold water!" said another.
>
> "Throwing on cold water!" said Mr. Himes; "I would throw on the Atlantic Ocean before I would be identified with such abominations as these, or suffer them in this place unrebuked."
>
> Starkweather immediately announced that "the saints" would thenceforth meet at another place than the Chardonstreet Chapel; and, retiring, his followers withdrew with him.
>
> From this time he was the leader of a party, held separate meetings, and, by extending his visits to other places, he gained a number of adherents. He was not countenanced by the friends of Mr. Miller; but the public identified him and his movement with Mr. Miller and his.
>
> This was most unjust to Mr. Miller . . . .—*Ibid.*, p. 233)

That it was. And it still is.

The *documentation package* gives no documentation for this charge whatsoever. Indeed, none can be found.

#9: [The picture used to illustrate #8, depicting fanatical adults crawling around like babies, and doing other inappropriate things.]

#9: This picture is of one of Miller's pre-October 22 meetings. It isn't at all, as any well-informed critic can verify. It was drawn to illustrate a description of a February *1845* meeting in Atkinson, Maine, when Miller was nowhere around.

The description appeared in an article in the March 7, 1845, issue of the *Piscataquis Farmer*. The article, which purports to be a condensed account of some court proceedings, is suspect because it was intentionally left anonymous, and the author was not present at the "fanatical" meeting in question. Additionally, he felt the need to excuse the errors of his account by calling it "imperfect" and by saying that he was "inexperienced." And since the article contains a number of contradictions regarding the meeting, what really happened is hard to determine.

We should remember that newspapers were not very unreliable in their statements regarding Millerites. Take for example an article in the November 5, 1844, issue of *The Daily Argus* of Portland, Maine. It reprints information from *The New York Commercial* of the previous Friday that said that Himes had renounced Millerism the previous Tuesday evening. However, the *Argus* adds this note: "Someone else must have been mistaken for Elder Himes, as he was in this city on Wednesday last."

In the picture in the video, Mrs. White is shown having a vision in the way the *Piscataquis* article described, but she had no visions before October 22. Her first vision came in December 1844. James White is shown standing behind her, yet they did not begin associating and working together until 1845 (Arthur L. White, *Ellen G. White*, vol. 1, pp. 70, 71, 77). He could not have stood behind her in this manner, therefore, in 1844.

Which leaves us with the question, Why does the video use this picture to illustrate an example of a pre-October 22 meeting of William Miller?

#10 & #11: "Ellen Harmon was a willing participant, though when Christ did not return when Miller predicted, she dissolved into tears and prayers and remained, as she said, in this hopeless condition for months."—David Snyder.

#10: She said this. There is no such statement anywhere in her writings.

The *documentation package* lists this as "Point 6," which provides as proof of the charge page 293 of *Life Sketches of James White and Ellen G. White*, 1880 edition. On this page we read, "My wife has for many years been subject to occasional, and sometimes protracted, seasons of the most hopeless despair." The immediate context clearly shows that this was written by Stephen Pierce about his wife, Almira. It isn't about Mrs. White at all! And the very next paragraph says that this depression started in May 1852, over seven years after October 22 (p. 294)!

"Point 6" also quotes from *Spectrum*, a theologically liberal journal that, unlike Mrs. White, does not advocate the concept of the infallibility of God's Word (cf. *Selected Messages*, bk. 1, p. 416). This quotation speculates that when Mrs. White later wrote about others going insane because of the teachings of fanatics, she was in fact writing about her own mental state. By no stretch of the imagination can this be used as proof that she ever said she was "in this hopeless condition for months."

#11: She felt that way. It simply isn't true. *Life Sketches of Ellen G. White* clearly says: "We were disappointed but not disheartened."—p. 61. If she was not disheartened, it is quite clear that she never "dissolved into tears and prayers" for months.

Like most young people, she was depressed at times. For instance, she felt in despair for a period of months around 1840. This was just prior to her conversion when she was but twelve years old (*Selected Messages*, bk. 3, pp. 324, 325). Many feel this way as they realize the depth of their sin and their need of a Savior.

In 1842 she was convicted that the Lord wanted her to pray publicly, but she didn't want to and stopped praying altogether. This resulted in a state of melancholy and despair that lasted three weeks or a little longer, until she followed through with what she believed was her duty (*Spiritual Gifts*, vol. 2, pp. 15-20).

Her second vision, soon after the first one of December 1844, instructed her to share what God had revealed to her. This troubled her. Being so young and in frail health, she shrank from the duty of traveling to share with others, dreading the scoffs, sneers, and opposition she would surely meet. She wrote:

> I really coveted death as a release from the responsibilities that were crowding upon me. At length the sweet peace I had so long enjoyed left me, and my soul was plunged in despair.—*Life Sketches*, 1880 ed., p. 195; cf. *Testimonies for the Church*, vol. 1, p. 63.

The words, "sweet peace I had so long enjoyed," indicate that she had no episodes of despair between the previous incident in 1842 and her second vision a few months after October 22, 1844. So she was not "in a hopeless condition" for months after October 22, and had no depression after Christ did not return when expected.

#12 & #13: "Ellen White just could not accept the fact that Christ did not return in 1843 or 1844. She could not admit her mistake. Interestingly enough, William Miller did."—David Snyder.

#12: She didn't admit her mistake. In actuality, both she and William Miller freely admitted that they were mistaken in thinking that Christ would return in 1843 or 1844. Yet they explained their mistake quite differently.

Mrs. White first admitted what she thought was a mistake, and then she admitted quite a different mistake. In 1847 her husband wrote,

> When she received her first vision, December, 1844, she and all the band [the group of Advent believers] in Portland, Maine (where her parents then resided) had given up the midnight cry, and shut door, as being in the past.—Arthur White, vol. 1, p. 61.

And Mrs. White wrote the same year, "At the time I had the vision of the midnight cry [December, 1844], I had given it up in the past and thought it future, as also most of the band had."—*Ibid.*

To comprehend these two statements we must first understand the terminology being used. During the seventh-month movement, the prophecies of Daniel 8 and 9 were connected to a number of other Scriptures, particularly the parable of the ten virgins of Matthew 25.

> And at *midnight* there was a *cry* made, Behold, the bridegroom cometh; go ye out to meet him. Then all those virgins arose, and trimmed their lamps. And the foolish said unto the wise, Give us of your oil; for our lamps are gone out. But the wise answered, saying, Not so; lest there be not enough for us and you: but go ye rather to them that sell, and buy for yourselves. And while they went to buy, the bridegroom came; and they that were ready went in with him to the marriage: and the *door* was *shut*. Afterward came also the other virgins, saying, Lord,

Lord, open to us. But he answered and said, Verily I say unto you, I know you not. (Mat. 25:6-12)

At the conclusion of the 2300 days of Daniel 8:14 (October 22), it was expected that the bridegroom would come, the wedding between Christ and his people would begin, and the "door" would be "shut." This all would occur after the "midnight cry," a term referring to the message being given during the seventh-month movement.

By Mrs. White initially giving up the idea that the midnight cry and shut door were past, she was repudiating the teaching that the 2300 days had already ended on October 22. This was a common conclusion among Millerites at that time.

After her first vision she realized that she had erred in calling the October 22 date a mistake. The real error she and fifty thousand other Millerites had made was in thinking that the beginning of the judgment and the ending of the 2300 days were synonymous with the second coming of Christ.

Daniel 8:14 had declared that the 2300 days ended with the cleansing of the "sanctuary." The popular belief among both Millerites and non-Millerites at that time was that this "sanctuary" was the earth or some part of it. Millerites therefore felt that the predicted cleansing of the sanctuary was Christ's cleansing of the earth by fire at His second coming.

They were mistaken that this was the predicted event of the prophecy, and this mistake Mrs. White was always willing to freely admit:

As the disciples were mistaken in regard to the kingdom to be set up at the end of the seventy weeks, so Adventists were mistaken in regard to the event to take place at the expiration of the 2300 days. In both cases there was an acceptance of, or rather an adherence to, popular errors that blinded the mind to the truth.—*Great Controversy*, p. 352.

Christ's disciples thought He would set up the kingdom of glory at His first coming, in which kingdom the Jews would rule the world and the Romans. When Christ died, they had a choice to make. Were they mistaken that Jesus was the true Messiah? Or were they mistaken about the kind of kingdom the Messiah was supposed to set up?

This observation prompts the question, Shall we reject the teachings of the apostles simply because they had erroneous views about prophecy, even as late as the time of Christ's ascension (Acts 1:6)? Of course not.

So Mrs. White made a mistake and freely admitted it. Are the contributors to this video willing to do the same regarding the mistakes it contains? To illustrate, under #103 and #104 is an allegation that a certain book was plagiarized in its entirety, resulting in a lawsuit. Since this allegation was proven to be fictitious more than half a century ago, would it not be well to freely admit this error to the Christian community? After all, Paul wrote, "Therefore thou art inexcusable, O man, whosoever thou art that judgest: for wherein thou judgest another, thou condemnest thyself; for thou that judgest doest the same things" (Rom. 2:21).

#13: Miller admitted his mistake. This is a gross oversimplification. To explain what Miller really admitted to would make the inclusion of this point in the video appear rather silly.

In a statement dated August 1, 1845, Miller identified his mistake:

But while I frankly acknowledge my disappointment in the exact time, I wish to inquire whether my teachings have been thereby materially affected. My view of exact time depended entirely upon the accuracy of chronology; of this I had no absolute demonstration; but as no evidence was presented to invalidate it, I deemed it my duty to rely on it as certain, until it should be disproved. Besides, I not only rested on received chronology, but I selected the earliest dates in the circle of a few years on which chronologers have relied for the date of the events from which to reckon, because I believed them to be best sustained, and because I wished to have my eye on the earliest time at which the Lord might be expected. Other chronologers had assigned later dates for the events from which I reckoned; and if they are correct we are only brought into the circle of a few years, during which we may rationally look for the Lord's appearing. As the prophetic periods, counting from the dates from which I have reckoned, have not brought us to the end, and as I cannot tell the exact time that chronology may vary from my calculations, I can only live in continual expectation of the event. I am persuaded that I cannot be far out of the way, and I believe that God will still justify my preaching to the world.—*Wm. Miller's Apology and Defense*, p. 34.

Thus the mistake that he admitted to was not the way he had interpreted and calculated the time prophecies of Scripture, but the dates of the human chronologers he had used to begin those time prophecies with.

The book shown in the video to illustrate this point is *Sketches of the Christian Life and Public Labors of William Miller*, written by James White and published in 1875. We already noticed how James's wife Ellen admitted her mistake. James did as well in this very book on *page 7*, the *third page* of text: "But Mr. Miller was mistaken in the event to occur at the close of the prophetic periods, hence his disappointment." This is just one of many examples where the video displays or quotes from books that disprove its claims.

The *documentation package* lists this point in its index as "Point 7." Turning to "Point 7," we find a page of a research paper dealing with the Albany Conference of April 1845, a meeting conducted by the principal Millerite leaders. This page allegedly describes what was voted at that Conference, but says nothing about whether Miller was in harmony with the vote or not. It also says nothing about what mistakes Miller allegedly admitted to making.

If one compares what was actually voted at the Albany Conference with this page from the research paper, one finds that they do not agree (Bliss, pp. 301-313). No, that conference did not endorse "the following positions":

1. "The movement had been mistaken in all attempts to set the date for Christ's coming."
2. "The use of parables as prophetic allegories was a mistake."

3. "Rejection of . . . the 'investigative judgement' theory."

Why, the investigative judgment theory wasn't really around yet (see #59; cf. #56). The paper also claims that the conference issued "a stern warning . . . primarily directed at a young, rising charismatic star among sabbatarian Adventists: Ellen Harmon-White." But it's a simple fact that she was not yet a Sabbatarian (see #163), and that her name did not appear in the voted statements. There was mention of those "making great pretensions to special illumination," but from the description given regarding the activities and teachings of that party, it is quite apparent that the statement wasn't talking about Ellen Harmon.

Far better would it have been if the compiler of the *documentation package* had provided the original source rather than an interpretation of it.

#14 & #15: "Instead she claimed she had a vision from God, the first of many. 'I have seen that the 1843 chart was directed by the hand of the Lord, and that it should not be altered; that the figures were as He wanted them, that His hand was over, and hid a mistake in some of the figures...' Early Writings p. 74."—David Snyder.

#14: This was her first vision. Not at all. This statement from *Early Writings* is from a vision that occurred on September 23, 1850, nearly six years *after* her first vision of December 1844 (*Early Writings*, pp. 13, 74; *Present Truth*, Nov. 1, 1850).

#15: God "covered up" the mistake. Under the next number, the narrator builds upon this out-of-context quotation.

Let's fill in the ellipsis and thus complete the quoted sentence: ". . . that His hand was over and hid a mistake in some of the figures, so that none could see it, until His hand was removed." Rather than God covering up His own alleged errors, He was instead not bringing the mistakes of others to their attention until just the right time. The connotation of the actual quote is thus different than what the video alleges.

#16: "Rather than admit she was in error, Ellen Harmon claimed that God was the one who had made the mistake, and had covered it up Himself."—Narrator.

#16: She said God made the mistake. She never said that God made a mistake then or at any other time, for God makes no mistakes.

We've all made mistakes, but why didn't we recognize it sooner? Why didn't God show it to us sooner? Just because He didn't, does that mean God made the mistake instead of us? By no means.

Besides, what Mrs. White is referring to here is not about October 22 being a mistake. Rather, she's talking about how the original date of 1843 was arrived at through a mathematical error. This is the "mistake in some of the figures" she was referring to.

As mentioned under #5, Miller and his many associates began the 2300 days in 457 BC and ended them in 1843. Sometime in the Jewish year 1843, Christ's coming was therefore expected. Yet instead of 1843, the year was really supposed to be 1844.

Two things were not understood in 1843 (Uriah Smith, *The Sanctuary and the Twenty-Three Days of Daniel VIII,14*, pp. 93-96). First, if the decree foretold in Daniel 9 went forth on the first day of the Jewish year 457 BC, the 2300 days could not end until the last day of the Jewish year 1843, for it takes 2300 full years to fulfill the prophecy. Thus, under such a scenario, the 2300 days could not end until the new moon of April 1844. Second, if the decree did not go forth until a certain number of days into 457 BC, then the 2300 days could not end until that same number of days into 1844.

After the Karaite Jewish year of 1843 had ended in April 1844, it was apparent that some sort of mistake had been made. Eventually it was discovered that the decree of 457 BC did not go forth, did not go into effect, until that fall. Thus the 2300 days could not end until the fall of 1844.

Another way to arrive at the same result is the following: Christ's death was believed to have occurred in the middle of Daniel 9's 70th week. Since Christ died in the spring, that would make the middle of the week to be the spring, and the beginning and ending of all the weeks to be the fall. Thus the 70 weeks had to commence in the fall, and the 2300 days, commencing at the same time, must likewise end in the fall. (See #20 for more on this interpretation, and a comparison of it with the most popular alternative view today.)

Of course, God knew that the math of the Millerites was off, and He permitted them to understand this after the fact.

While no mistake about the validity of the October 22 date is suggested in the quoted statement, Mrs. White's words indicate that there was some sort of divine purpose in what happened. Perhaps comparing the experience of the Millerites to that of the disciples can illuminate our understanding.

The disciples of Christ were tested severely at two different times, both relating to mistaken views about prophecy. John 6:66 indicates that many of Christ's disciples just up and left Him when He cryptically told them that His kingdom was a spiritual kingdom, not a kingdom in which they would rule the Romans. This was the first test, and it was hard. The second

one came at the crucifixion when all the hopes and dreams of the disciples for an earthly kingdom of power were dashed to pieces.

The Millerites likewise were tested twice. First, Christ did not come as expected during the Jewish year of 1843, for there was a mistake in their figures. Second, Christ did not come as expected on October 22, 1844, for the second coming does not occur at the same time as the judgment.

If the first and only test for the disciples had been at the crucifixion, and if it had been then when the majority of Christ's followers forsook Him, the test would have been much more overwhelming for the disciples. Having the previous test strengthened the disciples for the later one. Likewise, the first test strengthened the Millerites to be able to endure the second one.

Was God responsible for the mistaken views about prophecy that all those followers of Jesus had 2000 years ago, just because He didn't point out their errors sooner? Not at all. He revealed their mistakes at specific times for specific reasons. The same was true with the Millerites.

The *documentation package* gives no evidence that Mrs. White ever said that God made any mistake. Under "Point 8" and "Point 8a" it merely repeats Mr. Snyder's quote from *Early Writings*, and shows a picture of the 1843 chart referred to.

This is actually very common in the *documentation package*. Rather than substantiate the charges being made, it often resorts to only reproducing the identical paragraphs from which the video quoted, and sometimes not even the whole paragraph.

#17 & #18: "Ellen's controversial vision forced the re-adjustment of many Adventist dates and doctrines."—Narrator.

#17: This vision was controversial. Neither her first vision nor her vision of September 23, 1850 (see #14), should have been considered controversial at the time. Both appeared reasonable and middle of the road to their targeted audiences.

At some point after October 22, 1844, there were two major and opposite divisions of thought: 1) The 2300 days of Daniel 8:14 had not ended yet and Christ's literal and visible coming was yet future. 2) The 2300 days had ended and Christ had already returned in a spiritual way.

In contrast, Mrs. White's first vision indicated that the 2300 days had ended, but Christ's return was yet future and would be literal and visible like the Bible says. Thus it promoted a middle-of-the-road position between the two major camps.

Fifty thousand Millerites had felt moved by the Spirit of God during the seventh-month movement. Since her first vision indicated that that movement was indeed of God, this point too should have been considered non-controversial.

The 1850 vision the video quoted from, first published in November of that year, taught that:

1. There was nothing wrong with printing a periodical to proclaim the truth.
2. The word "sacrifice" in Daniel 8:12 was not in the original, but had been added by the translators (an indisputable fact).
3. "Time . . . will never again be a test." In other words, there should be no more setting dates for Christ's return.

4. Lots of money should not be spent sending people to Jerusalem, thinking that somehow this will help fulfill prophecy. (*Present Truth*, Nov. 1, 1850; *Early Writings*, pp. 74-76)

Nothing controversial here, though some who were setting dates might not have cared for the third point. However, she had already been opposing date setting for five years by that time, so this position was nothing new (see *Testimonies for the Church*, vol. 1, pp. 72, 73).

Those who wanted to go to Jerusalem probably didn't like the fourth point, but this wasn't controversial either, for it harmonized with what the Millerites had believed and taught prior to 1844. They did not believe that the Bible foretold a restoration of literal Israel, but felt that Israel today is composed of all believers, as the apostle Paul taught:

For he is not a Jew, which is one outwardly; neither is that circumcision, which is outward in the flesh: But he is a Jew, which is one inwardly; and circumcision is that of the heart, in the spirit, and not in the letter. (Rom. 2:28, 29)

Know ye therefore that they which are of faith, the same are the children of Abraham. . . .

If ye be Christ's, then are ye Abraham's seed, and heirs according to the promise. (Gal. 3:7, 29)

This teaching may be controversial today, but it definitely wasn't among Millerites in 1844.

#18: It caused a re-adjustment of many dates and doctrines. No dates were re-adjusted by either vision. The first vision didn't really introduce any new doctrines. The 1850 vision called for a moratorium on date setting, but that wouldn't constitute a re-adjustment of *many* doctrines, especially since she had already been advocating that position for five years. Going to Jerusalem not being a fulfillment of prophecy was already a standard Millerite doctrine, so this doctrine was not re-adjusted either.

#19 & #20: "Even though the 1843 date had now been adjusted to 1844, it was still an error."
—Narrator.

#19: It adjusted the 1843 date to 1844. Neither Mrs. White's first vision of December 1844 nor her 1850 vision had anything to do with the change of date from 1843 to 1844. The simple proof of this is the fact that the date was adjusted in the summer of 1844, long before she had either of these visions (see #6).

#20: The 1844 date was still an error. The *documentation package* is silent on quite a few points, including this one. The reason for silence here is simple: The theological understandings of those of any and every persuasion have yet to produce any valid objections to the basic interpretations of Scripture that lead to this date. No better date has yet been found.

If the 2300 days of Daniel 8:14 did not end in 1844, when did they end? Actually, this question is premature. Since Daniel 8 and 9 are tied together linguistically, a better question to start with is, When did the 490 days of Daniel 9 end?

Even though Gabriel had already explained *everything* except the 2300 days, Daniel says that "none understood" the "vision" (8:27). How could that be? The answer lies in the Hebrew text.

There are two different Hebrew words translated "vision" in chapter 8: *mar'eh* and *chazown*. *Chazown* occurs in verses 2, 13, 15, 17, and the last half of 26. *Mar'eh* occurs in verse 16, the first half of 26, and 27. The distinction between these two words is critical to a proper understanding of the chapter, for it is the *mar'eh* that "none understood," not the *chazown*.

When Gabriel says in verse 26 that the "vision [*mar'eh*] of the evening and the morning which was told is true," he provides the key to understanding the difference between the *chazown* and the *mar'eh*. Literally, the Hebrew for "2300 days" in verse 14 is "2300 evening-morning." So the vision or *mar'eh* of the evening-morning must specifically refer to the 2300 evening-morning, while the *chazown* refers to the entire vision.

Thus, when Daniel said none understood the vision or *mar'eh*, he was correct, for Gabriel had not explained the *mar'eh* of the 2300 days yet. Gabriel was specifically assigned the special task of making Daniel "to understand the vision," or *mar'eh*, but Daniel fainted a little too soon (vss. 16, 27).

In chapter 9 Gabriel returns, "the man" "whom I had seen in the vision" or *chazown* (vs. 21). Gabriel tells Daniel, "Consider the vision," or *mar'eh*, the 2300 days (vs. 23). The rest of what he says to Daniel in the chapter is connected to the time prophecy of the 70 weeks, or 490 days. Somehow, therefore, the 70 weeks are supposed to be an explanation of the 2300 days.

Nearly everyone agrees that the first 483 of the 490 days of Daniel 9 end at some point in the ministry of Christ, each day representing a year.

One troublesome problem in chapter 8 is that there is no starting point given for the beginning of the

2300 days. This problem is removed in chapter 9, for these time prophecies are said to begin with the decree to restore and build Jerusalem:

> Know therefore and understand, that from the going forth of the commandment to restore and to build Jerusalem unto the Messiah the Prince shall be seven weeks, and threescore and two weeks. (Dan. 9:25)

So we need to find a decree that both restores and builds. Adventists begin the 490 years with the decree of Artaxerxes' seventh year, or 457 BC. In that year the Jews' judicial system was "restored" to the point that they could even execute the death penalty against violators of God's law (Ezra 7:7, 8, 26). Isaiah 1:26 had predicted this restoration of the judges.

What about the "build" part of the decree? We need to understand that the giving of this decree was a process that took some time. It began with Cyrus commanding the building, and it ended with Artaxerxes restoring the judiciary (Ezra 6:14).

Ezra 1:2 records Cyrus's decree which commanded the building of the temple, but did Cyrus really fulfill Daniel 9:25 by also commanding the building of Jerusalem? Yes, he did. The Lord, calling Cyrus by name more than a century before his birth, said that he would command *Jerusalem* to be built (Is. 44:28; 45:13).

If we start the 70 weeks in 457 BC, then the first 69 weeks unto "Messiah the Prince" would end in 27 AD. Adventists identify this as being the year of Christ's baptism. At that time He was anointed with the Holy Spirit descending upon Him in the form of a dove (Luke 3:1, 22; Acts 10:38). Since the Hebrew word for "Messiah" and the Greek word for "Christ" both mean "the anointed one," it seems most logical to identify the coming of the Messiah of Daniel 9:25 with Christ's anointing at His baptism.

"And he shall confirm the covenant with many for one week: and in the midst of the week he shall cause the sacrifice and the oblation to cease" (Dan. 9:27). When Christ died after a ministry of 3½ years (31 AD), the veil of the temple was torn from top to bottom (Mat. 27:51). Thus Christ showed that the sacrifices were to cease, since the true sacrifice for sin had been offered.

This leaves but half a week left of the prophecy, 3½ years, stretching to 34 AD. In Acts 7 we find Stephen being stoned as the first Christian martyr. Immediately after this the gospel started going to non-Jews: Samaritans, the Ethiopian eunuch, and the Roman centurion Cornelius, along with his household (Acts 8:4-39; 10). Gabriel had told Daniel, "Seventy weeks are determined upon *thy people*" (Dan. 9:24). It therefore seems logical to end the 70 weeks with the stoning of Stephen, for at that point the gospel began to go to the Gentiles, not just Daniel's people, the Jews.

"And he shall confirm the covenant with many for one week" (Dan. 9:27). For one week (7 years) the gospel, the new "covenant," was "confirmed" with "many," the Jewish nation: 3½ years during the ministry of Christ, and 3½ years after His resurrection. After that, it went to the Gentiles.

The first 490 days of the 2300 thus ended in 34 AD. The remaining 1810 years can be added to 34 AD to arrive at 1844.

Before it can be said emphatically that 1844 is "an error," a better interpretation than the above must be found. None has been found to date.

The most popular alternative interpretation today is the following, which is more complex than what was above, which should tell you something: The first 69 weeks stretch from Artaxerxes' supposed twentieth year in 445 BC to about the death of Christ, and the 70th week is yet future.

Sir Robert Anderson proposed multiplying the 69 weeks, or 483 days, by 360 days to the year, and then dividing this product by 365.25 days per year. By this method he reduced the 483 years to just over 476 years, a total of 173,880 days. He then began the time period on March 14, 445 BC, what he supposed was the first day of the first Jewish month of Nisan that year. Then he ended it with April 6, 32 AD, what he supposed was Nisan 10, Palm Sunday, the week Christ was crucified. The 70th week of Daniel 9 Anderson put off into the future to a yet unknown time (*The Coming Prince*).

There are a number of serious problems with Anderson's theory:

1. In making this calculation, he mistakenly added three leap days too few, owing to his misunderstanding the differences between the Julian and the Gregorian calendars. 173,880 days should really end on Thursday, April 3, not Sunday, April 6.

2. Nisan 10 could not have been earlier than Wednesday, April 9, in 32 AD, and so could not have been April 6. This is because the sighting of the new moon which begins the new Jewish month could not have occurred as early as Anderson's theory demands.

3. Thus, Nisan 14 would have been on a Sunday or Monday in 32 AD, not on a Thursday as Anderson supposed. Anderson tied the last supper to Nisan 14, with Christ dying on the 15th. If Nisan 14 was on a Sunday or Monday, that would put Christ's death on a Monday or Tuesday in disagreement with the gospel accounts.

4. The Jews of Elephantine used accession-year reckoning for Artaxerxes, and the Jews of that time

used a fall-to-fall calendar (Horn and Wood, *The Chronology of Ezra 7*, pp. 75-90; Neh. 1:1; 2:1). A king's accession year ran from the date of his enthronement until the next New Year's day. In a fall-to-fall calendar this would be Tishri 1, sometime in September or October. Not till after the accession year did the king's first year of reign begin. In contrast, non-accession year reckoning has no accession year, but begins the first year of reign with the king's enthronement. Each year of reign still ends on New Year's day.

Xerxes was murdered sometime in 465 BC. An Aramaic papyri, *AP 6*, written on January 2, 464 BC, is still dated in Artaxerxes's accession year, meaning that his first year would not begin until Tishri 464 (*Ibid.*, pp. 98-115, 172-174). This makes Nisan in his twentieth year 444 BC, not 445. So Anderson's starting date was a year off.

5. Daniel 9 requires a "commandment to restore and build." While we have record of a decree from Artaxerxes' seventh year in Ezra 7, we have no record of a decree from his twentieth year. So how can we commence the 70 weeks with the twentieth year?

6. The reason Artaxerxes's twentieth year is chosen is because it is thought that then is when the Jews were commanded to build Jerusalem. However, Cyrus had commanded this long before (Is. 44:28; 45:13).

7. Putting the seventieth week of Daniel 9 into the future ignores the linguistic ties between chapters 8 and 9, and the resulting connection between the 2300 days and the 490 days.

8. The method of reducing the 69 weeks of 483 years to only 476 years ignores the Jewish seven-year cycle, since the 483 years no longer coincide with 483 actual years.

The Israelites were to work their fields for six years, and then let the land keep a sabbath for the seventh year (Lev. 25:2-7). It is easy to see an allusion to this practice in Daniel 9's "70 weeks," "7 weeks," "62 weeks," and "1 week." In fact, many scholars of various persuasions have recognized just such a connection. One's interpretation of the 70 weeks ought to therefore coincide with actual seven-year sabbatical cycles.

The Adventist way of reckoning them indeed does. The fall of 457 BC began the first year, and the fall of 34 AD ended the seventh year of a seven-year cycle (see "When Were the Sabbatical Years?" posted at http://www.pickle-publishing.com/papers). Thus, when 31 AD is identified as the date for Christ's crucifixion, the middle of the last week of seven years, it truly is the precise middle of a seven-year cycle.

Back to the original point: Until the critics find a better interpretation that fits all the data, they really shouldn't be so emphatic that the 1844 date is an error. Indeed, with the evidence as overwhelming as it is, the 1844 date is as solid as it gets.

The Role of Mrs. White and Her Writings

#21: "Because she claimed to have the spirit of prophecy, she came to be the visible, absolute authority figure for the initially small group of Adventist believers."—David Snyder.

#21: Mrs. White became the absolute authority figure. Sad to say, for the last 157 years, what she has written and said has often not been followed. Anyone acquainted with her writings would agree, and toward the end of the video this is even admitted by Sydney Cleveland (see #231). It is also admitted in Walter Rea's *The White Lie*, which is one of the primary exhibits used in this video against Mrs. White (see #196).

Was the situation different in the early days? Was she the authority figure back then? Actually, they were a bit overcautious on the matter. Consider what her husband James published in the *Review and Herald* of October 16, 1855:

> What has the REVIEW to do with Mrs. W.'s views [visions]? The sentiments published in its columns are all drawn from the Holy Scriptures. No writer of the REVIEW has ever referred to them as authority on any point. The REVIEW for five years has not published one of them.—p. 61.

The *Review and Herald* began being published in November 1850. Therefore, James White is saying that since the beginning of this paper, his wife's visions have not been printed in it. The only exception was in the Extra of July 21, 1851, when material from visions was printed that included a warning against setting dates for the second coming.

While the extreme policy of not printing any of Mrs. White's visions was later discontinued, it is interesting to consider the comments that followed the above quote from James. What he expresses below has not changed one bit.

> Its motto has been, "The Bible, and the Bible alone, the only rule of faith and duty." Then why should these men charge the REVIEW with being a supporter of Mrs. W.'s views?

> Again, How has the Editor of the REVIEW regarded Visions, and the gifts of the Gospel Church for more than eight years past? His uniform state-

ments in print on this subject will satisfactorily answer this question. The following is from a Tract he published in 1847:

> "The Bible is a perfect and complete revelation. It is our only rule of faith and practice. But this is no reason why God may not show the past, present, and future fulfillment of his word, in these last days, by dreams and visions, according to Peter's testimony. True visions are given to lead us to God, and to his written word; but those that are given for a new rule of faith and practice, separate from the Bible, cannot be from God, and should be rejected."

> Again, four years since, he wrote on the Gifts of the Gospel Church, re-published in the REVIEW for Oct. 3d, 1854, from which is taken the following:

> "Every Christian is therefore in duty bound to take the Bible as a perfect rule of faith and duty. He should pray fervently to be aided by the Holy Spirit in searching the Scriptures for the whole truth, and for his whole duty. He is not at liberty to turn from them to learn his duty through any of the gifts. We say that the very moment he does, he places the gifts in a wrong place, and takes an extremely dangerous position."

> Now if these paragraphs were not in print, his enemies might accuse him of changing his position; but as one was printed eight years since, and the other four, and re-printed one year since, they are nails driven in right places. Slanderous reports must fall powerless before facts of this character.

To the above we add one additional paragraph where James White describes precisely what this video is doing:

> But what deserves especial attention here, is the unrighteous use some are making of the Visions. They take the advantage of the common prejudices against Visions, misrepresent them, and those who are not ready to join them in anathematizing them as the work of Satan, then brand any view held by the body of Sabbath-keepers as the "Vision view," and not the Bible view of the subject. In this way an

unhallowed prejudice can be excited in the minds of some against any view, and even all the views held by that body of Christians called Advent Sabbath-keepers. This course has been, and is being pursued on the subjects of the Two-horned beast, Sanctuary, Time to commence the Sabbath and period of the establishment of the kingdom of God on the earth. It should be here understood that all these views as held by the body of Sabbath-keepers, were brought out from the Scriptures before Mrs. W. had any view in regard to them. These sentiments are founded upon the Scriptures as their only basis.

Solomon was right. There is nothing new "under the sun" (Eccl. 1:9).

#22: "Her writings grew to be seventeen times as large as the entire Bible."—David Snyder.

#22: They grew to be seventeen times larger. John Wesley, Martin Luther, Spurgeon, and others wrote a lot too. So?

The video endeavors to show that Adventists are supplanting the Bible with the writings of Mrs. White. That she wrote more words than what can be found in the Bible, like other religious leaders have, is supposed to somehow bolster this claim, but the amount she wrote is irrelevant to the point.

#23: "Her followers were to reference these 5000 articles, 49 books, plus 55,000 manuscript pages she claimed to write, and regard them as being as inspired as the Bible through Ellen White's pen of inspiration."—David Snyder.

#23: They regard them as being as inspired as the Bible. This statement is revealing. To believe that Mrs. White's writings are as inspired as the Bible is somehow wrong? It really doesn't make sense.

Seventh-day Adventists do not believe in degrees of inspiration. Someone's writings are either inspired or they are not. The first eleven chapters of Genesis are neither less inspired nor more inspired than the Gospel of Luke.

Since Adventists believe that *the Bible teaches* that the gifts of the Spirit did not end in the first century, and that *the Bible teaches* that the gift of prophecy would be manifested in the last days, they also believe that someone in the last days would deliver inspired messages like the Bible prophets did. Yet they have always maintained that the Bible must be the final authority. Any last day prophet that contradicts the Bible must be a false prophet.

This was true in the first century as well. If Agabus or Philip's four daughters (Acts 11:28; 21:9, 10) in their inspired messages had contradicted the Word of God, they would have had to be declared false prophets. As Paul wrote, "The spirits of the prophets are subject to the prophets" (1 Cor. 14:32).

So while there are not degrees of inspiration, there are degrees of authority. Agabus and Philip's four daughters were just as inspired as Moses or Matthew, James or Jeremiah, Micah or Mark, and John or Jonah. But the authority of the messages of Agabus and Philip's four daughters was always subordinate to that of Scripture.

#24: "To this day official publications of the church have used her writings as the last word on doctrine."—David Snyder.

#24: They're used as the last word on doctrine. This is simply not true. If the Bible is Adventism's "last word on doctrine," how can Mrs. White be?

After the Bible, who has the next-to-the-last word? Some super-smart scholar with seven Ph.D.'s who can quote the Bible from memory in the original languages backwards, or a divinely inspired prophet? The answer ought to be obvious to every Bible-believing Christian.

Having grown up in the wilderness, John the Baptist was considered inferior in education to the rabbis and scholars of his day, yet Jesus declared that there was no greater prophet than John (Mat. 11:11). In the journals of that day, who should have had the next-to-the-last word: the inspired prophet John the Baptist, or Dr. Nicodemus, Ph.D.?

What is really at issue here are two theological points:

1. Were the gifts of the Holy Spirit really to remain in the church till the end of time as Ephesians

4:11-14 and Joel 2:28-31 indicate?

2. Are the writings of one true prophet more inspired than the writings of another true prophet? Was the apostle Paul more inspired than the apostle James or the prophet Amos?

Seventh-day Adventists should not be faulted for taking the biblical position on these points.

No documentation whatsoever is given for this point in the *documentation package*. However, under "Point 17" is a page from a *Ministry* magazine article dated October 1981. The first paragraph says:

> For Seventh-day Adventists the one standard, rule, and ultimate authority for doctrine is the Bible. All

other doctrinal authorities are subordinate. "God will have a people upon the earth to maintain the Bible, and the Bible only, as the standard of all doctrines and the basis of all reforms," Ellen White wrote (*The Great Controversy*, p. 595). "The Bible, and the Bible alone, is to be our creed, the sole bond of union. . . . Let us lift up the banner on which is inscribed, The Bible our rule of faith and discipline." - *Selected Messages*, book 1, p. 416.

Well would it be if those responsible for the content of this video had read their own documentation.

#25 & #26: "In the twenty-seven points of fundamental beliefs, they state that the Bible is a source of authority. But they also say that her writings are a continuing and an authoritative source of truth."—David Snyder.

#25: They say that the Bible is *"a"* source of authority rather than *"the"* source of authority. This is simply not true. In the twenty-seven fundamental beliefs, the one about the Bible comes first. It says:

> The Holy Scriptures are the infallible revelation of His will. They are *the* standard of character, *the* test of experience, *the* authoritative revealer of doctrines, and *the* trustworthy record of God's acts in history. —*Seventh-day Adventists Believe*, p. 4, italics added.

#26: They say her writings are an authoritative source of truth. So? If one believes that the biblical gift of prophecy will be manifested in the last days, then one must also believe that the writings or talks of a person genuinely having that gift must have some degree of authority. Yet the Bible must always remain the ultimate authority.

Number seventeen of the twenty-seven fundamen-

tal beliefs deals with the gift of prophecy:

> One of the gifts of the Holy Spirit is prophecy. This gift is an identifying mark of the remnant church and was manifested in the ministry of Ellen G. White. As the Lord's messenger, her writings are *a* continuing and authoritative source of truth which provide for the church comfort, guidance, instruction, and correction. They also make clear that the Bible is *the* standard by which *all* teaching and experience must be tested.—*Seventh-day Adventists Believe*, p. 216, italics added.

The *documentation package* gives this quotation under both "Point 13" and "Point 94." Thus the *documentation package* proves that Adventists believe, and that Mrs. White taught, that the Bible is to be *the* standard by which all are to be tested, including Mrs. White herself!

#27 & #28: "They have, however, made her more embarrassing writings unavailable, locking them securely away in the White Estate vault."—David Snyder.

#27: They're unavailable, locked away in the vault. The vault protects her writings against theft, vandalism, and fire, but all her writings are available and are not "locked away," unless, of course, it is after hours.

All her published writings have been available on CD-ROM for a decade. There is an ongoing project of putting all her unpublished writings on CD-ROM as well. Until this project is completed, those interested in reading her unpublished writings can find them at

the White Estate's main office in Silver Spring, Maryland; three branch offices located at Andrews University, Loma Linda University, and Oakwood College; or one of eleven Research Centers operated throughout the world.

The *documentation package* lists "The White Estate Vault" as "Point 14." However, turning to "Point 14," we find but two selections that provide no evidence for the accusation. In fact, the two selections do not even once contain the word "vault."

#28: Her more embarrassing writings are the ones unavailable. More embarrassing? What makes them more embarrassing?

Sometimes Mrs. White was shown personal matters in vision which she was called upon to rebuke, like adultery, for example. Often these matters were not common knowledge then or now. It would be "embarrassing" to the family members of the persons involved if such communications were free to circulate around with the names of the offenders attached.

Out of Christian courtesy these writings were not published, or if they were, the names of the offenders were most often omitted. The original documents and letters were kept in the vault for safekeeping.

Enough time has passed so that the possibility of embarrassing someone no longer exists, for the offenders have all died, and there are typically a few generations between them and now. Therefore, the White Estate is working on putting every last thing on CD-ROM.

#29: "She claimed an angel stood by her bed near this chair in her bedroom."—David Snyder.

#29: She said she was visited by an angel. This really has no bearing on whether Adventism is a cult, for the Bible tells how an angel woke up Peter and came to visit Daniel (Acts 12:7; Dan. 9:21). All this point shows is that one of three possibilities is the case:

1. Mrs. White or Peter or Daniel was lying.

2. Mrs. White or Peter or Daniel was really visited by an angel of God.

3. Mrs. White or Peter or Daniel was actually visited by an evil angel in disguise.

The Bible tests of a prophet must be applied to determine which of the three possibilities Mrs. White's case falls into.

Her Predictions and Views

#30 & #31: "It's a matter of historical record that the following prophecies of Ellen G. White did not come true as she foretold. 'Then I was pointed to some who are in the great error of believing that it is their duty to go to Old Jerusalem, and think that they have work to do there before the Lord comes... I saw that Satan had greatly deceived some in this thing... I also saw that Old Jerusalem never would be built up...' Early Writings p. 75. The exact opposite of Ellen White's prediction has happened. Old Jerusalem has been greatly built up in the years since 1948 when Israel became a nation. She was absolutely wrong."—Sydney Cleveland.

#30: Her prophecies did not come true. Not one valid example is given by Mr. Cleveland in the discussion that follows.

#31: Her prediction about Jerusalem not being built up failed. Her words are being misconstrued.

A similar statement found on page 136 of her book *Maranatha* has this modern-day note attached: "Written in the early 1850's when 'the age-to-come' advocates taught that old Jerusalem would be built up as a center of Christian witness fulfilling certain prophecies of the O.T." Support for this meaning of the phrase "built up" can be found in the February 28, 1856, issue of *Review and Herald*. It gives the following statement which it goes on to refute:

> ISA.liv,1-10. The expressions in this chapter cannot refer to the New Jerusalem; the same that has been forsaken, desolate, &c., is to be built up in the future age. (See Age to Come, by J. Marsh, pp. 66,67.)—J. H. Waggoner, "Objections Answered," p. 169.

In the May 7, 1857, issue, Alvarez Pierce wrote:

> There is no one that regards the Sabbath here, yet there is one family right on the immortality question, but otherwise they are on the "Age-to-Come" doctrine, and that I cannot endorse. I believe that when Christ comes it will not be to restore the carnal Jew, and to build up old Jerusalem, but it will be to take vengeance on his enemies.—p. 6.

In the 1842 third volume of *Miller's Works*, Miller says, "Although our Judaizing teachers tell us the Jews are to be built up again, I believe them not."—p. 67. He didn't say *"Jerusalem."* He said *"Jews."* He's not talking about the number of buildings. Rather, he's talking about the Jews and Old Jerusalem occupying an extraordinarily special place in God's workings either in the last days or during the millennium.

The phrase "built up" is also found in the Psalms: "The LORD doth build up Jerusalem: he gathereth together the outcasts of Israel" (Ps. 147:2). What might this mean?

As pointed out under #17, the Millerites firmly believed in the Pauline teaching of spiritual Israel. Such concepts were inherited from them by the early Seventh-day Adventists. Thus, those who accept Christ were viewed as being grafted into Israel:

> And if some of the branches [literal Jews] be broken off, and thou [a Gentile], being a wild olive tree, wert graffed in among them, and with them partakest of the root and fatness of the olive tree . . . . Thou wilt say then, The branches were broken off, that I might be graffed in. Well; because of unbelief they were broken off, and thou standest by faith. (Rom. 11:17-20)

So what would Psalm 147:2 mean to a Millerite or early Seventh-day Adventist, if they had viewed it as a prophecy for the last days? It would have been considered a prediction of the gathering together of all believers, both Jew and Gentile, into either the New Jerusalem or the church.

Old Testament prophecies concerning literal Israel's return to Palestine were generally seen to be fulfilled when the Jews returned from Babylon in the sixth century BC. As Miller put it,

> As it respects the Jews return, I say there is not a text, promise or prophecy, written or given of God,

which was not given before their return from Babylon, and I believe was then literally fulfilled. —*Miller's Works*, vol. 1, p. 233.

Many feel that Jerusalem will be a center for God's activities in the last days, and so will disagree with the statement of Mrs. White that Mr. Cleveland quoted. But then it becomes an issue of a difference in theology rather than a false prophecy.

Encyclopædia Britannica has this to say in its article on Jerusalem: "By the mid-19th century half of the city's population was Jewish, and it was expanding beyond the walls."—"Jerusalem: History: Modern Jerusalem." Since Jerusalem was indeed inhabited, inhabitable, and growing when Mrs. White wrote the statement in question, the alternative meaning of the phrase "built up" is in order.

The simple fact is that Jerusalem is still not "built up" in the sense she was using the phrase. Until it has been, this statement by Mrs. White cannot truthfully be called a false prophecy.

#32: "Again, Mrs. White foretold in *Early Writings* that she would be among the living saints when Jesus returned. 'Soon our eyes were drawn to the East, for a small black cloud had appeared, about half as large as a man's hand, which we all knew was the sign of the Son of Man... the graves opened... and in the same moment we were changed and caught up together with them to meet the Lord in the air.' The Day-Star January 24, 1846. Mrs. White was not among the living saints seen in her vision. This event did not occur in her lifetime. We are still looking for the glorious return of our Lord Jesus Christ. Rather than being caught up with the living saints at Jesus's return, Mrs. White died on July 16, 1915, and was buried beside her husband James. Another one of her prophecies failed."—Sydney Cleveland.

#32: She said she would be among the living saints. She never said that. Moreover, this charge destroys the credibility of the Scriptures, for it in essence declares the apostle Paul to be a false prophet.

The reader will notice that this quotation from Mrs. White is very close in wording to 1 Thessalonians 4:16, 17, where Paul says essentially the same thing:

For the Lord himself shall *descend* from heaven with a shout, with the voice of the archangel, and with the *trump* of God: and *the dead* in Christ shall rise first: Then *we* which are alive and remain shall be *caught up together with them* in the clouds, *to meet the Lord in the air*: and so shall we ever be with the Lord.

Some portions of the quotation from *The Day-Star* that the video left out make the parallels with 1 Thessalonians 4 even more striking:

Then Jesus' silver *trumpet* sounded, as he *descended* on the cloud . . . . The graves opened, and *the dead* came up clothed with immortality. . . . and in the same moment we were changed and *caught up together with them to meet the Lord in the air.*—italics added.

If Paul can say, "We which are alive and remain shall be caught up," and not be a false prophet, then Mrs. White can too.

In the Bible, God chose to reveal events in vision to a prophet as if he were alive at the time the events were taking place, and sometimes as if he were even participating in those events. The book of Revelation gives a number of examples of this phenomenon. Thus, a prophet who saw future events in vision as if he were participating in those events is not necessarily a false prophet.

#33: "Like others of her time, Mrs. White taught the imminent end of the world to spur on her workers. In *Early Writings* in the 1850's she urged the new converts on, telling them they had only a few months to wait. '...But now time is almost finished, and what we have been years learning, they will have to learn in a few months.' A Sketch of the Christian Experience and Views of Ellen G. White p. 55."—Sydney Cleveland.

#33: She said Christ would return in a few months. She said no such thing. The careful reader will note that her statement merely says that believers will be learning more quickly than they previously did.

Mrs. White attached the date of June 27, 1850, to the vision this quote comes from (*Early Writings*, p. 64). In 1854 she wrote basically the same thing:

Truths that we have been years learning *must be learned in a few months* by those who now embrace the Third Angel's Message. We had to search and wait the opening of truth, receiving a ray of light here and a ray there, laboring and pleading for God to reveal truth to us. But now the truth is plain; its rays are brought together. . . . There is no need of milk after souls are convinced of the truth. . . . It is a disgrace for those who have been in the truth for years to talk of feeding souls who have been *months in the truth,* upon milk. It shows they know little of the leadings of the Spirit of the Lord, and realize not the time we are living in.—*Manuscript Releases*, vol. 1, p. 33, italics added.

Notice the similarities in thought of this passage and Hebrews 5:11-6:3. According to Mrs. White, it is disgraceful to think that new believers must spend years learning the basics, the milk. Paul likewise urged that believers move on from the "milk" to the "strong meat."

Generally speaking, the new believer learns today in a few months the truths of God's word that took years back then to hammer out. Mrs. White's words are literally true.

Besides, if she were predicting a date for Christ's return, she would be contradicting the statements she made during the same time frame that opposed setting dates for Christ's return (see #14 and #17).

Please note: The video quoted from her September 23, 1850, vision under #17, a vision that opposed date setting. The contributors to the video should have noticed this inconsistency in their logic. To quote from an 1850 vision that was against date setting, and then to unnecessarily portray another 1850 vision as setting dates does not make sense.

One other inconsistency: The statement in question was first published in 1851 in *Experience and Views*, and was then republished in *Early Writings* in 1882. Mr. Ratzlaff says on the video that embarrassing material was deleted in later publications (see #52, #53). Why then was this statement still included in *Early Writings* if it really means what Mr. Cleveland says it means?

#34: **"These were not isolated prophecies, but restated over and over again. In May 1856 at a church meeting in Battle Creek, Michigan, Mrs. White boldly stated, 'I saw that some of those present would be food for worms, some subjects for the seven last plagues, and some would be translated to heaven at the second coming of Christ, without seeing death.' Spiritual Gifts, Vol. 2 p. 208."**—Sydney Cleveland.

#34: This "food for worms" vision did not come true. Will the reader please note the sentences immediately following the portion quoted?

> Sr. [Clarissa] Bonfoey remarked to a sister as we left the meeting-house, "I feel impressed that I am one that will soon be food for worms." The conference closed Monday. Thursday Sr. B. sat at the table with us apparently well. She then went to the Office as usual, to help get off the paper. In about two hours I was sent for. Sr. B. had been suddenly taken very ill. My health had been very poor, yet I hastened to suffering Clara. In a few hours she seemed some better. The next morning we had her brought home in a large chair, and she was laid upon her own bed from which she was never to rise. Her symptoms

became alarming, and we had fears that a tumor, which had troubled her for nearly ten years, had broken inwardly. It was so, and mortification was doing its work.

> Friday about seven o'clock she fell asleep.—*Spiritual Gifts*, pp. 208, 209.

Within days of Mrs. White's statement, a lady who thought she would be one of those who would be "food for worms" was. Thus a remarkable fulfillment of the prophecy did take place.

What about the part of the vision that said some would still be alive when Jesus came? The next point will address this question.

#35: **"In biblical times she would have been stoned to death for being a false prophet."**—Sydney Cleveland.

#35: She was a false prophet for teaching that Christ would come in her day. This same charge is used by liberal theologians to undermine the authority of Scripture. The apostles, they say, believed and taught Christ would come in their day.

They were wrong, they say. Therefore, they say, the Bible contains errors.

There are some verses in the New Testament which seem to support this attack on Scripture, such as 1 Thessalonians 4:17. Paul in this passage appears to say that some believers alive in his day would still be alive when Jesus returned. Yet this interpretation of his words must be wrong, for Paul makes it crystal clear in 2 Thessalonians 2:1-4 that Christ's return was not imminent in his day.

Should Jonah have been stoned because he said Nineveh would be destroyed in forty days, but it wasn't (Jonah 3:4, 10)? Should Huldah have been stoned because she said Josiah would die in peace, but he didn't (2 Chr. 34:22-28; 35:20-24)? Is this what Mr. Cleveland is saying?

Jonah and Huldah were not false prophets, for their prophecies were based on the conditions of Nineveh's continued unrepentance and Josiah's continued obedience. Since Nineveh repented, it was not destroyed. Since Josiah disobeyed, the promised blessing of dying in peace could not be fulfilled.

> At what instant I shall speak concerning a nation, and concerning a kingdom, to pluck up, and to pull down, and to destroy it; If that nation, against whom I have pronounced, turn from their evil, I will repent of the evil that I thought to do unto them. And at what instant I shall speak concerning a nation, and concerning a kingdom, to build and to plant it; If it do evil in my sight, that it obey not my voice, then I will repent of the good, wherewith I said I would benefit them. (Jer. 18:7-10)

According to Jeremiah, some prophecies are therefore definitely conditional.

The Bible clearly says that the gospel must be preached in all the world before Christ returns (Mat. 24:14). If His people are lax in reaching the lost, then Christ's coming will be delayed. In 1883 Mrs. White explained that Christ's coming had been delayed for this very reason (*Evangelism*, p. 695), and she made similar statements over the years.

The 1883 statement was made just twenty-seven years after the 1856 one Mr. Cleveland quoted from. Since a good portion of those present at the 1856 conference were still strong and healthy in 1883, the latter statement is not an attempt to explain why the former prophecy "failed."

#36: "Mrs. White did not confine her prophesying to the events surrounding the coming of the Lord, but prophesied how foreign governments would act against the United States. In 1862 Ellen White predicted the downfall of the United States following a great war involving many nations."—Sydney Cleveland.

#36: She predicted the downfall of the United States. Not really. Technically, she predicted that *if* our nation remained divided, *then* it would fall:

> England is acquainted with the diversity of feeling among those who are seeking to quell the rebellion. She well knows the perplexed condition of our Government; she has looked with astonishment at the prosecution of this war—the slow, inefficient moves, the inactivity of our armies, and the ruinous expenses of our nation. The weakness of our Government is fully open before other nations, and they now conclude that it is because it was not a monarchial government, and they admire their own government, and look down, some with pity, others with contempt, upon our nation, which they have regarded as the most powerful upon the globe. Had our nation remained united it would have had strength, but divided it must fall.—*Testimonies for the Church*, vol. 1, pp. 259, 260.

It would be hard to refute such an assessment. But Mrs. White did not say that our nation would definitely remain divided.

In the same chapter she wrote at length about how the North had often mistreated escaped slaves and returned them to their southern masters, in direct violation of the Word of God (Deut. 23:15). Yet the government, rather than righting these wrongs, declared a day of fasting and prayer to ask God's blessing on the war effort!

> And yet a national fast is proclaimed! Saith the Lord: "Is not this the fast that I have chosen? to loose the bands of wickedness, to undo the heavy burdens, and to let the oppressed go free, and that ye break every yoke?" *When* our nation observes the fast which God has chosen, *then* will He accept their prayers as far as the war is concerned; but now they enter not into His ear. He turns from them, they are disgusting to Him. It is so managed that those who would undo the heavy burdens and break every yoke are placed under censure, or removed from responsible stations, or their lives are planned away by those who "fast for strife and debate, and to smite with the fist of wickedness."—*Ibid.*, p. 258, italics added.

Clearly, this is a conditional prophecy (see #35). *When* the North would seek to break every yoke, *then* God would hear their prayers and bless. But *if* the North remained divided over the slavery question, *then* it would fall.

#37: "During the Civil War she prophesied that England would declare war on the northern states, and humble them into the dust. 'Said the angel... when England does declare war, all nations will have an interest of their own to serve, and there will be general war, general confusion... this nation will yet be humbled in the dust...' *Testimonies for the Church* vol. 1 p. 259"—Sydney Cleveland.

#37: She predicted that England would declare war. Actually, this quotation was altered by someone. "This nation will yet be humbled in the dust..." is a complete sentence standing on its own. Rather than coming at the *end* of the selection, it is actually the sixth sentence *preceding* the sentence "When England does declare war . . . ." The intervening five sentences that were deleted neutralize the point being made:

England is studying *whether* it is best to take advantage of the present weak condition of our nation, and venture to make war upon her. She is weighing the matter, and trying to sound other nations. She fears, *if* she should commence war abroad, that she would be weak at home, and that other nations would take advantage of her weakness. Other nations are making quiet yet active preparations for war, and are hoping that England will make

war with our nation, for then they would improve the opportunity to be revenged on her for the advantage she has taken of them in the past and the injustice done them. A portion of the queen's subjects are waiting a favorable opportunity to break their yoke; but *if* England thinks it will pay, she will not hesitate a moment to improve her opportunities to exercise her power and humble our nation.—italics added.

Clearly, Mrs. White's prediction was what would happen *if* England declared war, not that England *would* declare war.

The *documentation package* merely gives under "Point 22" a copy of *Testimonies for the Church*, vol. 1, pages 259, 260. This copy adequately documents the fact that the quotation as it appears on the video isn't genuine, and that the context of the quotation neutralizes the point being made by the video.

#38 & #39: "History proves the utter error of this prophecy. England did not declare war on the northern states. Other nations did not join in."—Sydney Cleveland.

#38: Her prophecies about the Civil War were erroneous. The honest reader who peruses the context of the passage in question will be surprised at how solid the information really is.

"Had our nation remained united it would have had strength, but divided it must fall."—*Testimonies for the Church*, vol. 1, p. 260. Many today assume that the Civil War was fought over slavery. Historians declare, as Mrs. White has written, that this was not the initial motivation for the war. Rather, it was fought to maintain the Union. Many enlistees thought they were fighting to abolish slavery, but those in charge of the war had no such intention. We were a nation divided.

Once Lincoln passed the Emancipation Proclamation during the year after Mrs. White wrote these things, and the North became united in its goal of abolishing slavery, then the tide began to turn in favor of the North. We can thank the Lord that the North did unite so that our nation did not fall.

I was shown that if the object of this war had been to exterminate slavery, then, if desired, England would have helped the North. But England fully understands the existing feelings in the Government, and that the war is not to do away slavery, but

merely to preserve the Union; and it is not for her interest to have it preserved.—*Ibid.*, p. 258.

The *World Book Encyclopedia* says under "Emancipation Proclamation,"

As a result, it greatly influenced the North's victory in the war. . . .

As the abolitionists had predicted, the Emancipation Proclamation strengthened the North's war effort and weakened the South's. . . .

The Emancipation Proclamation also hurt the South by discouraging Britain and France from entering the war. Both of those nations depended on the South to supply them with cotton, and the Confederacy hoped that they would fight on its side. But the proclamation made the war a fight against slavery. Most British and French citizens opposed slavery, and so they gave their support to the Union.

World Book thus makes it crystal clear that England was considering entering the war. It was the North's uniting against slavery that prevented England from doing so, and this is precisely how Mrs. White described the political situation of those times.

There are other predictions that she made. For example, she predicted the demise of the South six months before their fortunes started sinking at Gettysburg:

> In regard to the South, I was referred to Deuteronomy 32:35-37: "To Me belongeth vengeance, and recompense; their foot shall slide in due time: for the day of their calamity is at hand, and the things that shall come upon them make haste."—*Testimonies for the Church*, vol. 1, p. 368.

Who told her that the "foot" of the South would "slide in due time" while they were still doing quite well? Who told her that that day was "at hand"?

Then there is Mrs. White's January 12, 1861, vision at Parkville, Michigan. After it she said:

> "Men are making light of the secession ordinance that has been passed by South Carolina. They have little idea of the trouble that is coming on our land. No one in this house has even dreamed of the trouble that is coming.
>
> "I have just been shown in vision that a number of States are going to join South Carolina in this secession, and a terrible war will be the result. In the vision I saw large armies raised by both the North and the South. I was shown the battle raging. I heard the booming of the cannon, and saw the dead and wounded falling on every side. I was then taken to hospitals, and saw the sufferings of the sick and wounded prisoners. I was taken in the vision to the homes of those who had lost sons, brothers, or husbands in the war. There was distress and mourning all over the land."
>
> . . . "There are men in this house who will lose sons in that war."—Arthur White, vol. 1, p. 463.

Only one state had seceded, and the general sentiment in the North was that the whole rebellion was going to vaporize. For most, war was nowhere on the horizon, and yet Mrs. White was already predicting a terrible civil war!

"There are men in this house who will lose sons in that war." Judge Osborne and Mr. Shellhouse were present. They thought her prediction utterly absurd, but one year later they wept at the mention of the vision. The one had lost his only son, and the other had lost one son, with a second son somewhere down South in jail.—John Loughborough, *Miracles in My Life*, p. 57.

#39: She predicted world war. Fascinating subject. She actually predicted two world wars, as we shall see.

> Other nations are making quiet yet active preparations for war . . . . When England does declare war, all nations will have an interest of their own to serve, and there will be general war, general confusion. . . . A portion of the queen's subjects are waiting a favorable opportunity to break their yoke . . . .—*Testimonies for the Church*, vol. 1, p. 259.

The phrases "general war," "general confusion," and "active preparations for war" of "other nations" bring to mind page 268 of the same book. On that page is a prediction of two times of world war separated by a little time of peace:

> Other nations are intently watching this nation, for what purpose I was not informed, and are making great preparations for some event. . . .
>
> I was shown the inhabitants of the earth in the utmost confusion. War, bloodshed, privation, want, famine, and pestilence were abroad in the land.
>
> My attention was then called from the scene. There seemed to be a little time of peace. Once more the inhabitants of the earth were presented before me; and again everything was in the utmost confusion. Strife, war, and bloodshed, with famine and pestilence, raged everywhere. Other nations were engaged in this war and confusion. War caused famine. Want and bloodshed caused pestilence. And then men's hearts failed them for fear, "and for looking after those things which are coming on the earth."

"When England does declare war, all nations will have an interest of their own to serve, and there will be general war, general confusion." Out of the twenty-eight nations or more that fought in World War I, England was the fifth or sixth to declare war. And in World War II, after a little time of peace, England was among the first six nations to declare war out of at least fifty-eight.

"A portion of the queen's subjects are waiting a favorable opportunity to break their yoke . . . ." England ruled about a fourth of the world's land and people, and then lost it all as her colonies sought their independence about the time of the world wars. How interesting that Mrs. White connected England's declaring war and world war with this very thing!

She never said, "When England does declare war *on the United States* . . . ." She said, "When England does declare war . . . ." There is a difference.

As Mr. Cleveland almost said, "History proves the utter" truth "of this prophecy."

#40: "The United States of America was not humbled into the dust in defeat. Mrs. White again clearly to the objective mind prophesied falsely."—Sydney Cleveland.

#40: She said the US would be humbled into the dust in defeat. She never said "in defeat." The facts are these:

1. Our nation had been proud.
2. Other nations were disgusted at how we were conducting the Civil War.
3. We were humbled into the dust.

Consider the following from her pen:

This war is a most singular and at the same time a most horrible and heartsickening conflict. Other nations are looking on with disgust at the transactions of the armies of both North and South. They see such a determined effort to protract the war at an enormous sacrifice of life and money, while at the same time nothing is really gained, that it looks to them like a strife to see which can kill the most men. They are indignant.—*Testimonies for the Church*, vol. 1, p. 367.

On January 20, 1863, the London *Times* reported the words of an American preacher who in prayer had "blessed the name of God for having so humbled the nation that it was compelled as a military necessity to ask the aid of the negro." On July 4th of the same year, the *Times* described that year's American Independence Day as "this day of festivity, now converted into a day of humiliation" (F. D. Nichol, *Ellen G. White and Her Critics*, p. 120).

Mr. Cleveland would have had a hard time convincing these "objective minds" that Mrs. White prophesied falsely.

#41: "Mrs. White in a vision also claimed to have traveled complete with wings to various planets which were full of inhabitants. She reported meeting Enoch on a distant planet during one of her journeys. Other times she saw angels using golden gate passes to go in and out of heaven." —Narrator.

#41: She went in vision to other planets. So? What difference does this make? Does this make her a false prophet?

Was John the Revelator a false prophet because he claimed that in vision he went to heaven and heard angels talking there (Rev. 4:1, 2; 5:11)? Was Ezekiel a false prophet because he claimed that in vision he was carried by a lock of his hair to another country (Ezek. 8:3)? Or was the apostle Paul a false prophet because he said he went to heaven, but whether he went there only in vision or actually with his body, he could not tell (2 Cor. 12:2-4, 7)?

Or is the problem the fact that she said there were other inhabited worlds? Does such a claim make her a false prophet? The Bible says that Christ made the "worlds," plural, using the Greek word *aion*, a word that does not mean uninhabited planets (Heb. 1:2; cf. 11:3). And Job says that the sons of God came for a special meeting. Satan got to be included because he claimed to be a representative from Earth, implying that the other participants in the meeting were also representatives from inhabited planets (Job 1:6, 7; 2:1, 2). Though one might disagree with these interpretations of Scripture, the matter cannot be construed into a clear-cut case for declaring someone to be a false prophet.

Under "Point 23" and "Point 24," the *documentation package* shows four quotations from two books proving that Mrs. White saw these things in vision. However, no evidence is offered to show why her seeing these things in vision is unscriptural, as claimed a few moments later (see #44).

#42 & #43: "Some of her so-called visions reflected her own racist views. For example, she believed that certain races of people [blacks are shown in the picture] were the result of sexual relations between man and animal, which she referred to as an amalgamation. 'Every species of animal which God had created were preserved in the ark. The confused species which God did not create, which were the result of amalgamation, were destroyed by the flood. Since the flood there has been amalgamation of man and beast, as may be seen in the almost endless varieties of species of animals, and in certain races of men.' Spiritual Gifts vol. 3 p. 75"—Narrator.

#42: She said that animals and people crossed sexually. She said no such thing. She never said that the amalgamation was through sexual relations.

Scientists today routinely mix the genes of various species, even putting animal genes into plants through genetic engineering. Since the Bible portrays man becoming more degenerate over time instead of more advanced, why could not ancient man have had such technology? It is evolution, not the Bible, that says that man is smarter today than he was back then.

While Mrs. White indicates that it was man doing the amalgamation before the Flood, she does not say who did it after the Flood. Elsewhere she does speak of Satan altering plants through some sort of process: "All tares are sown by the evil one. Every noxious herb is of his sowing, and by his ingenious methods of amalgamation he has corrupted the earth with tares."—*Selected Messages*, bk. 2, p. 288. So it is possible that it was Satan doing the post-Flood amalgamation instead of man.

As F. D. Nichol pointed out in his book *Ellen G. White and Her Critics*, she did not specifically say "amalgamation of man *with* beast." Thus there is room for his idea of there being amalgamation of man with man and beast with beast (pp. 308, 309).

What does this mean? Many interpret Genesis 6:2, which speaks of the sons of God marrying the daughters of men, to mean the same as what Mrs. White writes of in the August 23, 1892, issue of the *Review and Herald*:

> Those who profess to be followers of Christ, should be living agencies, co-operating with heavenly intelligences; but by union with the world, the character of God's people becomes tarnished, and through amalgamation with the corrupt, the fine gold becomes dim.

So amalgamation of man before the Flood could possibly mean intermarriage of believers with unbelievers, of the sons of God with the daughters of men.

Under "Point 25" the *documentation package* gives the identical quotation found on the video. It also gives another quotation that speaks of witnessing to "white people" in the South as well as for the "higher class." The compiler of the *documentation package*, being unacquainted with Mrs. White's writings, must

have equated the terms "white people" with "higher class," when in fact they mean something totally different. "Higher class" refers to economic and social status, not race (*Desire of Ages*, p. 550).

Mrs. White repeatedly encouraged witnessing to the wealthy class. Since the poor often seem more receptive than the wealthy, the latter are often neglected, but they need the gospel too, whether they be black or white.

Here are a few statements from her pen which were quite anti-racist:

> How little of the spirit of Christ has been manifested in the treatment given to the colored race in this so-called Christian country!—*Manuscript Releases*, vol. 4, p. 8.

> God has marked out no color line, and men should move very guardedly, lest we offend God. The Lord has not made two heavens, one for white people and one for colored people. There is but one heaven for the saved.—*Ibid.*, p. 33.

> When the Holy Spirit moves upon human minds, all petty complaints and accusations between man and his fellow man will be put away. . . . In our worship of God there will be no distinction between rich and poor, white and black. All prejudice will be melted away. When we approach God, it will be as one brotherhood.—*Selected Messages*, bk. 2, p. 487.

#43: As the picture illustrates, she taught that amalgamation produced the black race. Regardless of what she meant by "amalgamation," whether genetic engineering or intermarriage with unbelievers, she never said what races of men she was talking about. She never said "amalgamation" produced the black race. Why didn't the video use a picture of whites or Asians instead? Is it because it would not have been as inflammatory as a picture of blacks?

#44 & #45: "Despite the unbiblical nature of her visions, her followers continue to accept her as God's messenger and her writings as inspired as the Bible."—Narrator.

#44: Her visions are unbiblical. The video is begging the question here. So far not one aspect of her visions has been proven to be unbiblical. Visited by angels? Transported to heaven? So were the Bible writers.

One aspect of her visions that the video does not mention at all is the physical phenomena that occurred during them. Consider what Daniel wrote regarding a vision he had: "For how can the servant of this my lord talk with this my lord? for as for me, straightway there remained no strength in me, neither is there breath left in me" (Dan. 10:17). Daniel

while in vision did not breathe. Likewise, Mrs. White while in vision did not breathe. These visions would last from fifteen minutes to three hours. She was examined by physicians on several occasions while in vision, and their opinion was that she was not breathing. Consider this eyewitness account:

> The first is from M. G. Kellogg, M. D., who refers to the first vision given in Michigan, May 29, 1853, at a meeting held in the barn of Wm. Dawson, in Tyrone, Livingston Co. He says:-

> "Sister White was in vision about twenty minutes or half an hour. . . . Brother White arose and in-

formed the audience that his wife was in vision. After stating the manner of her visions, and that she did not breathe while in vision, he invited any one who wished to do so to come forward and examine her. Dr. Drummond, a physician, who was also a first-day Adventist preacher, who [before he saw her in vision] had declared her visions to be of mesmeric origin, and that he could give her a vision, stepped forward, and after a thorough examination, turned very pale, and remarked, *'She doesn't breathe!'*

"I am quite certain that she did not breathe at that time while in vision, nor in any of several others which she had when I was present. The coming out of vision was as marked as her going into it. The first indication we had that the vision was ended, was in her again beginning to breathe. She drew her first breath deep, long, and full, in a manner showing that her lungs had been entirely empty of air. After drawing the first breath, several minutes passed before she drew the second, which filled the lungs precisely as did the first: then a pause of two minutes, and a third inhalation, after which the breathing became natural." Signed, "M. G. Kellogg, M. D., Battle Creek, Mich., Dec. 28, 1890."—*General Conference Daily Bulletin*, Jan. 31, Feb. 1, 1893, pp. 59, 60.

While this aspect of her visions was very biblical, it must be pointed out that such phenomena do not prove that a prophet or vision is from God. They merely prove the supernatural character of those visions. The Bible tests of a prophet must then be applied to determine whether that supernatural source is God or Satan. This is a vital point, for Revelation 16:14 explicitly tells us that the devil can work miracles, and will work many at the end of time.

#45: Adventists claim her writings are as inspired as the Bible. The irrelevancy of this charge was already pointed out under #23.

Under "Point 26" the *documentation package* has an article from the December 23, 1982, issue of the *Review* to prove that Adventists believe that "her writings are as inspired as the Bible." But the article's ten affirmations and ten denials actually negate what the video is trying to prove:

Affirmations

1. We believe that Scripture is the divinely revealed Word of God and is inspired by the Holy Spirit.

2. We believe that the canon of Scripture is composed only of the 66 books of the Old and New Testaments.

3. We believe that Scripture is the foundation of faith and the final authority in all matters of doctrine and practice.

4. We believe that Scripture is the Word of God in human language.

5. We believe that Scripture teaches that the gift of prophecy will be manifest in the Christian church after New Testament times.

6. We believe that the ministry and writings of Ellen White were a manifestation of the gift of prophecy.

7. We believe that Ellen White was inspired by the Holy Spirit and that her writings, the product of that inspiration, are applicable and authoritative especially to Seventh-day Adventists.

8. We believe that the purposes of the Ellen White writings include guidance in understanding the teaching of Scripture and application of these teachings, with prophetic urgency, to the spiritual life.

9. We believe that the acceptance of the prophetic gift of Ellen White is important to the nurture and unity of the Seventh-day Adventist Church.

10. We believe that Ellen White's use of literary sources and assistants finds parallels in some of the writings of the Bible.

Denials

1. We do not believe that the quality or degree of inspiration in the writings of Ellen White is different from that of Scripture.

2. We do not believe that the writings of Ellen White are an addition to the canon of Sacred Scripture.

3. We do not believe that the writings of Ellen White function as the foundation and final authority of Christian faith as does Scripture.

4. We do not believe that the writings of Ellen White may be used as the basis of doctrine.

5. We do not believe that the study of the writings of Ellen White may be used to replace the study of Scripture.

6. We do not believe that Scripture can be understood only through the writings of Ellen White.

7. We do not believe that the writings of Ellen White exhaust the meaning of Scripture.

8. We do not believe that the writings of Ellen White are essential for the proclamation of the truths of Scripture to society at large.

9. We do not believe that the writings of Ellen White are the product of mere Christian piety.

10. We do not believe that Ellen White's use of literary sources and assistants negates the inspiration of her writings.

Pretty clear, isn't it? The contributors to the material in the video really ought to read this part of the *documentation package*. It would answer a lot of their questions.

The Investigative Judgment and Shut Door, and Their Ramifications

#46 & #47: "The investigative judgment doctrine that Seventh-day Adventists still cling to came from a reinterpretation of William Miller's failed prophecy that Christ would come to the earth on October 22, 1844."—Dale Ratzlaff.

#46: It's a reinterpretation. Not really. The whole Millerite movement was predicting that the day of judgment would occur around 1843 or 1844. That being so, it can't be a reinterpretation, for they already believed that.

Here's the evidence that Millerites were predicting the commencement of the judgment in the 1840's. First, we have William Miller as early as 1822 saying that he believed that the second coming and the judgment would take place at the same time:

> "ART. XVII. I believe in the resurrection, both of the just and of the unjust,—the just, or believers, at Christ's second coming, and the unjust one thousand years afterwards,—when the judgment of each will take place in their order, at their several resurrections; when the just will receive everlasting life, and the unjust eternal condemnation."—Bliss, p. 79.

From his "Lecture 1" printed in 1842, he clearly predicted the beginning of the judgment to take place about 1843. Included also is a bit of his appeal to sinners to give their hearts to Jesus:

> And now, my impenitent friends, what say you? . . . And are there no signs of the near approach of the Judgment Day? . . . "We say, 'You were very unwise to fix on the year 1843, or sooner, for this day to come; for it will not come; and then you will be ashamed." And I hope I may be able, by the grace of God, to repent. But what if it does come? You cannot with any propriety say positively it will not come, for you make no pretence to divination. But I say, what if it does come? Where will you be? No space then for repentance. No, no—too late, too late; the harvest is over and past, the summer is gone, the door is shut, and your soul is not saved. Therefore it can do you no harm to hear, and believe, and do those things which God requires of you, and which you think you would do, if you knew he would appear. First, I ask you to repent of your sins. Would this be

right? Yes. Next, I ask you to believe in God. Is this right? Yes. And I ask you to be reconciled to his will, love his law, forsake sin, love holiness, practice his precepts, obey his commands. Would these things be right? Yes, yes. And last of all, and not least, I ask you to "look for the blessed hope and the glorious appearing of the great God and our Savior Jesus Christ."—*Miller's Works*, vol. 2, pp. 26, 27.

The investigative judgment doctrine of Seventh-day Adventism came from a realization, not a reinterpretation, that the judgment did begin after all on October 22 as predicted, but that the second coming was yet future.

And it has to be something like that anyway, for Jesus said, "Behold, I come quickly; and my reward is with me, to give every man according as his work shall be" (Rev. 22:12). Since Jesus will have his rewards with Him when He comes, the judgment which determines what those rewards will be must have already taken place before He comes.

As the apostle Paul said, "Because he hath appointed a day, in the which he will judge the world" (Acts 17:31). Millerites before October 22 believed that the 2300-day prophecy of Daniel 8:14 pinpointed that "appointed" "day" (*Ibid.*, vol. 1, p. 129). And over 150 years later, Seventh-day Adventists still believe that the 2300 days pinpointed the commencement of the judgment.

#47: William Miller's prediction of October 22 failed. As brought out under #6, William Miller did not make the prediction, did not teach it, and never accepted it as the certain date when Christ would come.

But let's take a look at the whole question of the "failed prediction." Over and over again the video asks us to believe that the calculation of the 2300 days was in error. We have already looked at this question under #20, but let us look at it again.

Miller and the Millerites merely drew conclusions based on the teachings of some of the greatest scholars of several centuries. The general dates Miller arrived at could not be faulted. Consider the comments of one of his most learned opponents, Dr. George Bush of New York City University, from a letter to William Miller:

> I do not conceive your errors on the subject of chronology to be at all of a serious nature, or in fact to be very wide of the truth. In taking a day as the prophetical time for a year, I believe you are sustained by the soundest exegesis, as well as fortified by the high names of Mede, Sir Isaac Newton, Bishop Newton, Faber, Scott, Keith, and a host of others, who have long since come to substantially your conclusions on this head. They all agree that the leading periods mentioned by Daniel and John do actually expire about this age of the world; and it would be strange logic that would convict you of heresy for holding in effect the same views which stand forth so prominently in the notices of these eminent divines. . . .
>
> Your results in this field of inquiry do not strike me as so far out of the way as to affect any of the great interests of truth or duty.—*Advent Herald*, Mar. 6 and 13, 1844.

This opponent of Miller freely admits that many famous scholars of old agreed that the prophetic periods of the prophecies would end in Miller's day! What problem, then, did Dr. Bush see with Miller's interpretation? Why did he not become a Millerite if he thought his calculations were correct?

> Your error, as I apprehend, lies in another direction than your chronology. . . .
>
> You have entirely mistaken the nature of the events which are to occur when those periods have expired. This is the head and front of your expository offending. . . .
>
> The great event before the world is not its physical conflagration, but its moral regeneration. Although there is doubtless a sense in which Christ may be said to come in connection with the passing away of the fourth empire and of the ottoman power, and his kingdom to be illustriously established, yet that will be found to be a spiritual coming in the power of His gospel, in the ample outpouring of His spirit, and the glorious administration of His providence.—*Ibid.*

Dr. Bush didn't believe that Christ would literally come. He believed that the Scriptures that speak of Christ's coming should be taken symbolically, not literally. We cannot fault Miller for believing that the second coming would be literal like the Bible says, instead of spiritual like Dr. Bush believed.

That William Miller had a firm biblical footing for his teachings is attested by his basic agreement with the conclusions of multitudes of scholars spanning decades and centuries. Though his ideas were not free from error, the date of October 22, 1844, was correct. Or at least, no solid evidence to the contrary has been presented by his opponents back then or now.

#48 & #49: "At first Adventists believed that the door of mercy was shut on that date."—Dale Ratzlaff.

#48: They believed in a "shut door" of mercy. It's not hard to see why.

"As has been stated, Adventists were for a short time united in the belief that the door of mercy was shut. This position was soon abandoned."—Ellen White, *Spirit of Prophecy*, vol. 4, p. 271. When one understands what was happening in those days, this charge becomes irrelevant. Additionally, since Seventh-day Adventism did not yet exist, this is really an argument against the Millerite Movement and first-day Adventism, if it be an argument at all. ("First-day Adventists" is a general term for post-1844, Sunday-keeping Millerite groups.)

America has been called a Christian nation, yet we haven't acted very Christ-like at times. We used to own slaves. After we freed them, we had lynchings and cross burnings. Blacks couldn't eat in the same restaurants, use the same restrooms, or drink at the same water fountains as whites.

As the expected time for Christ to come approached and passed, a spirit seemed to take hold of those who did not believe in Miller's views. Reports include: meetings broken up by mobs; stones, eggs, snowballs, and spikes thrown at the speakers at meetings; some believers publicly whipped; and a lecturer almost tarred and feathered by a minister and mob (Eugene Durand, *Yours in the Blessed Hope, Uriah Smith*, p. 21; Bliss, p. 353; James White, *Life Incidents*, pp. 77, 78; *Bible Adventism*, p. 193; John N. Loughborough, *Great Second Advent Movement*, pp. 176, 177, 525).

Albert Barnes, the noted Presbyterian author of *Barnes' Commentary*, told of the spiritual declension of those times:

At a recent meeting of the Presbytery of Philadelphia, Rev. Mr. Barnes, pastor of the 1st Presbyterian Church in Philadelphia, whose notes are so extensively used in our families and Sabbath-schools, stated that he had been in the ministry for twenty years, and never till the last communion had he administered the ordinance without receiving more or less to the church. But now there are no awakenings, no conversions, not much apparent growth in grace in professors, and none come to his study to converse about the salvation of their souls. With the increase of business, and the brightening prospects of commerce and manufactures, there is an increase of worldly-mindedness. Thus it is with all denominations. —*Congregational Journal*, May 23, 1844.

The spiritual condition of the nation as a whole and the churches in particular had reached a low ebb. Consider also the words of revivalist Charles Finney and an unknown author:

In the month of February of the same year, Professor Finney of Oberlin College said: "We have had the fact before our minds, that, in general, the Protestant churches of our country, as such, were either apathetic or hostile to nearly all the moral reforms of the age. There are partial exceptions, yet not enough to render the fact otherwise than general. We have also another corroborated fact: the almost universal absence of revival influence in the churches. The spiritual apathy is almost all-pervading, and is fearfully deep; so the religious press of the whole land testifies. . . . Very extensively, church members are becoming devotees of fashion,—join hands with the ungodly in parties of pleasure, in dancing, in festivities, etc. . . . But we need not expand this painful subject. Suffice it that the evidence thickens and rolls heavily upon us, to show that the *churches generally are becoming sadly degenerate*. They have gone very far from the Lord, and He has withdrawn Himself from them."

And a writer in the *Religious Telescope* testified: "We have never witnessed such a general declension of religion as at the present. Truly, the church should awake, and search into the cause of this affliction; for as an affliction everyone that loves Zion must view it. When we call to mind how 'few and far between' cases of true conversion are, and the almost unparalleled impertinence and hardness of sinners, we almost involuntarily exclaim, 'Has God forgotten to be gracious? or, Is the door of mercy closed?' "—*Great Controversy*, p. 377.

It sure seemed like it.

As pointed out under #12, the term "shut door" comes from the parable of the ten virgins. It is also derived from the following verse:

When once the master of the house is risen up, and hath shut to the door, and ye begin to stand without, and to knock at the door, saying, Lord, Lord, open unto us; and he shall answer and say unto you, I know you not whence ye are. (Luke 13:25)

These parables indicate that at some point the bridegroom who is Christ will come, and the door to the wedding feast will be shut. Then the five foolish virgins will try to get in and won't be able to.

The Millerites had been teaching that Christ would come on October 22, and that probation, the door of mercy, would then close. It was only natural for them to think that it had indeed closed on that date, especially given the spiritual declension of the churches and the continual harassment by mobs. No more sinners wanted to hear their preaching, so why should they think they still had a mission to preach to sinners?

#49: They've got to be wrong if they believed this. Besides being irrelevant, this whole objection is an inadvertent attack on the New Testament. Those who have read through the book of Acts will remember that the early church was of the opinion that no Gentile could be saved. Before the door of mercy could be opened for a Gentile, that Gentile had to become a Jew.

To convince them otherwise, God sent Peter the vision recorded in Acts 10. This vision corrected his misunderstanding that the door of mercy was shut to the Gentiles, and he went and preached to Cornelius, the Roman centurion.

When he got back to Jerusalem, the elders met with him to reprimand him, for they were certain that Gentiles could not repent and be saved. Peter recounted his vision and his experience at Cornelius's house, after which the record says, "When they heard these things, they held their peace, and glorified God, saying, Then hath God also to the Gentiles granted repentance unto life" (Acts 11:18).

To be consistent, if we must automatically reject Mrs. White and first-day Adventism for their misunderstanding, we must reject the apostles and Christianity as well, for they made the same error.

Many Christians still believe something similar today. Calvinists teach that everyone is already predestinated to be saved or lost, and there really isn't anything anyone can do about it. The door of mercy for the strict Calvinist is shut to all those who have been predestinated to damnation.

This writer doesn't agree with such a teaching, but he isn't going to call all the Calvinist churches cults because they teach such.

#50: "Ellen G. White with prophetic authority supported both this date and the shut-door belief."—Dale Ratzlaff.

#50: She supported the shut-door-of-mercy doctrine. While she did support the date of October 22, she never had a vision supporting the shut-door-of-mercy belief:

> With my brethren and sisters, after the time passed in forty-four I did believe no more sinners would be converted. But I never had a vision that no more sinners would be converted. And am clear and free to state no one has ever heard me say or has read from my pen statements which will justify them in the charges they have made against me upon this point.
>
> It was on my first journey east [February 1845] to relate my visions that the precious light in regard to the heavenly sanctuary was opened before me and I was shown the open and shut door. We believed that the Lord was soon to come in the clouds of heaven. I was shown that there was a great work to be done in the world for those who had not had the light and rejected it. Our brethren could not understand this with our faith in the immediate appearing of Christ. Some accused me of saying that my Lord delayeth His coming, especially the fanatical ones. . . .
>
> I never have stated or written that the world was doomed or damned. I never have under any circumstances used this language to any one, however sinful. I have ever had messages of reproof for those who used these harsh expressions.—*Selected Messages,* bk. 1, p. 74.

From this quotation it appears that she believed in no more mercy for sinners for a period of time between October 1844 and February 1845. And for part of even that short period, she had given up the idea that the "shut door" had already occurred (see #12).

As pointed out under #49, it was a vision that corrected the apostolic church and Peter's false idea that the door of mercy was shut for Gentiles. Likewise, it was the vision of February 1845 that corrected the misunderstanding of first-day Advent-

ists. One difference though: Mrs. White was mistaken for a few months at most. Peter and the apostles, it would appear, were mistaken for a few years. They were mistaken for a much longer period of time than Mrs. White.

Despite Peter's vision, some early Christians still held onto their false concepts for years, necessitating the council of Acts 15 at least fourteen years later (Gal. 2:1). Still the idea did not die, and Paul had to write his epistle to the Galatians even later.

If a few former Millerites were likewise a bit slow in properly comprehending Mrs. White's visions on this topic, let it be remembered that some members of the early church were even slower.

Mrs. White had another vision along the same lines in 1847. In this one she was shown a large, future evangelistic thrust:

> I saw that God had children, who do not see and keep the Sabbath. They had not rejected the light on it. And at the commencement of the time of trouble, we were filled with the Holy Ghost as we went forth and proclaimed the Sabbath more fully.—*Word to the Little Flock,* p. 19; also in *Early Writings,* p. 33.

On January 5, 1849, came still another vision which taught that every case had not yet been decided for salvation or damnation. God's wrath had not been and could not be poured out upon the wicked because Christ's intercession had not yet ceased (*Present Truth,* Aug. 1849; *Early Writings,* p. 36). Over and over again, "Ellen G. White with prophetic authority" opposed "the shut-door[-of-mercy] belief."

Under "Point 27" in the *documentation package,* the quotation under #51 is given, but neither in it nor in its full context does Mrs. White once mention a "door of mercy," whether open or shut. No proof is given that she ever had a vision endorsing the idea that there was no more mercy for sinners.

#51: "Her first vision contained a fearful judgment on Adventists who had given up the 1844 message called the midnight cry. She said they had fallen off the path to heaven. 'It was just as impossible for them to get on the path again and go to the city as all the wicked world which God had rejected...' The Day-Star January 24, 1846."—Dale Ratzlaff.

#51: Her first vision taught the shut-door-of-mercy doctrine. This is not true.

The first published account of her vision in the January 24, 1846, issue of *The Day-Star* is taken from a letter written by Mrs. White to Eli Curtis, the editor

of that journal. The last sentence of her letter says, "This was not written for publication; but for the encouragement of all who may see it, and be encouraged by it." We may therefore expect that the wording is not perfect.

Mrs. White testified:

> These two classes are brought to view in the vision—those who declared the light which they had followed a delusion, and the wicked of the world who, having rejected the light, had been rejected of God. No reference is made to those who had not seen the light, and therefore were not guilty of its rejection.—*Selected Messages*, bk. 1, p. 64.

Therefore, her first vision was not teaching that there was no more mercy for sinners. The statement in question is only dealing with those who had *rejected* light, not those who had never yet seen the light. This thought is also expressed in the quote about her February 1845 vision cited under #50.

To the contrary, her first vision taught that there was still mercy for sinners. In that vision she saw "the living saints, 144,000 in number," who were alive at the second coming. The 144,000 are mentioned a total of six times, yet there were only 50,000 Millerites in 1844, and her vision pictured many of these falling off the path. Obviously, since there would have to be a lot of evangelism to get the number up to a literal 144,000, the door of mercy could not yet be shut.

The Jewish leaders of Jesus's day rejected light and hardened their hearts to the point that they could no longer be reached with the gospel. Likewise, those who rejected the light to that point in 1844, the light regarding Christ's coming being literal and soon, could no longer be reached.

#52: "Years later, when her first vision was reprinted, even though the preface stated that no changes were made in idea or sentiment, the portion of her vision which taught the shut door to salvation was just left out. [Picture of the July 21, 1851, issue of *Review and Herald* shown.]"—Dale Ratzlaff.

#52: The preface said there was no change. The entire preface to the reprinted vision can be read, and one will fail to find any such statement saying that there were no changes in idea or sentiment. Instead, one will read:

> Here I will give the view that was first published in 1846. In this view I saw only a very few of the events of the future. More recent views have been more full. I shall therefore leave out a portion and prevent repetition.

We leave it with the reader to determine whether a statement saying that a portion was left out should be used to prove that there were no changes in idea or sentiment.

Under "Point 28" in the *documentation package*, the only evidence for this charge is a secondary source which quotes the last two sentences of the paragraph quoted above. Thus the *documentation package* substantiates that the preface said "a portion" was left out. It also substantiates that it is the 1851 reprinting the video is referring to, not a later one.

On January 4, 2000, Dale Ratzlaff emailed the present writer a few answers to his questions regarding parts of the video. He began by saying, "A few quick answers but first a note or two: I was not the one to edit this video. I would have done it much differently. I feel that some of the material would have been better left out or changed."

Would Mr. Ratzlaff have left out his own referral to a statement that does not exist?

The vision in question was first published in the January 24, 1846, issue of *Day-Star*. Then it was printed in a broadside on April 6 of that year. In May 1847 it was printed in *A Word to the Little Flock*. These printings all contained the sentence that Mr. Ratzlaff under #51 found so objectionable, though each did contain other sorts of minor editorial changes.

The next printing in the *Girdle of Truth, and Advent Review*, Extra, of January 20, 1848, indeed left the sentence out. This printing was done by Eli Curtis, not James or Ellen White.

In the July 1851 *Review* Extra the vision was reprinted once again, with a "portion" left out that included the sentence in question. Why was the sentence left out? Did the version of the vision being reprinted already have the sentence deleted? Such is possible. Or, were the Whites trying to avoid folk giving the sentence a meaning it was never intended to have? This too is possible.

One month later, *Sketches of the Christian Experience and Views of Mrs. E. G. White* was published. It included the version of the vision printed in the *Review* the month before. "Years later," in 1882, *Early Writings* was published, which reprinted *Experience and Views* along with two other works. The "publisher's preface" of this 1882 reprinting stated:

> "Aside from [footnotes and an appendix], no changes from the original work have been made in the present edition, except the occasional employment of a new word, or a change in the construction of a sentence, to better express the idea, and no portion of the work has been omitted. No shadow of change has been made in any idea or sentiment of the original

work, and the verbal changes have been made under the author's own eye, and with her full approval."
—*Early Writings*, 1945 ed., III, IV.

Of course that's true. There were no changes in "idea or sentiment" in *Early Writings*, for *Experience and Views* already contained the deletion in question!

The "change" appeared by 1851, and the 1882 reprinting was an authentic copy of the one of 1851.

Thus in the end we succeed in finding the elusive words that Mr. Ratzlaff used, words written thirty-one years later than what the video alleges, words that do not help the video's case at all.

#53 & #54: "After 1851 the other shut door passages were either dropped or reinterpreted."—Dale Ratzlaff.

#53: There were other shut door passages. What other passages? The *documentation package* does not mention any other alleged shut-door passages in Mrs. White's writings. Indeed, there really aren't any that speak of a shut door of mercy, that say that no more sinners will ever be converted.

Not that some don't try to manufacture others. Take for example the place where she speaks of apostate ministers who no longer had a burden for souls (*Early Writings*, pp. 42-45). Immediately after writing this out in March of 1849, she penned the following: "We know we have the truth, the midnight cry is behind us, the door was shut in 1844 and Jesus is soon to step out from between God and man."—*Manuscript Releases*, vol. 5, p. 200. Now if Jesus is soon to step out from between God and man, He must still be there now, and thus there must still be mercy for sinners!

#54: They were reinterpreted after 1851. The "reinterpretations" referred to surfaced long before 1851, for it is a simple fact that the term "shut door" amongst Millerites meant a number of different things:

1. A shut door of mercy for all sinners.
2. A shut door of mercy for those who have persistently rejected truth.
3. A shut door of access to the people to present God's message.
4. A shut door to the Holy Place of the heavenly sanctuary, since Christ's ministry is now in the Most Holy Place.

When one reads the term "shut door" in a Millerite publication, one has to be careful to choose the correct definition of the term. If the context does not indicate which meaning is intended, it may not be possible to know for sure what the speaker or writer meant.

Further explanations of these four usages follow, taken in part from P. Gerard Damsteegt's *Foundations of the Seventh-day Adventist Message and Mission*, pages 106 ff.

1. Shut "door of mercy" for all sinners. While this was the initial view of the subject, "it was soon abandoned" (*Spirit of Prophecy*, vol. 4, p. 271). Enoch Jacobs opposed it in November of 1844, claiming it was unbiblical (*Western Midnight Cry*, Nov. 29, 1844, p. 20). Himes similarly advocated preaching to "lost and perishing sinners" in late December 1844 (*Advent Herald*, Jan. 15, 1845, p. 182). This gives us an idea of what "soon abandoned" means.

But there were some who adopted strange positions, and incorporated an ongoing version of this view into their theology. According to John Loughborough, Joseph Turner was the originator of this (*Great Second Advent Movement*, pp. 220 ff.). Loughborough cites Himes's eye-witness account of Turner's views as of the spring of 1845. Turner taught that Christ really had come after all, that now it was a sin to work, and that the door of mercy was shut.

Ellen White was directed by God to oppose Turner's views. Someone had to, for as she described the situation, "honest, precious souls had been rejected by these fanatics, and by them told that they were rejected of God."—Arthur White, vol. 1, p. 83; *Spiritual Gifts*, vol. 2, pp. 49-51. Turner's retaliation for the rebuke was most unkind.

2. Shut "door of mercy" for only those who have rejected truth. In contrast to number 1, this view related only to those who had had opportunity to hear the message of a soon-coming Savior, and had rejected it.

J. B. Cook came out strongly for this view in the January 30, 1845, issue of *Western Midnight Cry*. This was the position that Mrs. White took, and it is biblical. The Bible contains a number of examples of people who rejected truth to the point that they could no longer be reached with the gospel. Even Paul said, "It is impossible . . . to renew them again unto repentance" (Heb. 6:4-6).

3. Shut "door of access" to preach the gospel. This view was often espoused along with number 2, and sometimes with number 1. No longer were there the opportunities to preach the gospel that there once had been, for the Lord had shut the "door of access." Scriptures from the New Testament supporting this meaning of "shut door" are found under #58.

Enoch Jacobs, J. B. Cook, and J. D. Pickands were all using the term "door of access" in 1845. Joseph Bates in his 1847 *Second Advent Way Marks and High Heaps* says the same while using different words (pp. 109, 110).

4. Shut door to the Holy Place of the heavenly sanctuary, God's temple in heaven. Mrs. White described her vision of March 24, 1849, using language like this (*Early Writings*, pp. 42, 86; *Manuscript Releases*, vol. 5, p. 200). The previous January Joseph Bates was also using such language (*A Seal of the Living God*, p. 20), language derived from Jesus's message to Philadelphia:

> And to the angel of the church in Philadelphia write; These things saith he . . . that openeth, and no man shutteth; and shutteth, and no man openeth . . . . I have set before thee an open door, and no man can shut it . . . . Him that overcometh will I make a pillar in the temple of my God. (Rev. 3:7-12)

The door to the Holy Place of the heavenly sanctuary was shut in 1844, but the door to the Most Holy Place was then opened, and Christ's intercession continued there.

Chapter 3 isn't the only place where Revelation alludes to these two doors.

> After this I looked, and, behold, a door was opened in heaven. (Rev. 4:1)
> And out of the throne proceeded lightnings and thunderings and voices: and there were seven lamps of fire burning before the throne, which are the seven Spirits of God. (Rev. 4:5)
> And another angel came and stood at the altar, having a golden censer; and there was given unto

him much incense, that he should offer it with the prayers of all saints upon the golden altar which was before the throne. (Rev. 8:3)
> And the temple of God was opened in heaven, and there was seen in his temple the ark of his testament. (Rev. 11:19)

In Revelation 4:1, John sees "a door" "opened in heaven." After going up to heaven he sees seven lamps of fire in 4:5 and a golden altar of incense in 8:3, 4. Since the seven lamps and the golden altar were pieces of furniture in the Holy Place (Ex. 40:24, 26), the first door opened must have been the door to the Holy Place of the heavenly temple. When the temple is "opened" in Revelation 11:19, John sees the ark, a piece of furniture from the Most Holy Place (Ex. 40:21). This opening would therefore be of the second door, the door to the Most Holy Place.

The strong possibility also exists that a Millerite's use of the term "shut door" might refer to the validity of the date October 22, 1844, and nothing more. In other words, some Millerites undoubtedly had a conviction that something was shut on that date, but were not sure what exactly was shut.

It is a fact that not believing in a shut door of some sort was a repudiation of the idea that October 22 was a fulfillment of prophecy. Therefore, belief in a shut door was synonymous with belief in the 2300 days ending in 1844, but not necessarily synonymous with a shut door of mercy.

Let's conclude by returning to the idea of post-1851 "reinterpretations" of non-existent shut-door passages in Mrs. White's writings. As we have seen, definitions 2 and 3 surfaced by 1845, and definition 4 by 1849. So having "reinterpretations" after 1851 is a bit late.

#55: "An explanation for the 1844 disappointment had to be found. Two Millerites, Hiram Edson and Mr. Crosier, introduced a new sanctuary theology which taught that instead of Christ coming visibly to earth in 1844, He entered for the first time the Most Holy Place in heaven. This new teaching gave them a way out of their dilemma without actually admitting their error."—Dale Ratzlaff.

#55: They never admitted their error. To the contrary, they did admit their error.

Daniel 8:14 said that at the end of the 2300 days the sanctuary would be cleansed. The Millerites taught that on October 22, 1844, Christ would return. Something obviously went wrong.

There were primarily two possible alternatives: 1) Admit that there was *an error in the predicted date* of the event of Christ's return. 2) Admit that there was

an error in the predicted event for the date of 1844.

Edson and Crosier chose the second alternative. They freely admitted their error in thinking that the predicted cleansing of the sanctuary was the second coming.

That the first alternative, admitting that the date was wrong, was not really plausible, please see #20 and #47.

#56: "Ellen G. White immediately put God's endorsement on this new explanation for the date October 22nd, 1844. 'The Lord shew me in vision more than one year ago that Brother Crosier had the true light of the cleansing of the sanctuary.' A Word to the Little Flock p. 12."—Dale Ratzlaff.

#56: She immediately put God's endorsement on their explanation. Actually, she put God's endorsement on Edson and Crosier's explanation before she heard that they had found an explanation, and even before they had had time to publish it.

Edson and Crosier's findings were printed in the February 7, 1846, issue of the *Day-Star*, published in Cincinnati. Their findings may have also appeared in an issue of the Canandaigua, New York, *Day Dawn* in March or April of 1845, though opinions vary on this (*Lest We Forget*, 3rd qtr., 1994, p. 5; "Day-Dawn" and "Crosier, Owen Russell Loomis," *Seventh-day Adventist Encyclopedia*).

However, in mid-February of 1845, Mrs. White had a vision at Exeter, Maine, during her first journey east, the same vision referred to under #50. This vision endorsed Edson and Crosier's ideas:

While in Exeter, Maine . . . . It was then I had a view of Jesus rising from His mediatorial throne and going to the Holiest as Bridegroom to receive His kingdom. They were all deeply interested in the view. They all said it was entirely new to them. . . . Previous to this I had no light on the coming of the Bridegroom, but had expected Him to [come to] this earth to deliver His people on the tenth day of the seventh month. I did not hear a lecture or a word in any way relating to the Bridegroom's going to the Holiest.—*Manuscript Releases*, vol. 5, pp. 97, 98.

There was no way she could have heard of Edson and Crosier's study at the time she had this vision.

Typically, someone else found a doctrine in the Bible, and then her visions endorsed it. In this case her visions endorsed the doctrine before she heard of it.

#57: "All doctrines were soon adjusted to fit 1844 as the cleansing of the sanctuary and the beginning of the investigative judgment. [#58:] The shut door had to be opened to allow salvation for their own children who had been born after 1844 and to evangelize others into Adventism. [#59:] Salvation for everyone, even those who lived in Bible times, had to be conditional on this judgment, and so soul sleep was introduced. [#60:] The prophecies of Daniel and Revelation had to be reinterpreted to fit the investigative judgment. [#61:] It was a time of turmoil and doctrinal reversal, but the investigative judgment doctrine survived with Ellen White's stamp of approval."—Dale Ratzlaff.

#57: All doctrines were soon adjusted. And what doctrines were these? The *documentation package* doesn't explain this statement or list any "adjusted" doctrines. What follows in Mr. Ratzlaff's list doesn't include any doctrines "adjusted" to fit the cleansing of the sanctuary or the investigative judgment.

#58: That shut door of mercy had to be opened. The shut door was dealt with under #48–#54. We'll add another point here.

What made it so obvious to at least some of the apostolic Christians that the door of mercy was not shut to Gentiles was the fact that the door of access to reach them was now open. After Stephen's stoning in Acts 7, they could preach to Samaritans, Ethiopian eunuchs, and Roman centurions, something they had not been able to do before. So if Peter's vision of Acts 10 wasn't enough to correct their theology, the early church also had the simple fact that now the "door" of access was "opened":

And when they were come, and had gathered the church together, they rehearsed . . . how [God] had opened the door of faith unto the Gentiles. Acts 14:27)

But I will tarry at Ephesus until Pentecost. For a great door and effectual is opened unto me. (1 Cor. 16:8, 9)

Furthermore, when I came to Troas to preach Christ's gospel, and a door was opened unto me of the Lord. (2 Cor. 2:12)

Withal praying also for us, that God would open unto us a door of utterance, to speak the mystery of Christ. (Col. 4:3)

If Adventists holding shut-door-of-mercy beliefs allowed it to, Mrs. White's vision of February 1845 corrected their theological misunderstanding. Also, the sanctuary doctrine explained what doors were opened and shut in 1844, and how there was still an open door of mercy into the Most Holy Place. But even though the "door of mercy" was still open, the "door of access" definitely was not.

At first the vast majority of non-Millerites, like the Gentiles in the days of the apostles, had no interest in hearing Adventists preach. The door indeed was shut. But at some point, like in the early church, a change came. The door was opened, and people wanted to listen.

Such an opening of the door would not be an adjustment because of the cleansing of the sanctuary and investigative judgment doctrines, but rather the result of the providence of God and the workings of His Spirit. It was the result of a change in the climate for evangelism, not an "adjustment" of doctrine.

#59: Soul sleep was introduced because of the investigative judgment. This is not true, and the context of a statement found in the *documentation package* proves it.

Under "Point 33" is a selection from page 49 of *Life Sketches* describing Mrs. White's hearing of a sermon on soul sleep some months after a conversation between her and her mother on the same subject. Both the conversation and the sermon took place before October 22, 1844, as the context clearly shows.

Yet the doctrine of the investigative judgment, as understood today, did not come along until after October 22. Thus soul sleep could not have been introduced because of the investigative judgment doctrine.

The phrase "investigative judgment" was coined by Elon Everts in a letter dated December 1856, which was published in the January 1, 1857, issue of *Review and Herald* (p. 72). It was at this time that the doctrine of the investigative judgment was crystallized, though hints of some of its fundamental concepts had surfaced previously.

Prominent Millerite leader, Josiah Litch, suggested as early as 1840 that there had to be a trial phase of judgment before an executive phase. Occasionally, Sabbatarian Adventists would refer to Christ's wearing the "breastplate of judgment" on the Day of Atonement or to judgment beginning at the end of the 2300 years, but at other times they would declare that the Day of Judgment could not begin before the second advent. Not until 1857 was a solid understanding of the subject arrived at by Sabbatarian Adventists (C. Mervyn Maxwell, "The Investigative Judgment: Its Early Development," in *The Sanctuary and the Atonement*, pp. 545-581).

So while soul sleep was introduced *before* October 22, 1844, the doctrine of the investigative judgment was not crystallized and fully formulated until over twelve years *after*.

Who introduced the concept of soul sleep or, as it is also known, conditional immortality among the pre-1844 Millerites?

Deacon Henry Grew of Philadelphia became a believer in conditional immortality while serving as a Baptist preacher. He later wrote a tract on the subject which was read by George Storrs, a Methodist preacher, in 1837. Storrs then wrote his own tract in 1841, and published six sermons on the subject in 1842. Copies of his six sermons eventually amounted to 200,000, and even reached England.

Just after their publication he heard of Miller's teachings and became a Millerite preacher himself. He preached to thousands in New York, Indiana, and Ohio. A number of Millerite ministers joined with him in his belief on conditional immortality.

Miller, Josiah Litch, I. E. Jones, and the *Signs of the Times* all came out against his views on conditional immortality, so his views were anything but unanimously held. But the point is that the idea of conditional immortality was definitely introduced *before* a consensus was reached among Sabbatarian Adventists regarding the investigative judgment (Froom, vol. 4, pp. 805-807; *Conditionalist Faith of Our Fathers*, vol. 2, pp. 300-315).

As earlier mentioned, Joseph Bates, James White, and Ellen White are viewed as being founders of the Seventh-day Adventist Church. Both Bates and James White were members of the Christian Connection, which "as a body rejected the inherent-immortality-of-the-soul-position" (*Ibid.*, pp. 283, 672, 675). Bates and James were therefore acquainted with the idea long before Storrs introduced the subject among Millerites.

The Bible says:

1. We are to *seek* immortality (Rom. 2:7).
2. We put on immortality at the resurrection (1 Cor. 15:53, 54).
3. Only God has immortality (1 Tim. 6:16).

If we must seek it, it must be something we do not yet have. And obviously we don't yet have it. Immortality means "unable to die," and we presently can and do die.

Only upon *condition* that we accept Jesus as our Savior do we receive *immortality* at the *resurrection*. For this reason, "soul sleep" is called "conditional immortality."

#60: The prophecies of Daniel and Revelation were reinterpreted to fit the investigative judgment. This accusation doesn't really make sense. Once the doctrines of the cleansing of sanctuary and the investigative judgment were formulated, what prophecies needed to be reinterpreted to fit them?

The basic interpretations of Daniel and Revelation were already worked out before October 22, 1844. This was before Edson and Crosier published their study on the cleansing of the sanctuary in 1845 or 1846. It was definitely before Elon Everts helped crystallize the subject of an investigative judgment in 1857.

The *documentation package* lists this as "Point 34." Under "Point 34" are two pages out of *The Great Controversy*, but nothing on these two pages refers to a reinterpretation of the prophecies of Daniel and Revelation to fit the investigative judgment.

#61: It was a time of doctrinal reversal. What doctrines were reversed? The shut door? But Adventists were definitely actively preaching to non-Millerites long before 1857, the "door of access" having opened a number of years earlier. A change in the time to keep the Sabbath (see #164-#174)? Changing by minutes or an hour when to commence the Sabbath wouldn't constitute a doctrinal reversal.

#62 & #63: "The terms of this new investigative judgment doctrine, or sanctuary doctrine as it came to be known, were harsh. It taught that a recording angel now kept track of every move, even to the extent of recording wasted moments, where one might want some leisure time. 'Every man's work passes in review before God and is registered for faithfulness or unfaithfulness. Opposite each name in the books of Heaven is entered with terrible exactness every wrong word, every selfish act, every unfulfilled duty, and every secret sin, with every artful dissembling. Heaven-sent warnings or reproofs, neglected, wasted moments, unimproved opportunities, the influence exerted for good or evil, with its far reaching results; all are chronicled by the recording angel.' Great Controversy 482."—Dale Ratzlaff.

#62: The idea of an angel recording everything is harsh. In essence, this statement asserts that the Bible's teachings are harsh.

That there are books of record in heaven is clearly taught by the following verses:

> A fiery stream issued and came forth from before him: thousand thousands ministered unto him, and ten thousand times ten thousand stood before him: the judgment was set, and the books were opened. (Dan. 7:10)
> And I saw the dead, small and great, stand before God; and the books were opened: and another book was opened, which is the book of life: and the dead were judged out of those things which were written in the books, according to their works. (Rev. 20:12)

That these books used in the judgment must contain everything we have ever done can be seen from the fact that we will be judged by everything we have ever done: "For God shall bring every work into judgment, with every secret thing, whether it be good, or whether it be evil" (Eccl. 12:14). Jesus took it one step further by declaring that that includes everything we have ever said as well. So every word we have ever spoken must be recorded too:

> But I say unto you, That every idle word that men shall speak, they shall give account thereof in the day of judgment. For by thy words thou shalt be justified, and by thy words thou shalt be condemned. (Mat. 12:36, 37)

So according to the Bible, the video's declaration that this basic Bible teaching is harsh has been recorded in the books of record in heaven. According to Jesus, the makers of this video will have to "give account thereof in the day of judgment" for this very statement.

#63: This doctrine teaches that you can't have leisure time. There is a typographical error in the above quotation that makes it less understandable. The video mistakenly added a comma. "Heaven-sent warnings or reproofs, neglected, ..." should be "Heaven-sent warnings or reproofs neglected, ..."

As far as wasted moments and leisure time go, technically, the question is how we should spend our leisure time, not whether or not we should have any. Mrs. White was not against people having leisure time. That this must be the case is clear from the following statement written by her in 1867:

> I was shown that Sabbathkeepers as a people labor too hard without allowing themselves change or periods of rest. Recreation is needful to those who are engaged in physical labor and is still more essential for those whose labor is principally mental. It is not essential to our salvation, nor for the glory of God, to keep the mind laboring constantly and excessively, even upon religious themes.—*Testimonies for the Church*, vol. 1, p. 514.

Consistently, she advocated using one's leisure time in activities that were beneficial and useful:

> As a rule, the exercise most beneficial to the youth will be found in useful employment. The little child finds both diversion and development in play; and his sports should be such as to promote not only physical, but mental and spiritual growth. As he

gains strength and intelligence, the best recreation will be found in some line of effort that is useful. That which trains the hand to helpfulness, and teaches the young to bear their share of life's burdens, is most effective in promoting the growth of mind and character.—*Education*, p. 215.

Who would argue with this? Notice also her concern for children:

> Give some of your leisure hours to your children; become acquainted with them; associate with them in their work and in their sports, and win their confidence. Cultivate friendship with them. In this way you will be a strong influence for good.—*Review and Herald*, May 26, 1910.

And her concern for ministers:

> If a minister, during his leisure time, engages in labor in his orchard or garden, shall he deduct that time from his salary? Certainly not, any more than he should put in his time when he is called to work over hours in ministerial labor. Some ministers spend many hours in apparent ease, and it is right that they should rest when they can; for the system could not endure the heavy strain were there no time for letting up. There are hours in the day that call for severe taxation, for which the minister receives no extra salary, and if he chooses to chop wood several hours a day, or work in his garden, it is as much his privilege to do this as to preach. A minister cannot always be preaching and visiting, for this is exhaustive work.—*Evangelism*, p. 660.

While Mrs. White was all for people having leisure time, she was against wasting time. Yet she was not the only Christian leader to call upon believers not to waste time, even moments of time. Consider this selection from Charles Spurgeon, who called wasting time a sin:

> I need not stop to mention the various sins of which ye have been guilty. . . . Oh, do you not think within yourselves, ". . . Have I not wasted many hours within this week that I might have spent in winning souls to him? Have I not thrown away many precious moments in light and frivolous conversation which I might have spent in earnest prayer?"—*The Spurgeon Sermon Collection*, vol. 1, p. 1027.

The revivalist Charles Finney called upon the members of the church to use their leisure time in soul winning:

> If [church members] have any leisure time, let them then make extraordinary efforts for the conversion of sinners and the sanctification of the Church. This is reasonable, this is right, and I see not how this can be neglected without sin.—*Letters on Revival, or Revival Fire*, pp. 66, 67.

Would not the world be a better place if every Christian utilized their leisure time in spreading the gospel, helping the poor, teaching their children Bible truths, meditating upon the Word of God, etc.? However, the time many professed Christians spend in some activities of pleasure benefits no one, not even themselves.

#64 & #65: "Truly this doctrine of investigative judgment, unique to Seventh-day Adventists, has colored every other doctrine in the Movement. There has been much controversy and debate since it cannot be supported from the Scriptures."—Dale Ratzlaff.

#64: It's unique to Seventh-day Adventists. This is a bit of an oversimplification, for almost all of the basic elements of this doctrine were taught by others who were neither Seventh-day Adventists nor Millerites:

1. The work of judgment includes an investigation. It seems pretty obvious that the judgment the Bible talks about must include an investigation, or else it really wouldn't be a judgment. The word "investigation" was used by Lactantius (d. 330 AD) in his description of the judgment in *Divine Institutes*:

> Nor, however, let any one imagine that souls are immediately judged after death. For all are detained in one and a common place of confinement, until the arrival of the time in which the great Judge shall make an *investigation* of their deserts. Then they

whose piety shall have been approved of will receive the reward of immortality; but they whose sins and crimes shall have been brought to light will not rise again, but will be hidden in the same darkness with the wicked, being destined to certain punishment.—*Ante-Nicene Fathers*, vol. 7, p. 445, 446, italics added.

2. The righteous and wicked receive their rewards after the judgment, not before. Adam Clarke, a prominent Wesleyan commentator from Ireland, said as much in the articles of faith he wrote out not too long after 1783:

> XXIX. There will be a general judgment; after which all shall be punished or rewarded, according to the deeds done in the body; and the wicked shall be sent to hell, and the righteous taken to heaven.—J. W. Etheridge, *The Life of Rev. Adam Clarke, LL.D.*, p. 68.

3. The Day of Atonement was a day of judgment. The Puritan writer John Owen back in 1680 listed three tasks that the Old Testament high priest did on the Day of Atonement: " '1. To offer sacrifices to God for the people. 2. To bless the people in the name of God. 3. To judge them.' "—Bryan Ball, *The English Connection*, p. 303.

4. Judgment begins with the professed people of God, and the judgment of the wicked takes place later. Barton W. Johnson was a Disciples of Christ commentator. In his 1891 *People's New Testament*, in a comment on 1 Peter 4:17, he wrote: **"The time for judgment is come.** It begins at the house of God, the church. In Matt., chapter 25, the righteous are judged first."

5. The 2300 days of Daniel 8:14 are 2300 years. The list on this point would get a bit long if it included everyone. Here is a sample of individuals who held this view: the writer of the anonymous pamphlet *De Semine* in 1205 AD; Villanova in the 1290's; Nicholas of Cusa in 1440; Sir Isaac Newton in 1727; and Judge John Bacon, a Congregational clergyman from Massachusetts, in 1799. Jewish expositors who held the same view include: Nahawendi in the 8th or 9th century; Bar Hiyya about the 11th century; and Abravanel about the 15th century.

6. The 70 weeks of Daniel 9 are part of the 2300 years. The notes found in the *Berlenburg Bible*, which was finished in 1739, state the same. This Bible was popular among German Baptists, and has the honor of being the first Bible printed in America, in 1743.

7. The 70 weeks and the 2300 days begin at the same time. This sounds similar to point 6, but while the *Berlenburg Bible* taught point 6, it did not teach this point. Besides Johann Petri in 1768 (see #5), this view was held by: William C. Davis, Presbyterian minister from South Carolina, in 1811; Dr. Joshua L. Wilson, Presbyterian minister and General Assembly moderator from Ohio, in a sermon first preached in 1828; Alexander Campbell, founder of the Disciples of Christ, in an 1829 debate in Ohio; and Samuel M. M'Corkle, a Disciples of Christ layman from Tennessee, in 1830.

Did any of these folk get their ideas from William Miller? No, for Miller didn't start preaching until 1831.

8. The 70 weeks begin with the seventh year of Artaxerxes. This view was held by: Samuel Osgood, American soldier, legislator, and Postmaster General, in 1794; George Stanley Faber, prebendary of Salisbury Cathedral, in 1811; and Thomas Scott, Church of England commentator, in 1812.

9. The 70 weeks begin in 457 BC. This view was held by: Robert Reid, Reformed Presbyterian minister of Pennsylvania and president of Erie Academy, in 1828; and Miss Harriet Livermore, "first woman ever to speak publicly within the walls of the U.S. Congress," in 1839.

10. The first 69 weeks of the 70 end with Christ's baptism. The *1599 Geneva Bible*'s footnote for Daniel 9:25 plainly teaches this.

11. The 2300 days end around 1843. This view was held by: John A. Brown of England in 1811; Archibald Mason, Reformed Presbyterian minister in Scotland, in 1820; and William Cuninghame, Esquire of Lainshaw in Scotland, in 1826.

Many, many expositors could be added who felt that the 2300 days would end in 1843, 1844, or 1847, three dates that were essentially the same. The 1843 group started with Artaxerxes' seventh year in 457 BC and calculated forward to 1843. The 1844 group took into account the fact that there was no year 0, making 2300 full years end in 1844 instead of 1843 (cf. #16). The 1847 group thought Christ was born in the year 0 instead of 4 BC. They then calculated back from Christ's time to determine when was Artaxerxes's seventh year, and arrived at 453 BC instead of 457 BC. Beginning the 2300 days at this four-year-off date, they then arrived at 1847 AD.

12. Daniel 8:14 is talking about a) the antitypical Day of Atonement services in b) the heavenly sanctuary. Of all the basic aspects of the investigative judgment doctrine, these appear to be the only ones that are truly unique to Seventh-day Adventists. Yet they are very natural conclusions if one already believes the other aspects.

(Information above not already referenced is taken from Leroy Froom's *Prophetic Faith of Our Fathers*. See the summary charts in vol. 1, pp. 894, 895; vol. 2, pp. 156, 157, 194, 784, 785; vol. 3, pp. 252, 253, 744, 745; vol. 4, 396, 397, 404, 405. See also the pages in Froom cited in these charts.)

#65: The doctrine of the investigative judgment cannot be supported by the Scriptures. Let's see if that's true.

The Bible teaches that before God hands down a sentence or executes judgment, He always investigates the facts of the case, even though He already knows everything. First He searches hearts, then He rewards:

> And the LORD God called unto Adam, and said unto him, Where art thou? And he said, I heard thy voice in the garden, and I was afraid, because I was naked; and I hid myself. And he said, Who told thee

that thou wast naked? Hast thou eaten of the tree, whereof I commanded thee that thou shouldest not eat? (Gen. 3:9-11)

And the LORD said unto Cain, Where is Abel thy brother? And he said, I know not: Am I my brother's keeper? (Gen. 4:9)

And the LORD came down to see the city and the tower, which the children of men builded. (Gen. 11:5)

And the LORD said, Because the cry of Sodom and Gomorrah is great, and because their sin is very grievous; I will go down now, and see whether they have done altogether according to the cry of it, which is come unto me; and if not, I will know. (Gen. 18:20, 21)

And I will kill her children with death; and all the churches shall know that I am he which searcheth the reins and hearts: and I will give unto every one of you according to your works. (Rev. 2:23)

Repeatedly, Jesus foretold that God will separate the wheat from the tares, the good fish from the bad, the sheep from the goats, the righteous from the wicked (Mat. 13:30, 48; 25:32, 33). One would think He would precede this with an investigation too, just like He did with Adam, Cain, Babel, and Sodom. Indeed, Jesus foretold that right before the wedding, just such an investigation will occur of all professed believers, all who respond to the gospel:

So those servants went out into the highways, and gathered together all as many as they found, both bad and good: and the wedding was furnished with guests. And when the king came in to see the guests, he saw there a man which had not on a wedding garment: And he saith unto him, Friend, how camest thou in hither not having a wedding garment? And he was speechless. Then said the king to the servants, Bind him hand and foot, and take him away, and cast him into outer darkness; there shall be weeping and gnashing of teeth. For many are called, but few are chosen. (Mat. 22:10-14)

This wedding occurs at the end of time (Rev. 19:7-9). So near the end of time before the rewards are passed out, an investigative judgment will occur. But that's not all.

Daniel 7 discusses a succession of empires and ends with the judgment. Daniel 8 discusses a succession of empires and ends with the cleansing of the sanctuary. Would not therefore the judgment and the cleansing of the sanctuary be the same event?

"And there was given me a reed like unto a rod: and the angel stood, saying, Rise, and measure the temple of God, and the altar, and them that worship therein" (Rev. 11:1). What does it mean to measure the worshippers? "For with what judgment ye judge, ye shall be judged: and with what measure ye mete,

it shall be measured to you again" (Mat. 7:2). So measuring the temple, altar, and worshippers means that the temple, altar, and worshippers are being judged.

It just so happens that these same three entities being judged in Revelation 11 are the same three entities being cleansed on the Day of Atonement in Leviticus 16. Revelation is thus tying together the Day of Atonement's cleansing of the sanctuary with the judgment.

In fact, the Hebrew word for "cleansed" in Daniel 8:14 is used in Deuteronomy 25:1 to refer to judicial acquittal. Daniel 8:14 might therefore be interpreted to mean, "then shall the sanctuary be acquitted in court." Thus Daniel 8:14 itself suggests a connection between the judgment and the cleansing of the sanctuary.

And if all that's not enough, take a look at Revelation 10.

And I saw another mighty angel come down from heaven, . . . And he had in his hand a little book open: . . . And the angel . . . lifted up his hand to heaven, And sware by him that liveth for ever and ever, . . . that there should be time no longer. (Rev. 10:1-6)

Now compare this with Daniel 12.

But thou, O Daniel, shut up the words, and seal the book, even to the time of the end: . . . How long shall it be to the end of these wonders? And I heard the man clothed in linen, . . . when he held up his right hand and his left hand unto heaven, and sware by him that liveth for ever that it shall be for a time, times, and an half all these things shall be finished. . . . And he said, Go thy way, Daniel: for the words are closed up and sealed till the time of the end. . . . But go thou thy way till the end be: for thou shalt rest, and stand in thy lot at the end of the days. (Dan. 12:4-13)

Several facts may be noted.

1. The two passages are connected, since in both we have an angel lifting his hand to heaven and swearing by Him who lives forever. This suggests that the open book of Revelation 10 is the book of Daniel, once closed but now unsealed.

2. Daniel is told that his book is to be sealed until the "time of the end." Then he hears the question asked, When will that end be?

3. The answer given involves the 1260-day time prophecy, a prophecy found seven times in Daniel and Revelation. Sometimes it is said to be 1260 days, sometimes 42 months, and sometimes 3½ years ([1] time + [2] times + ½ time = 3½ times or years; cf. Rev. 12:6, 14).

4. After giving this answer, the angel tells Daniel a second time that his book will be sealed till the time of the end, and then he connects this time of the end with the "end of the days."

What part of Daniel was sealed so that it could not be understood until the end of the 1260-day time prophecy? The head of gold in chapter 2 was identified as being Nebuchadnezzar's kingdom of Babylon. Daniel 8 identifies the next two empires as being that of Medo-Persia and Grecia. These things were never sealed. They've always been understood.

But there was one part that was specifically said to be sealed:

> And he said unto me, Unto two thousand and three hundred [evening-morning]; then shall the sanctuary be cleansed. . . . Understand, O son of man: for at the time of the end shall be the vision. . . . And the vision of the evening and the morning which was told is true: wherefore shut thou up the vision; for it shall be for many days. . . . and I was astonished at the vision, but none understood it. (Dan. 8:14-27)

Thus the one part specifically said to be sealed until the end of the 1260 days is the 2300-day prophecy of Daniel 8:14. It is that prophecy, therefore, that is unsealed and opened in Revelation 10. When the angel in Revelation 10:6 declares, "There should be time no longer," he must therefore be announcing the approaching end of the 2300 days.

Do you see the point? While Revelation 11:1 ties together the judgment with Leviticus 16's cleansing of the sanctuary, Revelation 10 ties both these subjects together with the 2300 days of Daniel 8:14.

Before moving on, we should address a few questions that are sometimes raised regarding the identity of the horn that desolates the sanctuary in Daniel 8. The four universal kingdoms brought to view in chapters 2 and 7 of the book of Daniel, as most agree, are Babylon, Medo-Persia, Grecia, and Rome. In Daniel 8, since the ram and goat are identified by Gabriel as being Medo-Persia and Grecia, one would think that the horn that comes after them and waxes "exceeding great" should be the next kingdom in the series, Rome. Some, however, identify this horn as being Antiochus Epiphanes, a Grecian king of the Seleucid dynasty. Yet there are some problems with this view:

> [The ram] became great. . . . Therefore the he goat waxed very great . . . . a little horn, which waxed exceeding great, toward the south, and toward the east, and toward the pleasant land. (Dan. 8:4-9)

Clearly, the little horn must become greater than either Medo-Persia or Alexander's Grecian empire in three directions *in a precise order*. Antiochus's conquests, pseudo-conquests, and failures never attained to the glory of Cyrus the Great or Alexander. He went east last, not second, and perished there. In stark contrast, Rome excelled all in might, annexing Carthage to its south first, Macedonia, Syria, and Egypt to the east second, and Judea third. Thus Rome fulfilled the prophecy to a "T," even getting the order of conquest right.

The position that Daniel 8's little horn had something to do with pagan and/or papal Rome was held by such greats in the past as Martin Luther (1522), Philip Melanchthon (1543), Heinrich Bullinger (1557), George Downham (1603), Sir Isaac Newton (1727), the *Berlenburg Bible* (1743), Thomas Newton (1754), and John William Fletcher (1800) (Froom, vol. 2, pp. 269, 270, 289, 290, 343, 535, 662, 685, 688, 703, 784, 785).

> In the typical service only those who had come before God with confession and repentance, and whose sins, through the blood of the sin offering, were transferred to the sanctuary, had a part in the service of the Day of Atonement. So in the great day of final atonement and investigative judgment the only cases considered are those of the professed people of God.—*Great Controversy*, p. 480.

If one reads through the first chapters of Leviticus, one finds that through the blood of the sin offerings, the sins of the repentant were transferred to the sanctuary throughout the year. It was these sins that the sanctuary was cleansed of on the Day of Atonement. All this in Old Testament times was but a symbol of the gospel. The sins of the penitent are transferred to the heavenly sanctuary through the blood of Jesus. It is these sins that the sanctuary is being cleansed of during the investigative judgment.

"But," says the objector, "it is the little horn that defiles the sanctuary in Daniel 8, not the sins of God's people." To this we reply that as the above quote indicates, Adventists have always said that the investigative judgment involves "the professed people of God." Rome during most of its 2000 years of dominance in international affairs (c. 200 BC - 1798 AD) definitely qualified as being part of that group.

Moreover, the only passage that describes the Day of Atonement services prefaces that description with, "And the LORD spake unto Moses after the death of the two sons of Aaron, when they offered before the LORD, and died" (Lev. 16:1). The two sons of Aaron were Nadab and Abihu, two priests that went astray by substituting the wrong kind of fire for what God had specified to be used in His worship services (Lev. 10:1, 2).

Daniel 8 prefaces the cleansing of the sanctuary with a description of the little horn. The authorities referred to above identified this little horn as being, at least in part, priests who had gone astray by substituting a different form of worship than the one God had specified in the Bible. Thus we have yet another connection between Daniel 8 and the Day of Atonement services of Leviticus 16.

Most certainly, the doctrine of the investigative judgment can be "supported from the Scriptures."

#66, #67, & #68: "This central Adventist doctrine, which states that the judgment of believers' works will determine their salvation, is blatantly unbiblical, and is not taught by any legitimate Christian denomination."—Narrator.

#66: They teach that the judgment of believers' works determines their salvation. Technically, using the way evangelicals popularly use the term "saved," this charge is not true.

A lot depends on how we define the term "salvation." The plan of redemption includes a number of aspects:

1. Justification: pardon and conversion.
2. Sanctification: the believer's daily growth in Christ.
3. Glorification: the "redemption of our body" (Rom. 8:23), when we receive bodies that will never die.

Each of these three is a miracle of divine grace and is based on the finished work of Christ on Calvary's cross, not on our own works. Each is likewise made possible today through the intercession of Christ.

Some use the word "salvation" to mean only justification, while others use it to mean both justification and sanctification, while still others use it to mean all three. Later on, the video explicitly uses the term "saved" to mean only justification (see #143). But that cannot be the meaning here, for this statement mentions "believers' works." If they are already believers, then they must be already justified and converted, as well as daily growing in grace. So the video itself is using more than one definition of the word "saved," and the viewer should take note of this fact.

A major problem is that most evangelicals who hear the above statement from the video will think of justification when the video is really referring to glorification.

Adventists do not believe that works determine justification for the simple reason that individuals cannot perform good works (in the New Testament sense) until they are justified and converted. Until that point, all works are tainted by selfishness and are essentially "works of the flesh" (see Gal. 5:16-25).

They do believe, however, that justification occurs *on condition* of repentance and confession, and most nearly everyone agrees. Repentance and confession do not *buy* justification and conversion, but they are *conditions* for receiving this free gift of God.

Adventists also believe that glorification, and the retaining forever of justification and sanctification, are conditional. The investigative judgment determines who has complied with the conditions and who has not. What those conditions are is dealt with under the next point.

Many evangelicals disagree with the concept that glorification is conditional, since many believe that justification cannot be lost. We respect those who disagree, and we hope they will likewise respect us, for this Adventist belief is by no means uncommon in Christianity.

Does one have to accept Christ in order to have one's name written in the book of life?

> He that believeth on the Son hath everlasting life: and he that believeth not the Son shall not see life. (John 3:36)
> He that hath the Son hath life; and he that hath not the Son of God hath not life. (1 Jn. 5:12)
> He that believeth on him is not condemned: but he that believeth not is condemned already. (John 3:18)

These texts indicate that the answer is yes. Only the names of believers are written there. Once written, can they ever be blotted out?

> Yet now, if thou wilt forgive their sin—; and if not, blot me, I pray thee, out of thy book which thou hast written. And the LORD said unto Moses, Whosoever hath sinned against me, him will I blot out of my book. (Ex. 32:32, 33)
> Let them be blotted out of the book of the living, and not be written with the righteous. (Ps. 69:28)
> He that overcometh, the same shall be clothed in white raiment; and I will not blot out his name out of the book of life, but I will confess his name before my Father, and before his angels. (Rev. 3:5)
> And if any man shall take away from the words of the book of this prophecy, God shall take away his part out of the book of life, and out of the holy city, and from the things which are written in this book. (Rev. 22:19)

So it is possible to have one's name blotted out of the book of life. And where do those whose names do not appear there end up? "And whosoever was not found written in the book of life was cast into the lake of fire" (Rev. 20:15).

It is apparent, then, that an individual can be justified, and then later turn away from God and be lost. This concept explains the following Scripture, which is difficult to explain otherwise:

> Of how much sorer punishment, suppose ye, shall he be thought worthy, who hath trodden under foot the Son of God, and hath counted the blood of the covenant, wherewith he was sanctified, an unholy thing, and hath done despite unto the Spirit of grace? (Heb. 10:29)

So someone can be sanctified by the blood of Christ, and then be lost. This is why Peter says, "Wherefore the rather, brethren, give diligence to make your calling and election sure" (2 Pet. 1:10). Just being called and chosen isn't enough. We have to "make" them "sure."

And yet we have Jesus saying:

> My sheep hear my voice, and I know them, and they follow me: And I give unto them eternal life; and they shall never perish, neither shall any man pluck them out of my hand. My Father, which gave them me, is greater than all; and no man is able to pluck them out of my Father's hand. (John 10:27-29)

Notice that it is those that the Father gives to Jesus who can't be taken out of His hand. Now consider the following: "While I was with them in the world, I kept them in thy name: those that thou gavest me I have kept, and none of them is lost, but the son of perdition; that the scripture might be fulfilled" (John 17:12). The Father gave the disciples to Jesus, and "no man" could take them out of Jesus's hand. Yet one was lost, Judas Iscariot. It would appear, then, that "no man" does not include the one who is in the hand. While no one can take us out of Jesus's hand, we can take ourselves out!

#67: This is blatantly unbiblical. Not so. The Bible clearly says that obedience and holiness are condi-

tions for the retention of justification and the reception of glorification:

> Follow peace with all men, and holiness, without which no man shall see the Lord. (Heb. 12:14)
>
> For the hour is coming, in the which all that are in the graves shall hear his voice, And shall come forth; they that have done good, unto the resurrection of life; and they that have done evil, unto the resurrection of damnation. (John 5:28, 29)

And from the same book in which Paul is so adamant about our not being able to work our way to heaven:

> Now the works of the flesh are manifest, which are these; Adultery, fornication, uncleanness, lasciviousness, Idolatry, witchcraft, hatred, variance, emulations, wrath, strife, seditions, heresies, Envyings, murders, drunkenness, revellings, and such like: of the which I tell you before, as I have also told you in time past, that they which do such things shall not inherit the kingdom of God. (Gal. 5:19-21)

Clearly, while we cannot work our way to heaven and we are not saved by works, glorification and the retention of justification are conditional upon obedience and holiness.

#68: The investigative judgment is not taught by any legitimate Christian denomination. Obviously, this begs the question. If the Adventist Church is a Christian denomination, then this statement cannot be true.

Besides, Dan Snyder says under #232, "The last three years have been the most spiritually rewarding of my thirty-one years as a Christian." Will the narrator please take note: Mr. Snyder testifies that he was a Christian for twenty-eight years before leaving the Adventist Church. Therefore, according to the video itself, the Seventh-day Adventist Church must be a Christian denomination.

#69, #70, #71, #72, & #73: "This doctrine teaches at some point in time between 1844 and the second coming of Christ, every believer's name will come up in judgment. At that point in time, if one has any unconfessed sins, even forgotten sins, or if one does not demonstrate perfect obedience to the Ten Commandments, especially the fourth, he will be lost. This teaching is diametrically opposed to the New Testament gospel of grace."—Dale Ratzlaff.

#69: It teaches that believers will be lost if they have unconfessed sins. How can an individual be forgiven if he has not confessed his sins? The Bible declares: "If we confess our sins, he is faithful and just to forgive us our sins, and to cleanse us from all unrighteousness" (1 Jn. 1:9). How can an individual

be taken to heaven who has not confessed his sins, and has therefore not been forgiven? Does not the idea that people can be saved without confessing their sins strike at the very heart of the New Testament gospel of grace?

#70: And that includes even forgotten sins. One will fail to find the phrase "forgotten sins" either in Mrs. White's published and released writings or in the writings of early Adventists found on the *Words of the Pioneers* CD. The one exception is a single reference to the theology of another denomination, not of Seventh-day Adventists.

The *documentation package* lists this point as "Point 37." Under "Point 37" is only a single paragraph from volume 4 of *Spirit of Prophecy*, page 312. This paragraph contains the phrase "forgetfulness of the Saviour's claims," a far cry from "forgotten sins."

If there are forgotten sins that the sincere believer needs to confess, surely God will bring these sins back to his or her remembrance. But again, neither Mrs. White nor the pioneers of the Adventist Church ever said that sincere believers who had never confessed *forgotten sins* would be lost.

#71: It teaches that you have to have perfect obedience to the Ten Commandments. That the Ten Commandments are the standard in the judgment is clear. Equally clear is that God requires obedience to *all* His commandments:

> For whosoever shall keep the whole law, and yet offend in one point, he is guilty of all. For he that said, Do not commit adultery, said also, Do not kill. Now if thou commit no adultery, yet if thou kill, thou art become a transgressor of the law. So speak ye, and so do, as they that shall be judged by the law of liberty. (James 2:10-12)

Since the word "perfect" is a bit scary because of its present-day connotations, a better word to use might be "complete." That's what we're talking about anyway, the necessity of complete obedience.

If this concept bothers you, just ask yourself which commandment you plan to break today. Are you going to hate or kill? Are you going to covet or steal? Are you going to lust or run around on your spouse? Which commandment do you plan on not "completely" keeping, on breaking just a little bit?

When people say that we cannot keep the Ten Commandments even if God helps us, they are dishonoring the Lord and calling the Bible a lie:

> For this is the love of God, that we keep his commandments: and his commandments are not grievous. (1 Jn. 5:3)
>
> For my yoke is easy, and my burden is light. (Mat. 11:30)
>
> And hereby we do know that we know him, if we keep his commandments. He that saith, I know him, and keepeth not his commandments, is a liar, and the truth is not in him. (1 Jn. 2:3, 4)

Under "Point 38" in the *documentation package*, the substantiation for this charge is the fourth paragraph from the October 26, 1897, issue of the *Review and Herald*. Of the 193 words of this paragraph, 112 words are New Testament Bible verses!

#72: Especially the fourth. This is not true.

While James says that if we break one commandment we are "guilty of all" (2:10), he also says, "Therefore to him that knoweth to do good, and doeth it not, to him it is sin" (4:17). Clearly, if we do not know what God has said about the Sabbath, we are not held accountable for it. Other Scriptures on this include:

> Jesus said unto them, If ye were blind, ye should have no sin: but now ye say, We see; therefore your sin remaineth. (John 9:41)
>
> For until the law sin was in the world: but sin is not imputed when there is no law. (Rom. 5:13)

This is what Seventh-day Adventism has always taught. Regarding the beneficiaries of Christ's final intercession, Mrs. White herself testified: "It includes all who died trusting in Christ, but who, not having received the light upon God's commandments, had sinned ignorantly in transgressing its precepts."—*Early Writings*, p. 254.

Many believers in ages past did not know of the claims of the fourth commandment. Adventists agree with the Bible on this one. Such will not be held accountable for their violations of this commandment. In fact, it isn't hard to imagine that most believers who will be vindicated in the investigative judgment will be those who knew nothing about the true claims of the fourth commandment.

#73: This teaching is diametrically opposed to the gospel of grace. The reader may judge for himself from the points under this section, as well as the Scriptures given under #67, whether this statement is true or not.

Let us remember what the gospel of grace and the New Covenant really are:

> For I am not ashamed of the gospel of Christ: for it is the power of God unto salvation to every one that believeth. (Rom. 1:16)
>
> And thou shalt call his name JESUS: for he shall save his people from their sins. (Mat. 1:21)
>
> Whosoever committeth sin transgresseth also the law: for sin is the transgression of the law. (1 Jn. 3:4)
>
> The blood of Jesus Christ his Son cleanseth us from all sin. (1 Jn. 1:7)
>
> This is the covenant that I will make with them after those days, saith the Lord, I will put my laws into their hearts, and in their minds will I write them. (Heb. 10:16)

Did you notice how John defined sin? He said that sin is breaking God's commandments. So Jesus came to save us from our breaking of the commandments. He shed His blood to cleanse us from all sin, to bring us back into obedience to God's holy law.

The gospel of grace is a beautiful message about the power of God which both forgives sin and transforms the life. As Jesus said, "Sin no more" (John 5:14; 8:11). Simply put, this means, "Break the commandments no more."

To say that a person may continue to knowingly practice sin and still go to heaven, or to say that a person may still go to heaven even though he has never had the law written in his heart and mind, this is what is diametrically opposed to the gospel of grace.

Bible Versions and Footnotes

#74, #75, #76, & #77: "In all man-made religions the authority of God's Scripture and unchanging word is challenged. The Seventh-day Adventists are no exception. They have their own version of the Bible, known as *The Clear Word Bible*, which inserts the words and ideas of Ellen G. White directly into the biblical text."—Narrator.

#74: Adventism is a man-made religion. This is another point that begs the question. It also shows that the narrator does not understand Adventist history very well, for a knowledge of the providences that brought Adventism into existence would make it hard to call it "man made."

#75: They have their own version of the Bible. Not so. Jack Blanco's *paraphrase* is not in any sense an official Adventist version. As the *documentation package* under "Point 49a" proves, *The Clear Word*'s copyright is held by Dr. Blanco, not by the denomination or one of its presses. "Blanco" is the only name that appears on the spine, since he is both the author and the publisher. Thus, while it is true that Dr. Blanco has his own paraphrase, it is a falsehood to say that Seventh-day Adventism has its own version.

This writer has never owned a copy. If most members owned copies and regularly used them, that fact might be construed into evidence to support this charge. But the truth of the matter is that a minority of members regularly use this paraphrase, though it is likely more popular than *Philip's* or *The Living Bible*.

Under "Point 39" in the *documentation package* are two pages of the three-page preface to *The Clear Word*, but the first page is missing. The first page of the preface begins with these two sentences: "This is not a new translation but a paraphrase of the Scriptures. It is not intended for in-depth study or for public reading in churches." The second edition adds but one word: "This is not a new translation but an interpretive paraphrase . . . ." *The Clear Word* is crystal clear. Why didn't the contributors to the video read the very first sentences of the preface? On the other hand, how could they not have?

#76: It's known as *The Clear Word Bible*. Not any more. Dr. Blanco wanted to avoid misunderstandings, so he had the title changed for the second edition. It now carries the title, *The Clear Word*, not *The Clear Word Bible*.

Did the contributors to the video know about the change of title for the second edition? Yes they did, for the *documentation package* shows a photocopy of its cover under "Point 49a."

Additionally, when the video's footage shows a picture of Mr. Ratzlaff holding the first edition, the viewer can read on its cover, "A Paraphrase to Nurture Faith and Growth." Yet Mr. Ratzlaff at that moment calls Dr. Blanco's paraphrase "An *Expanded* Paraphrase to Nurture Faith and Growth" (see #80). The word "expanded" appears on the cover of the second edition, not the first. This indicates that either Mr. Ratzlaff, or the writer of the script he memorized, well knew about the second edition.

#77: The words and ideas of Mrs. White were inserted into the biblical text. Actually, it's the words and ideas of theologian and college professor Jack Blanco, not Mrs. White. Anyone comparing Dr. Blanco's paraphrase with her writings can see that he inserts words that didn't come from her.

In the two pages of the preface reproduced under "Point 39" in the *documentation package*, Dr. Blanco uses the word "paraphrase" six times. Twice he says that he interpreted and once that he "inserted information." While he not once refers to Mrs. White, he does say this:

> There were times when certain words and expressions from commentaries, translations, word studies, periodicals and conversations with colleagues

were found to be more appropriate and accurate than my own.

Rest assured that the authors of all these sources didn't borrow their wording from Mrs. White.

Is interpreting and inserting the words of "colleagues" and "commentaries" in paraphrases sinister?

Not at all. That's what paraphrases are all about, for they are not true to the biblical text. The paraphraser weaves in his understanding into the passage.

True, Dr. Blanco's paraphrase is more than just the average paraphrase. That's why it now says *expanded paraphrase* on the cover.

#78: "For example in the ninth chapter of the book of Daniel, 300 words have been added to the Holy Scriptures."—Narrator.

#78: 300 words were added. If the reader will peruse Daniel 9 in *The Clear Word*, he will see that Dr. Blanco's additions are not the words of Mrs. White. He will also see that the additions are in harmony with the method of interpreting Daniel 8 and 9 that has been popular for centuries (see #64). Indeed, many of his "added" words are simply *a rephrasing of the Hebrew text.*

The *documentation package* lists this as "Point 40 & 40a." Under these points is a research paper by a minister. The first page quotes page 446 of *Great Controversy* where it says that "The second commandment forbidding image worship has been dropped from the law" by the Catholic Church. Then the paper goes on to say how this is wrong because the Catholic Church claims that it hasn't changed the second commandment, and that the so-called second commandment is really part of the first.

But the very next sentences in *Great Controversy* after the one quoted say:

> But papists urge, as a reason for omitting the second commandment, that it is unnecessary, being included in the first, and that they are giving the law exactly as God designed it to be understood. This cannot be the change foretold by the prophet. An intentional, deliberate change is presented: "He shall *think* to change the times and the law." The change in the fourth commandment exactly fulfills the prophecy.

So the author of the research paper says a sentence in *Great Controversy* is wrong, and to prove it he gives points that the very next sentences in *Great Controversy* acknowledge to be so!

#79 & #80: "A blatant example of this type of alteration can be seen in Daniel chapter 8 verse 14 which in the King James Version simply reads, 'Unto two thousand and three hundred days; then shall the Sanctuary be cleansed.' However in the Adventist *Clear Word Version*: 'After two thousand, three hundred prophetic days (or two thousand, three hundred years), God will step in, proclaim the truth about Himself, and restore the ministry of the Sanctuary in heaven to its rightful place. This is when the judgment will begin, of which the cleansing of the earthly sanctuary was a type.' Daniel 8:14 The Clear Word Version."—Narrator.

#79: Look at all those "alterations" in Daniel 8:14! When one stops to examine Dr. Blanco's "alterations," it is hard to see what the problem really is.

First of all, Dr. Blanco says that the 2300 days are years. This used to be a popular interpretation among those of many faiths (see points 5-7 and 11 under #64). If most today think these views sound totally new, that is no fault of Dr. Blanco.

Second, the idea that the cleansing of the sanctuary is connected to the judgment is a very natural conclusion when one parallels Daniel 7 and Daniel 8 (see #65).

Third, the idea that the sanctuary is "restored" comes from the fact that the Hebrew word used for "cleanse" in Daniel 8:14 can be translated that way.

There are essentially three different connotations this Hebrew word can have, and this is one of them.

Fourth, the idea about God proclaiming the truth about Himself is derived from Romans 3:4. In some sort of way, according to this text, God is on trial. During the judgment His character is being vindicated, and Satan's lies are being exposed. No, He isn't a vengeful tyrant. No, He isn't overindulgent. He has been loving, merciful, and just with every sinner.

Matthew 18:15 says, "Moreover if thy brother shall trespass against thee, go and tell him his fault between thee and him alone." Why? For one reason, if there is a misunderstanding, then it can be explained before the party feeling injured begins publicly making false statements. It would have been wise if the narrator had followed Jesus's instruction on this one, thus saving himself some embarrassment.

#80: It's the Adventist *Clear Word Version*. The makers of the video took it upon themselves to change the title of Dr. Blanco's paraphrase from *The Clear Word* to *The Clear Word Version*.

As the preface's first sentence said, "This is not a new translation but an interpretive paraphrase of the Scriptures." If it isn't a "new translation," it can't be a "version," for *Webster's* defines "version" as being "a translation from another language; *esp*: a translation of the Bible or a part of it."

To be sure, by calling Dr. Blanco's paraphrase *The Clear Word Version*, a better case against Seventh-day Adventists can be made, but such a title has no basis in fact.

#81 & #82: "One can see the extent to which Seventh-day Adventists are prepared to go to support their prophetess, even to the manipulation of Scripture. *The Clear Word Bible* published in 1994 as an expanded paraphrase to nurture faith and growth is nothing more than added distortions to the Word of God to support Adventist theology."—Dale Ratzlaff.

#81: *The Clear Word* supports "their prophetess." Since the words and ideas of Dr. Blanco, not Mrs. White, are inserted in *The Clear Word*, it isn't supporting "their prophetess."

Dr. Blanco did this as a devotional exercise. The end result appeared worthy of publishing, and so it was.

#82: *The Clear Word* manipulates and distorts Scripture. Paraphrases contain by their very nature the inclusion of interpretations into the text. Dr. Blanco admitted freely in its preface what he had done, calling *The Clear Word* an "interpretive paraphrase." This charge is therefore totally unfounded.

Let's talk about the *New International Version* for a moment. Is it a paraphrase or a translation? Is it true to the biblical text, or does it contain the interpretations of its authors?

The NIV rendering of Hebrews 10:1 is, "The law is only a shadow of the good things that are coming." The *King James* rendering is, "For the law having a shadow of good things to come." Which is correct? Is the law a shadow, or does it "have" a shadow?

The Greek text clearly contains the Greek word for "have," which the NIV translators ignored. Thus they made the verse sound like the Ten Commandments are the shadow, and that we don't have to worry about keeping them anymore.

In actuality, the Ten Commandments "have" a shadow. This shadow was the ceremonies and sacrifices which pointed forward to Christ, as can clearly be seen from Hebrews 8:4, 5.

Maybe we should call the NIV the *New International Paraphrase* instead of the *New International Version*, since the translators apparently "distorted" the biblical text to reflect their own interpretations. However, it would be going way too far to call all the translators of the NIV cultists, non-Christians, and members of "man-made religions" simply because they added such a "distortion" to the biblical text. Likewise, the statements on this video are going too far.

Mr. Ratzlaff said that *The Clear Word* was published in 1994. If Adventists need a "manipulated" and "distorted" Bible to support their beliefs, why did they wait 150 years before publishing one?

#83, #84, & #85: "They have also published their *Study Bible* with Ellen G. White quotes included as an inspired commentary."—Dale Ratzlaff.

#83: Adventists have published their *Study Bible*. This point contradicts and proves false the previous charges. This study Bible is not *The Clear Word*. It's a *King James Version*. If *The Clear Word* was Adventism's official version, why would this Bible be a *King James Version*?

#84: The *Study Bible* is theirs. This is not true. Like *The Clear Word*, this study Bible is not published by the denomination, but by Mission Publishing, a private organization operated by laymen. It is not the denomination's study Bible.

#85: The *Study Bible* contains quotes from Mrs. White. For centuries, individuals and organizations have published Bibles containing footnotes, study helps, and commentary. Were all these folk and organizations sinning by doing so? Were they cultists and non-Christians? Did they belong to man-made religions?

True, sometimes the footnotes in these other Bibles are treated as if they are inspired when they are not. Some people will even ignore the plain meaning of a text in favor of the interpretation offered by the footnote, thus placing the authority of the footnote above the Word of God. But that is no fault of the authors of those footnotes, or their publishers.

So, are other Bibles that contain footnotes and comments all right as long as no one thinks that they are inspired? In other words, is it only those who have had visions, only those who have the biblical gift of prophecy, that cannot have their comments printed as footnotes?

Other Doctrines; the Jehovah's Witnesses

#86, #87, & #88: "Other heretical Adventist doctrines include the teaching that Christ's atonement for sins on the cross was incomplete, that Jesus Christ is Michael the Archangel, and that there is no hell."—Narrator.

#86: Adventists teach that Christ's atonement on the cross was incomplete. This is not true. If Adventists did teach this, they would be contradicting Mrs. White:

> The great sacrifice of the Son of God was neither too great nor too small to accomplish the work. In the wisdom of God it was complete; and the atonement made testifies to every son and daughter of Adam the immutability of God's law.—*Signs of the Times*, Dec. 30, 1889.

> God has accepted the offering of his Son as a complete atonement for the sins of the world.—*Youth's Instructor*, Sept. 20, 1900.

The only evidence for this point offered by the *documentation package*, under "Point 43," is a comment by Mrs. White cited in *The Seventh-day Adventist Bible Commentary* (vol. 7, p. 933). This comment doesn't say that Christ's atonement *on the cross* was incomplete. If it did say this, then we would have her contradicting herself. Rather, it merely refers to the Day of Atonement services, which Adventists feel did not end at the cross. Thus the charge stands totally unproven.

What is meant by "did not end" is this: The sacrifice offered on the Day of Atonement was fulfilled at the cross, just like all sacrifices were. However, Adventists believe that what the priest did after the sacrifice largely concerns events after October 22, 1844.

Technically, the correct way to view the atonement is probably to consider "the" atonement to be the entire plan of salvation, composed of several different facets. Each of these facets could be called "an" atonement. "The" atonement would thus be made up of a number of "an" atonements.

For instance, biblically speaking, Christ's intercessory work that He began when He ascended to heaven after His resurrection could be called "an" atonement. So while the sacrifice of Christ on the cross is "a" complete atonement, so also is His intercessory work "a" complete atonement.

According to Leviticus 4 and 5, an atonement was made *after* the sin offering was slain. The sacrifice provided the atoning blood, which the priest then used to make an atonement for the sinner. This suggests that there was some sort of atoning work for Christ to engage in after His death on Calvary, which at least consisted of His intercession for us.

While Christ's atonement on the cross was complete, the plan of salvation was not over at that point. As Paul said, "If Christ be not raised, your faith is vain; ye are yet in your sins" (1 Cor. 15:17). All must therefore agree that the plan of salvation was not yet completed until at the very least Christ's resurrection, even though His atonement on the cross was complete three days before.

#87: The idea that Michael the Archangel is Christ is heresy. So is the video calling Charles Spurgeon a heretic?

> Let the Lord Jesus Christ be for ever endeared to us . . . . He it is whose camp is round about them that fear Him; He is the true Michael whose foot is upon the dragon. All hail, Jesus! thou Angel of Jehovah's presence, to Thee this family offers its morning vows.—*Morning and Evening Daily Readings*, p. 556.

> *Michael will always fight*; his holy soul is vexed with sin, and will not endure it. Jesus will always be the dragon's foe, and that not in a quiet sense, but actively, vigorously, with full determination to exterminate evil.—*Ibid*. p. 673.

Is the video calling the learned Baptist commentator, John Gill, a heretic? Commenting on Jude 9 he wrote:

Yet Michael the archangel, &c.] By whom is meant, not a created angel, but an eternal one, the Lord Jesus Christ; as appears from his name Michael, which signifies, "who is as God": and who is as God, or like unto him, but the Son of God, who is equal with God? and from his character as the archangel, or Prince of angels, for Christ is the head of all principality and power; and from what is elsewhere said of Michael, as that he is the great Prince, and on the side of the people of God, and to have angels under him, and at his command, Dan. 10:21, 12:1; Rev. 12:7. So Philo the Jew {o} calls the most ancient Word, firstborn of God, the archangel . . . .—*Gill's Expositor and the Body of Divinity.*

Notice how Gill equated "archangel" with "Prince of angels." Indeed, *archo* is a Greek word that means "to rule," so "ruler of the angels" is an acceptable definition of "archangel."

Commenting on Revelation 12:7, Gill wrote:

Michael and his angels fought against the dragon: by whom is meant not a created angel, with whom his name does not agree, it signifying "who is as God"; nor does it appear that there is anyone created angel that presides over the rest, and has them at his command . . . .—*Ibid.*

Commenting on Daniel 12:1, he wrote:

And at that time shall Michael stand up, &c.] The Archangel, who has all the angels of heaven under him, and at his command, the Son of God, our Lord Jesus Christ; who is as God, as the name signifies, truly and really God, and equal in nature, power, and glory, to his divine Father . . . .—*Ibid.*

Another writer of a popular commentary was Matthew Henry. Is the video calling him a heretic too?

Daniel 12:1
Vs. 1-4: Michael signifies, "Who is like God," and his name, with the title of "the great Prince," points out the Divine Savior.—*Concise Commentary*, p. 1128.
Michael and his angels fight against the devil and his angels, who are defeated. (7-12) . . . .
Revelation 12:7

Vs. 7-11: The attempts of the dragon proved unsuccessful against the church, and fatal to his own interests. The seat of this war was in heaven; in the church of Christ, the kingdom of heaven on earth. The parties were Christ, the great Angel of the covenant, and his faithful followers; and Satan and his instruments.—*Ibid.*, p. 1719.

Is the video also calling the writer of the notes of the 1599 *Geneva Bible* a heretic?

Even though God could by one angel destroy all the world, yet to assure his children of his love he sends forth double power, even Michael, that is, Christ Jesus the head of angels.—note for Dan. 10:13.
The angel here notes two things: first that the Church will be in great affliction and trouble at Christ's coming, and next that God will send his angel to deliver it, whom he here calls Michael, meaning Christ, who is proclaimed by the preaching of the Gospel.—note for Dan. 12:1.

There must be some reason why these great Bible students of old, as well as many others, felt that Michael was another name for Christ, the divine Son of God. We'll revisit this issue under #93 and #207 ff.

#88: Adventists teach that there is no hell. To the contrary, Adventists have always taught that there is a hell.

If this charge be true, why did Mrs. White write, "Few believe with heart and soul that we have a hell to shun and a heaven to win"? (*Desire of Ages*, p. 636). The phrases "heaven to win" and "hell to shun" are found together at least 36 times in her writings.

This charge is "substantiated" under "Point 45" in the *documentation package* by a paragraph from *Mind, Character, and Personality*, volume 2, page 454. In this quotation Mrs. White suggests that some have worried so much about burning eternally for their sins that they have lost their reason. Yet while she thus calls into question the doctrine of an *eternally-burning* hell, she nowhere denies the reality of hell with its literal fire. More will be said on this later under #160, but suffice it to say for now, the charge stands unproven in the *documentation package*.

#89: "During the mid-1800's, within a few years of each other, Mormons, Jehovah's Witnesses, Christian Scientists, and Seventh-day Adventists were all presenting doctrines contrary to those held by traditional Bible believers."—Narrator.

#89: They teach doctrines contrary to tradition. The same could be said about nearly every church in existence today. They each proclaimed doctrines contrary to the traditions of the times. When the popular churches rejected the new doctrines discov-

ered in the Bible, the people who wanted to stay true to Scripture started a new church.

Even Jesus opposed the traditional beliefs of His day:

He answered and said unto them, Well hath Esaias prophesied of you hypocrites, as it is written, This people honoureth me with their lips, but their heart is far from me. Howbeit in vain do they worship me, teaching for doctrines the commandments of men. For laying aside the commandment of God, ye hold the tradition of men, as the washing of pots and cups: and many other such like things ye do. And he said unto them, Full well ye reject the commandment of God, that ye may keep your own tradition. For Moses said, Honour thy father and thy mother; and, Whoso curseth father or mother, let him die the death: But ye say, If a man shall say to his father or mother, It is Corban, that is to say, a gift, by whatsoever thou mightest be profited by me; he shall be free. And ye suffer him no more to do ought for his father or his mother; Making the word of God of none effect through your tradition, which ye have delivered: and many such like things do ye. (Mark 7:6-13)

The most basic principle of Protestantism is *Sola Scriptura*, or, the Bible and the Bible only. It used to be that tradition was considered subordinate to the authority of Scripture by Protestants. Alas, times have changed to the point that churches are being condemned on videos if they don't follow tradition.

Yet notice the contradiction: Michael being a name for Christ the Son of God was a popular traditional belief (see #87). If teaching doctrines contrary to tradition is wrong, then this video is wrong in calling the idea that Michael is Christ a heresy. It is also wrong for condemning the idea that the 2300 days would end around 1844 (see #64).

By associating Adventism with Mormons, Jehovah's Witnesses, and Christian Scientists, the video apparently is trying to suggest that if these other groups aren't Christian, then neither is Adventism. But that isn't necessarily true.

#90 & #91: "Many of the doctrines of Jehovah's Witnesses and Seventh-day Adventists are similar. This is because they had common roots. The founder of Jehovah's Witnesses, Charles Taze Russell, even co-authored a book called *The Three Worlds* with N. H. Barbour, an early Adventist."—Leslie Martin.

#90: Many doctrines are similar. Find a Jehovah's Witness who knows what Adventists believe, and see if he agrees that "many" of their doctrines are similar. You'll be hard pressed.

The use of the word "many" is a gross exaggeration. It's like saying that "many" of the beliefs of a particular church are similar to those of Jehovah's Witnesses simply because both believe that we will spend the millennium on earth. Out of Christian courtesy, such exaggerations should be avoided.

Some groups do not believe that the New Jerusalem is a literal city with walls and gates, just like the Jehovah's Witnesses. Likewise many groups believe that the six days of creation were not literal days, just like the Jehovah's Witnesses. Do these similarities justify the statement that "many" of their doctrines are similar?

For the reader's information, Adventists disagree with Jehovah's Witnesses on each of the above three doctrinal points: the millennium, the nature of the New Jerusalem, and the days of creation. They do agree with them regarding baptism by immersion, as do the Baptists and other groups.

Jehovah's Witnesses use Sunday as their major meeting day, just like most other churches. Does this make "many" of their doctrines similar?

Their theology has changed over the years, as has the theology of many Protestant denominations.

Adventism used to be more in agreement with all of them, but their theology has changed.

#91: N. H. Barbour was an early Adventist. What does Mrs. Martin mean by early Adventist? Does she mean a Millerite? A first-day Adventist? A Seventh-day Adventist? She later calls Uriah Smith an "early Adventist" as well. Smith was a Millerite for a *few months* at the age of *twelve* after being baptized in the early summer of 1844. After October 22 he lost interest in religion, but later became a Sabbath-keeping Adventist in 1852. It would therefore appear that Mrs. Martin is calling Barbour an early Seventh-day Adventist. However, there is no evidence whatsoever that Barbour was ever a Seventh-day Adventist.

Barbour was a part of a group that was predicting that Christ would return in 1874. When Christ did not come as expected, Barbour decided that He really had come, only invisibly. He convinced Russell of this unscriptural doctrine in 1876 (Charles Taze Russell in *The Finished Mystery*, p. 54).

If Barbour had accepted the Sabbath, the sanctuary message, and the investigative judgment doctrine as taught by Seventh-day Adventists, he would not have predicted Christ's return in 1874. He also would not have given up his faith in the literal return of Christ. Hence, he would not have led Russell astray by convincing him that Christ had come after all in 1874. The truth of the matter is, if Barbour had become a Seventh-day Adventist, Russell would never have started the Jehovah's Witnesses!

While "Point 46" in the *documentation package* proves that Barbour co-authored a book with Russell, it says nothing about him being an early Adventist (see also #98).

#92 & #93: "Both Adventists and Jehovah's Witnesses still cling to the heresies of soul sleep and Michael the Archangel being Jesus."—Leslie Martin.

#92: Soul sleep is a heresy. Yet this makes a heretic out of Martin Luther, father of the Protestant Reformation. Hear what he had to say on the subject:

"For just as one who falls asleep and reaches morning unexpectedly when he awakes, without knowing what has happened to him, so we shall suddenly rise on the last day without knowing how we have come into death and through death." "We shall sleep, until He comes and knocks on the little grave and says, Doctor Martin, get up! Then I shall rise in a moment and be happy with Him forever."—Froom, *Conditionalist Faith*, vol. 2, pp. 74, 75.

Commenting on Ecclesiastes 9:10, Luther wrote: "Another proof that the dead are insensible."—*Ibid.*, vol. 2, p. 77. Quite strong was the following:

But I permit the Pope to make articles of faith for himself and his faithful, such as [1] *The Bread and wine are transubstantiated in the sacrament.* [2] *The essence of God neither generated, nor is generated.* [3] *The soul is the substantial form of the human body.* [4] *The Pope is the emperor of the world, and the king of heaven, and God upon earth.* [5] THE SOUL IS IMMORTAL, with all those monstrous opinions to be found in the Roman dunghill of decretals . . . .—*Ibid.*, vol. 2, p. 73.

But if Martin Luther is a heretic, he's in good company, for John Wycliffe was of the same opinion about death (*Ibid.*, vol. 2, pp. 57-59). So was William Tyndale: "And ye, in putting them [departed souls] in heaven, hell, and purgatory, destroy the arguments wherewith Christ and Paul prove the resurrection."—*Ibid.* vol. 2, p. 94. And the apostle Peter:

Men and brethren, let me freely speak unto you of the patriarch David, that he is both dead and buried, and his sepulchre is with us unto this day. . . . For David is not ascended into the heavens. (Acts 2:29, 34)

Many more names could be added of Baptists, Anglicans, Lutherans, Catholics, and Presbyterians who believed the same. Even Pope John XXII in the fourteenth century believed that the soul of the deceased does not stand in the presence of God until after the resurrection (*Ibid.*, vol. 2, pp. 35-37).

Unlike Seventh-day Adventists, Jehovah's Witnesses believe that there are some today who do not sleep when they die, but go straight to heaven. This group they identify as the 144,000.

#93: Michael being Christ is a heresy. There are two problems with this charge.

First, it dispenses with and declares worthless one of the most potent arguments to convince the Jews about the deity of Christ. Various rabbis have taught that Michael the Archangel is a divine being, a being named "Jehovah," the high priest of the heavenly sanctuary, the mediator and deliverer of Israel, and one who sits at the right hand of God (Robert Leo Odom, *Israel's Angel Extraordinary*). Sounds like Christ, doesn't it?

This concept explains why we have so many Old Testament Scriptures talking about an "angel" who is God. More obvious examples of such Scriptures include:

And the angel of God spake unto me in a dream, saying, Jacob . . . . I am the God of Bethel. (Gen. 31:11, 13)

And he blessed Joseph, and said, God, before whom my fathers Abraham and Isaac did walk, the God which fed me all my life long unto this day, The Angel which redeemed me from all evil, bless the lads. (Gen. 48:15, 16)

And the angel of the LORD appeared unto him in a flame of fire out of the midst of a bush . . . . God called unto him out of the midst of the bush, and said, Moses, Moses. . . . Moreover he said, I am the God of thy father, the God of Abraham, the God of Isaac, and the God of Jacob. And Moses hid his face; for he was afraid to look upon God. And the LORD said . . . . (Ex. 3:2-7)

The word "LORD" in all caps in the *King James Version* indicates that the Hebrew word is *Yahweh*, commonly pronounced "Jehovah." Therefore, in this last passage "the angel" is plainly called both "God" and Jehovah.

But the angel of the LORD did no more appear to Manoah and to his wife. Then Manoah knew that he was an angel of the LORD. And Manoah said unto his wife, We shall surely die, because we have seen God. (Judg. 13:21-23)

The next two passages must be put together:

And Jacob was left alone; and there wrestled a man with him until the breaking of the day. . . . And he said unto him, What is thy name? And he said, Jacob. And he said, Thy name shall be called no more Jacob, but Israel: for as a prince hast thou power with God and with men, and hast prevailed. . . . And Jacob called the name of the place Peniel: for I have seen God face to face, and my life is preserved. (Gen. 32:24-30)

Yea, he had power over the angel, and prevailed: he wept, and made supplication unto him: he found him in Bethel, and there he spake with us; Even the LORD God of hosts; the LORD is his memorial. (Hos. 12:4, 5)

According to Genesis, Jacob wrestled with God. According to Hosea, he wrestled with "the angel" who is called *Yahweh.* Over and over again we have a divine Angel appearing who is called God and *Yahweh.* Could this "angel" who is God be God the Father? Not according to the New Testament:

No man hath seen God at any time; the only begotten Son, which is in the bosom of the Father, he hath declared him. (John 1:18)

And the Father himself, which hath sent me, hath borne witness of me. Ye have neither heard his voice at any time, nor seen his shape. (John 5:37)

The Greek and Hebrew words for "angel" simply mean "messenger." Sometimes they are used in Scripture to refer to human messengers, sometimes to Christ, and sometimes to the angels of heaven. The angels of heaven are called "angels" because their primary function is that of being "messengers" for God.

Indisputably, the supreme messenger of all is Christ: "Neither knoweth any man the Father, save the Son, and he to whomsoever the Son will reveal him" (Mat. 11:27). And this is precisely who King Nebuchadnezzar said the "angel" was:

He answered and said, Lo, I see four men loose, walking in the midst of the fire, and they have no hurt; and the form of the fourth is like the Son of God. . . . Then Nebuchadnezzar spake, and said, Blessed be the God of Shadrach, Meshach, and Abednego, who hath sent his angel, and delivered his servants that trusted in him. (Dan. 3:25, 28)

The second problem with calling these ideas heretical is that one can slip into the heresy of polytheism. If this divine "angel" the Bible speaks about is not Christ, who is it? If we have the Bible calling mere angels "god" and *yahweh,* then we have the Bible teaching that there is more than one God!

Unlike Seventh-day Adventists, most Jehovah's Witnesses will protest strongly to the following ideas:

1. Jesus is divine.
2. Jesus is God.
3. Jesus can be called Jehovah.

Want to read more of what *the Bible* says on the subject? Check out "An 'Angel' Named Yahweh" and "The Divine Christ in the Old Testament" posted at http://www.pickle-publishing.com/papers.

#94: "Early prominent Adventists, including James White and Uriah Smith, denied the deity of Jesus Christ, as do the Jehovah's Witnesses."—Leslie Martin.

#94: Uriah Smith and James White denied the deity of Christ. This is simply not true. The *documentation package* under "Point 48" and "Point 48a" gives no evidence to support such a claim. To the contrary, it cites James White as writing in 1877 that "ultra Unitarianism that makes Christ inferior to the Father is worse. Did God say to an inferior, 'Let us make man in our image?' "

James White repeatedly called Jesus "the divine Son of God" (*Bible Hygiene*, pp. 192, 203; *The Law and the Gospel*, p. 14; *Life Incidents*, p. 357; *The Redeemer and Redeemed*, p. 46). Uriah Smith called him "God's divine Son" (*The Biblical Institute*, p. 140). Smith emphatically stated that Christ is not a created being, and opposed such a teaching (*Daniel and the Revelation*, pp. 400, 430; *Looking Unto Jesus*, pp. 3-4, 10, 12, 18, 20-21).

White, Smith, and others reacted against certain speculations of their time regarding the Godhead. Their reactions are assumed to be a denial of belief in what the Bible teaches about the Trinity, making this charge in the video all too common. But such an assumption is unwarranted in light of three popular speculations about the Godhead that they reacted against.

1. A catechism from one church and a book from another taught the following: God is composed of three persons and is "without body or parts," but the second person definitely has a body! This view was criticized in the March 7, 1854, issue of the *Review and Herald*, page 50.

Early Seventh-day Adventists advocated taking the Bible literally unless there was an obvious symbol used. They saw such views of the Godhead as not doing this, since the Bible describes God as having a form and sitting on His throne in Heaven (e.g. Rev. 4:2, 3).

Just as they rejected views that spiritualized away the literalness of the second coming, so also they rejected views that spiritualized away the personality of God.

2. Some views of the Trinity did not make the Father and Christ to be separate persons. This can readily be concluded from the *documentation package*'s "Point 48." Joseph Bates is quoted as writing: "Respecting the trinity, I concluded that it was an impossibility for me to believe that the Lord Jesus Christ, the Son of the Father, was also the Almighty God, the Father, one and the same being."

3. The orthodox view of the Trinity includes an aspect that speculates regarding when Christ was begotten. Most believers are unaware of this aspect called the "processions." It teaches that the Son proceeded forth from the Father, and the Holy Spirit proceeded forth from both the Father and the Son. Yet, since God is outside of time, there never was a time when one of the three did not exist. So Jesus was begotten and proceeded forth, but that's not to say that He hasn't always been.

Pope John Paul II's views, found in Hogan and LeVoir's *Faith for Today* (complete with Imprimatur), describes this position pretty well. John Paul believes that the Father's self-concept, unlike our self-concept, is real. In God's "consciousness" was "an identical image of Himself," and that is how the Son was begotten. "The consciousness of the Father and the Son contains an inner reflection and image of Their act of Love," and that is how the Holy Spirit proceeded forth (pp. 12-14).

A 1933 English translation of a standard Dutch catechism, published in India, describes the processions in essentially the same way (J. F. De Groot, *Catholic Teaching*, pp. 99, 100).

A priest this writer heard lecture on the right to life included material in his talk about the Trinity. He said that when the Father and Son looked at each other, they had love for each other, and they sighed, and that was "the Holy Sigh."

And yet, though the Son and the Spirit came forth, They always have been, since God and the processions are outside of time (Hogan and Levoir, p. 14). Sounds a bit contradictory? These early Seventh-day Adventists thought so.

They apparently had no problem with the general idea of the processions, judging from what little they wrote on that topic, but they just couldn't be dogmatic about both God and the processions being outside of time. So can we with a clear conscience call men cultists and non-Christians who wanted to take the Bible just as it reads and not speculate like this?

#95 & #96: "Both Jehovah's Witnesses and Seventh-day Adventists have produced their own altered versions of the Bible to reflect their aberrant doctrines. Both have set false dates for the return of Jesus Christ, and failed miserably to prophesy correctly."—Leslie Martin.

#95: Both have produced altered versions of the Bible. The version used by the Jehovah's Witnesses is called the *New World Translation*. In its very title it thus claims to be a version or translation, while *The Clear Word*'s preface distinctly says that it is not such. This charge is therefore false (see #80).

The *documentation package* under "Point 49" clearly proves that the Watch Tower Society, the organization behind the Jehovah's Witnesses, has produced its own official version. It is the publisher and it holds the copyright. In contrast, "Point 49a" proves that Dr. Blanco's *The Clear Word* is but a paraphrase, and that he is the publisher and copyright holder, not the church. Therefore, it can't even truthfully be said that the Seventh-day Adventist Church has produced its own *paraphrase*.

While paraphrases by their very nature interweave interpretations into the text, translations are not supposed to. However, as in the case of the *New World Translation*, they sometimes do.

#96: Both have set dates for Christ's return. Mrs. Martin would be hard pressed to prove that Seventh-day Adventists have ever set dates for Christ's return, other than a renegade member now and then. Ever since they were organized as a denomination in 1863, they have never predicted a date for the second coming.

So is Mrs. Martin referring to some incident before 1863? Let's examine the historical facts.

In the July 21, 1851, *Review* Extra, Mrs. White published a vision of the previous September that opposed predicting dates for Christ's return (cf. *Early Writings*, p. 75), a vision the video itself quoted from under #14. Before even this, in 1845 we have her opposing some first-day Adventists who were setting dates (*Early Writings*, p. 22; Arthur White, vol. 1, p. 91). That takes us just about back to 1844.

And what about 1844? In January of that year there were no Sabbath-keeping Adventists, all Millerites being Sunday keepers. Sometime between that spring and the end of the year, a single congregation in Washington, New Hampshire, began to keep the Sabbath.

James and Ellen White did not become Sabbatarian Adventists until 1846. So before Ellen White became a *Seventh-day* Adventist, she was already opposing the setting of dates for the second coming.

It was Methodists, Baptists, Congregationalists, and Presbyterians who predicted the dates of 1843 and October 22, 1844, not Seventh-day Adventists. The group that became the Seventh-day Adventist Church was the group of Millerites which took a firm position against setting any more dates for Christ's coming.

In contrast, Jehovah's Witnesses, or more correctly, the Watchtower Society, set a number of dates from 1914 to 1975. Yet the video is even wrong here. Not one of the Watchtower dates was a prediction of Christ's return. When Barbour convinced Russell that Christ had really come in 1874 after all, it was already 1876, and the Watchtower Society did not yet exist. Likewise, the 1914 date for Christ's coming did not replace 1874 until the early 1930's. So with both the 1874 and the 1914 dates, the Watchtower adopted them as dates for Christ's return *after* the fact. They were *not* predictions.

Mrs. Martin wouldn't likely be an expert at Watchtower doctrines, even though the video presents her as such. But the one who wrote the script should be. Lorri MacGregor used to be a Jehovah's Witness, and her ministry is dedicated to disseminating "facts" about Watchtower doctrines.

Under "Point 50," the *documentation package* is supposed to prove that the Watchtower set dates for Christ's coming. However, it instead proves that they continued to teach as late as 1929 that Christ had come in 1874, thus showing that the Watchtower never predicted Christ's return in 1914. Regarding their predicting Christ's return in 1874, not one pre-1874 publication of the then non-existent Watchtower Society is cited.

#97: "Both have covered up their errors and claimed to be the only remnant church in the world."—Leslie Martin.

#97: Both claim to be the only remnant church. Under "Point 52a" in the *documentation package* is proof that Jehovah's Witnesses do not teach that they are the remnant church, contrary to what Mrs. Martin just said.

Jehovah's Witnesses teach that the 144,000 are the only ones who go to heaven, few of these still being on earth today. The rest of the redeemed they believe will stay on earth. The photocopy under "Point 52a" plainly says that this latter group, the "earthly class" or "bridesmaids," are not the remnant. Only the 144,000, the "heavenly class" or "bridal congregation," are:

> Of course these figurative bridesmaids do not expect to go to heaven with the "remnant," but they honor the heavenly King and his Bridegroom Son, and show due respect for the remnant of the Bridal congregation.—*The Watchtower*, Nov. 15, 1974.

Thus Witnesses teach that only a very minute portion of their numbers are the remnant. How minute? Of 10,650,158 Witnesses who attended the 1991 Memorial Service (communion service), only 8,850 believed they were part of the 144,000 (E. B. Price, *Our Friends the Jehovah's Witnesses*, p. 47). That means that in 1991, only .0831% of Jehovah's Witnesses were the remnant while 99.9169% were not, according to their own beliefs. And since the remaining 144,000 are quite advanced in years, this proportion decreases every passing year.

Seventh-day Adventists base their teaching of the remnant primarily on Revelation 12:17. "And the dragon was wroth with the woman, and went to make war with the remnant of her seed, which keep the commandments of God, and have the testimony of Jesus Christ" (Rev. 12:17). First of all, what does this woman symbolize? All through Scripture, a woman is used to symbolize God's people or church:

> Turn, O backsliding children, saith the LORD; for I am married unto you. (Jer. 3:14)
> For the husband is the head of the wife, even as Christ is the head of the church: and he is the saviour of the body. Therefore as the church is subject unto Christ, so let the wives be to their own husbands in every thing. Husbands, love your wives, even as Christ also loved the church, and gave himself for it; (Eph. 5:23-25)

We therefore have in Revelation 12:17 a picture of God's last day people, His remnant church. They are described as keeping God's commandments and having the testimony of Jesus. What is Jesus's testimony? How does He testify to us when He isn't here in person?

> Yet the LORD testified against Israel, and against Judah, by all the prophets, and by all the seers, saying, Turn ye from your evil ways, and keep my commandments and my statutes. (2 Kings 17:13)

Yet many years didst thou forbear them, and testifiedst against them by thy spirit in thy prophets. (Neh. 9:30)

Of which salvation the prophets have enquired and searched diligently, . . . Searching what, or what manner of time the Spirit of Christ which was in them did signify, when it testified beforehand the sufferings of Christ, and the glory that should follow. (1 Pet. 1:10, 11)

So when Jesus is not here in person to give His testimony, He testifies by His Spirit through a prophet. This is why the book of Revelation equates the "testimony of Jesus" with the "spirit of prophecy":

I am thy fellowservant, and of thy brethren that have the testimony of Jesus: worship God: for the testimony of Jesus is the spirit of prophecy. (Rev. 19:10)

Then saith he unto me, See thou do it not: for I am thy fellowservant, and of thy brethren the prophets. (Rev. 22:9)

Thus the remnant church is a church that keeps all of God's commandments and has the gift of prophecy. Find a church that meets that description, and you have found the remnant church of Bible prophecy.

Jehovah's Witnesses, Cont.; Plagiarism

#98 & #99: "Both have been guilty of plagiarism of earlier works without giving credit to the previous authors."—Leslie Martin.

#98: Both plagiarized. If this charge is true, it can't be proven by the "evidence" in the *documentation package*.

In the index under "Point 53," it says: "Both SDA's and JW's are guilty of plagiarism of earlier works. The SDA section is documented under point 54 and the JW plagiarism is listed here." When one turns to "Point 53," one finds a single sheet put together by a Mr. Gary Busselman from South Dakota. This sheet purports to contain an outline of history about the Witnesses. The only evidence that one finds on this sheet even remotely connected to this charge is the following:

> **John Aquila Brown**: published in book, *Even-Tide* (1823), his interpretation of the "seven times" of Daniel, by means of the day-year formula, to produce 2520 years, in exactly the same way as the Watchtower Society does today, except he started with 604 BC and ended up with 1917 AD. This 29 years before C. T. Russell was born, 47 years before C. T. Russell started his Bible study group, and 50+ years before the book *"Three Worlds"* was written.

A major problem with this is that Brown was from Britain. Did Russell ever hear of Brown's work, let alone read it? The *documentation package* is advertised as "substantiating the information contained in this program." Yet no demonstration of a connection between Brown's book and any Watchtower publication is even attempted. If the Watchtower really plagiarized Brown's book, where is the evidence?

Besides, Busselman's sheet is unreliable. It says that "Ellen G. White . . . founded the Second Advent Movement, the present Seven-Day [sic] Adventist group" after splitting off from the "Miller move-ment." However, the Millerite Movement *was* the "Second Advent Movement," or at least a very prominent part of it, and Mrs. White didn't found it. She was only four years old when Miller started preaching!

Busselman's sheet also says that "William Miller" "quit the movement he founded when his predictions, called the 'great disappointment of 1844,' failed." This is very slightly true. He officially quit the movement in December 1849 when he *died*. As he was dying he said to "Brother Bosworth": "Tell them (the brethren) we are right. The coming of the Lord draweth nigh; but they must be patient, and wait for him."—Bliss, p. 377.

Perhaps Busselman's sheet is the reason why the video leaves the impression that N. H. Barbour was a Seventh-day Adventist. The sheet identifies Barbour, Paton, and Wendell as being Second Adventists. Since it says that Mrs. White started the "Second Advent Movement," this leaves the impression that Barbour, Paton, and Wendell were Seventh-day Adventists. In actuality, they were Advent Christians, not Seventh-day Adventists.

#99: Both were "guilty" of this crime. One other problem with claiming that the Witnesses were "guilty" of plagiarizing Brown's book is this: Since Brown was from Britain, his book was fully in the public domain. There was no copyright protection in America on British books written prior to July 1, 1891 (Nichol, pp. 454, 455). Thus it is incorrect for anyone to say that the Witnesses were "guilty" of plagiarizing Brown's book.

#100: "In 1982 an Adventist pastor, Walter T. Rea, released this book, *The White Lie*. It was dedicated to all those who would rather believe a bitter truth than a sweet lie. He loved Mrs.

White's writings and thought that he should read what she read. He began to see huge amounts of plagiarism in her writings."—Wallace Slattery.

#100: The book tells you about a bitter truth. The bitter "truth" that *The White Lie* teaches is a "truth" that is totally repugnant to evangelicals who believe in the final authority of Scripture:

> Used in all Seventh-day Adventist schools and colleges as authoritative on Old Testament matters, *Patriarchs and Prophets* has been accepted by Adventists as the final word. No deviation from this norm is accepted in matters of ideas concerning *Creation, geology,* theology, or Christology.—p. 73, italics added.

This statement by Mr. Rea strongly suggests that he does not believe what the Bible says about Creation and Noah's Flood. Otherwise, why would he be critical of Adventist schools that do not allow deviations from Mrs. White's endorsement of the biblical accounts of a six-day creation and the origin of the geologic column?

When the present writer asked Lorri MacGregor, the video's script writer, about evidence for the long-ago debunked lawsuit myth (see #103–#105), she suggested that he call Mr. Rea. In talking with him, this writer asked if his reasons for not believing in Mrs. White could also be applied to the Bible. He proceeded to say that he:

1. does not take the Bible literally,
2. does not believe in a world-wide flood,
3. does not believe that God told Abraham to offer up Isaac, and
4. does not believe God told the Israelites to slay the Canaanites.—Jan. 4, 2000.

Mrs. White wrote:

> It is Satan's plan to weaken the faith of God's people in the *Testimonies*. Next follows skepticism in regard to the vital points of our faith, the pillars of our position, then doubt as to the Holy Scriptures, and then the downward march to perdition.—*Testimonies for the Church*, vol. 4, p. 211.

Whether one believes in Mrs. White or not, she had a point. Many of those who like Mr. Rea have given up faith in her writings have also come not to believe what the Bible says. It is no longer the authority to them that it once was. This kind of thing is all too common.

And why is this? Because the same arguments used against Mrs. White's inspiration either can be or are used against the Bible's inspiration too (see #101).

Seventh-day Adventists take the Bible just as it reads:

1. They believe that Jesus created the world in six literal days about 6000 years ago.
2. They believe that sin entered the world at the fall of Adam and Eve, and that death did not exist until after the Fall.
3. They believe that there was a world-wide flood in Noah's day that buried everything.
4. As a very natural conclusion of the above three Bible-based beliefs, they also believe that the fossils in the earth must be those of the creatures that were buried during the Flood.

Mrs. White's writings clearly endorse the above Bible-based beliefs. This is why some Adventists of a liberal bent would like to see Adventism jettison her writings. Generally, Adventists think she was a prophet. Since she endorsed what the Bible says about Creation and the Flood, faith in her writings is a major obstacle to liberal Adventists who would rather see the church adopt evolution. Thus her writings must be attacked.

Too bad every denomination doesn't have someone who spoke "with prophetic authority" about how we should take what the Bible says about Creation and the Flood literally. We would then not have so many denominations today openly teaching that evolution is a fact and that the Bible accounts are a lie. You see, Mrs. White's writings have helped the Adventist Church retain its conservative stance on these issues.

Do you really want to accept the bitter "truth" that *The White Lie* endorses?

To be fair to Mr. Rea, it should be added that despite his views on Mrs. White's inspiration, he still considers her writings to be very inspirational. He particularly enjoys her *Christ's Object Lessons* on the parables of Jesus, and *Thoughts from the Mount of Blessing* on Christ's Sermon on the Mount. Grab a copy and see if you can figure out why he likes them so much.

#101: "Through diligent research it was discovered that her supposed inspiration from God had been borrowed from other authors without proper credit being given to the original sources."—Narrator.

#101: Her inspiration was borrowed from others without giving credit. The problem with this argument is that it directly undermines the authority of the Scriptures.

Anyone reading Matthew, Mark, and Luke can tell that someone borrowed from someone without giving credit. Does that mean that Luke got his "supposed inspiration" from Matthew? Should we conclude that Luke was therefore a false prophet?

The books of Kings and 2 Chronicles are awfully similar in many places, and some of Chronicles's genealogies are found elsewhere. Parts of Jeremiah are just like 2 Kings and 2 Chronicles, and 1 Chronicles is nearly identical to 2 Samuel in places. Joshua 15:16-19 is the same as Judges 1:12-15. Someone was borrowing from someone.

The similarities between 2 Peter and Jude are another very striking example:

2 Peter	Jude
Simon Peter, a servant and an apostle of Jesus Christ, to them that have obtained like precious faith with us through the righteousness of God and our Saviour Jesus Christ. (1:1)	Jude, the servant of Jesus Christ, and brother of James, to them that are sanctified by God the Father, and preserved in Jesus Christ, and called. (1)
Grace and peace be multiplied unto you. (1:2)	Mercy unto you, and peace, and love, be multiplied. (2)
Wherefore I will not be negligent to put you always in remembrance of these things, though ye know them. (1:12)	I will therefore put you in remembrance, though ye once knew this. (5)
. . . there shall be false teachers among you, who privily shall bring in damnable heresies, even denying the Lord that bought them, and bring upon themselves swift destruction. (2:1)	For there are certain men crept in unawares, who were before of old ordained to this condemnation, ungodly men, turning the grace of our God into lasciviousness, and denying the only Lord God, and our Lord Jesus Christ. (4)
For if God spared not the angels that sinned, but . . . delivered them into chains of darkness, to be reserved unto judgment. . . . The Lord knoweth how . . . to reserve the unjust unto the day of judgment to be punished. (2:4, 9)	And the angels which kept not their first estate, but left their own habitation, he hath reserved in everlasting chains under darkness unto the judgment of the great day. (6)
And turning the cities of Sodom and Gomorrha into ashes condemned them with an overthrow, making them an ensample unto those that after should live ungodly. (2:6)	Even as Sodom and Gomorrha, and the cities about them in like manner, giving themselves over to fornication, and going after strange flesh, are set forth for an example. (7)
But chiefly them that walk after the flesh in the lust of uncleanness, and despise government. . . . they are not afraid to speak evil of dignities. (2:10)	Likewise also these filthy dreamers defile the flesh, despise dominion, and speak evil of dignities. (8)
Whereas angels, which are greater in power and might, bring not railing accusation against them before the Lord. (2:11)	Yet Michael the archangel, when contending with the devil . . . durst not bring against him a railing accusation. (9)
But these, as natural brute beasts . . . speak evil of the things that they understand not; and shall utterly perish in their own corruption. (2:12)	But these speak evil of those things which they know not: but what they know naturally, as brute beasts, in those things they corrupt themselves. (10)
Spots they are and blemishes, . . . while they feast with you. (2:13)	These are spots in your feasts of charity, when they feast with you. (12)
Which have forsaken the right way, and are gone astray, following the way of Balaam the son of Bosor, who loved the wages of unrighteousness. (2:15)	Woe unto them! for they have gone in the way of Cain, and ran greedily after the error of Balaam for reward, and perished in the gainsaying of Core. (11)
These are wells without water, clouds that are carried with a tempest. (2:17)	Clouds they are without water. (12)
To whom the mist of darkness is reserved for ever. (2:17)	To whom is reserved the blackness of darkness for ever. (13)
That ye may be mindful of the words which were spoken before by the holy prophets, and of the commandment of us the apostles of the Lord and Saviour. (3:2)	But, beloved, remember ye the words which were spoken before of the apostles of our Lord Jesus Christ. (17)
Knowing this first, that there shall come in the last days scoffers, walking after their own lusts. (3:3)	How that they told you there should be mockers in the last time, who should walk after their own ungodly lusts. (18)

If Jude "copied" from Peter, then he "borrowed" a total of 14 out of 25 verses!

"But Jude and Peter were both Bible writers. Mrs. White copied from people who weren't." Talk to the right skeptic, and he'll try to convince you that the Bible writers did that too. For example, compare the following selections from the book of 1 Enoch with 2 Peter 2:4, 9, and Jude 6:

> And again the Lord said to Raphael: "Bind Azazel hand and foot, and cast him into the darkness: . . . . and let him abide there for ever, and cover his face that he may not see light. And on the day of the great judgement he shall be cast into the fire."—10:4-7, in *The Apocrypha and Pseudepigrapha of the Old Testament.*

> And there mine eyes saw how they made these their instruments, iron chains of immeasurable weight. And I asked the angel of peace who went with me, saying: "For whom are these chains being prepared?" And he said unto me: "These are being prepared for the hosts of Azazel, so that they may take them and cast them into the abyss of complete condemnation."—54:3, 4, *Ibid.*

Four points should be noted. First of all, is the book of 1 Enoch inspired or is it not? Its seventh chapter tells us that angels married people, and that their kids grew to be "three thousand ells" tall. Then when men ran out of food to feed these giants, the giants started eating people. These and other doings led to the fallen angel Azazel and his cronies getting the punishment described above. Now you know why the book of 1 Enoch never became part of Scripture.

Second, did either Peter or Jude, in borrowing the wording of this uninspired source, say anything that was not factually and doctrinally accurate? Not at all.

They simply referred to the fact that the angels who rebelled against God will be punished on the day of judgment. These angels are on death row in prison, as it were. Moreover, neither Peter nor Jude endorsed the idea that these angels had fathered giants who ate up all the food.

Third, did either Peter or Jude "plagiarize"? Using a modern definition given by *Encyclopædia Britannica,* let's see.

> **plagiarism,** the act of taking the writings of another person and passing them off as one's own. . . .

> If only thoughts are duplicated, expressed in different words, there is no breach of contract.

No, they didn't plagiarize. They didn't copy 1 Enoch verbatim and then pretend that they had written the material themselves. Instead, they borrowed a few words to use when expressing their own thoughts.

Fourth, did Jude or Peter fail to give "proper credit"? It is safe to assume that they did whatever was considered "proper" by society at that time.

God inspired Peter and Jude with divine thoughts, and they then put those thoughts into the best human words they could find.

Evangelicals, Bible-believing Christians everywhere, if a prophet cannot borrow some of the words of another writer without giving credit and still be considered divinely inspired, then the Bible is not inspired!

Surely Jeremiah Films could not have known that this video they were making at the behest of former Adventists would strike right at the heart of the authority of Scripture.

#102: "Her major books, including *Patriarchs and Prophets, The Desire of Ages, The Spirit of Prophecy, The Great Controversy, Selected Messages, The Acts of the Apostles, Christ's Object Lessons, Counsels on Stewardship, Evangelism, Fundamentals of Christian Education, Gospel Workers, Messages to Young People, the Ministry of Healing, My Life Today, Prophets and Kings, Sons and Daughters of God, Steps to Christ, Testimonies to the Church, Thoughts from the Mount of Blessing,* **and others contain plagiarized material stolen from earlier writers."**—Narrator.

#102: All these books contain "stolen" material. A major problem is the use of the word "stolen." In order for Mrs. White to have "stolen" words and thoughts from another writer, those words and thoughts had to legally belong to them and not to her. You can't steal what you already own.

Until 1909, portions of the words and thoughts of other writers, along with the general flow of topics in a manuscript, were in the public domain. They did not belong solely to the writer, and so could not be

"stolen" from him or her. While the entire work belonged to the writer, some wording and thoughts could be used by another without "stealing."

Perusal of *The White Lie* indicates that what Mrs. White did at times, in the borrowing of some words and thoughts from other writers (like the Bible writers did), was to make a "derivative work." A derivative work is not one that has been copied verbatim. It is a work that is based on and derived from another work.

From the previous section it is clear that either Jude or Peter made a derivative work based on the other's epistle. Either Jude or Peter took thoughts from the other and utilized them in writing his own work. That's a derivative work, not a plagiarized work.

Making a derivative work without permission from the original author became illegal in 1909. Interestingly, as *The White Lie* points out on page 49, 1909 was the very year that Mrs. White requested that credit to the historians quoted from in *Great Controversy* be added in the next edition. This suggests that when it *first* became possible to steal material in this manner, Mrs. White took the needed precautions to prevent such occurrences.

Though the term "proper credit" took on a new definition that year, 1909 wasn't the first time she expressed concern about such issues. This is indicated by her comments in the April 14 issue of *Review and Herald*, comments regarding "proper credit" that was given to a particular author. Oh, the year? *1868.*

Rest assured that whatever "proper credit" meant at the time, Mrs. White endeavored to make sure it was given. It's just that society didn't consider any sort of credit necessary when making a derivative work.

The list of books that the narrator gave, with two exceptions, comes from pages 173-175 of *The White Lie,* photocopies of which appear under "Point 54a" and "Point 54b" in the *documentation package.* These photocopies also give a list of "plagiarized" sources. At the top of the list on page 175 is this entry:

Nichols, Francis Davis, Ed.
The S.D.A. Bible Commentary
Washington, D.C., Review & Herald
Pub., 7 vol., 1953-1957

So according to *The White Lie,* Mrs. White even borrowed from books published 38-42 years after her death? Must be a typo, but that's what it says.

If *The White Lie* had been written to provide answers rather than to raise doubts, some of its content would be radically different. Take for example this statement on page 147:

Please observe that the artists' signatures on the drawings have been altered. In some cases, *Pacific Press, Oakland, Cal.,* has been inserted in place of the artist's signature; in others, the signatures have either been obliterated or cut off, and *Pacific Press, Oakland, Cal.* added below.

Then follows five examples of artwork appearing in the 1886 printing of volume 4 of *Spirit of Prophecy,* artwork that was taken from Wylie's *History of Protestantism.*

In the last of the five examples of artwork, "Swain SC" is substituted with "Pacific Press, Oakland, Cal." "SC" is an abbreviation for the Latin word *sculpsit,* a word meaning "he engraved it." Since Pacific Press had to re-engrave the picture before they could print it, Swain was no longer the engraver, and they had every right to replace his name with theirs.

Now let's examine some of the other pictures in light of this discovery. In both the second and fourth examples of the five, the artist's initials in the lower right-hand corner are retained in Pacific Press's copy. Only the engraver's signature in the lower left of both pictures was replaced. No credit being given?

Whether Mr. Rea discovered these "stolen" pictures on his own, or whether he borrowed the idea from a 1930's issue of E. S. Ballenger's *The Gathering Call,* his book does not say. But it is a simple fact that the White Estate produced documents to answer such charges in the 1930's, proving that the right to use the artwork had been *paid for.*

Cassell and Company, who owned the rights to the illustrations in question, had offices in London, New York, and Melbourne. Mrs. White's son, W. C. White, coordinated negotiations with all three offices. By giving specific credit to Cassell for every picture used, they saved themselves 40% of the price when using them in the British Adventist paper. But for *Spirit of Prophecy,* volume 4, they opted for paying the full price and omitting the credits ("Did The Great Controversy Contain Stolen Illustrations?").

So the Whites endeavored to do everything appropriately, but even if something got overlooked, we shouldn't crucify them for it. The best of us sometimes goof.

Take for example the video's jacket, copyrighted by an organization associated with Mark Martin, the video's executive producer. In the upper left corner is a translucent, ghost-like picture of Mrs. White behind a church. This picture apparently was first published in 1960, having been "recently discovered" at that time (*The Spirit of Prophecy Treasure Chest,* p. 172). That being so, Mr. Martin should have enquired with the White Estate before using it. Since the White Estate has no recollection of such an enquiry, and Mr. Martin declines to comment, apparently Mr. Martin forgot to ensure that he was not violating any copyright laws. Perhaps it was just an oversight.

#103, #104, & #105: "One book, *Sketches from the Life of Paul*, was plagiarized in its entirety by Ellen G. White. It resulted in a lawsuit and the book was quickly taken out of print."—Narrator.

#103: It was plagiarized in its entirety. This writer has both Mrs. White's 1883 book and Conybeare and Howson's book, and this wild charge is simply not true. As well as being different in both wording and size, the books definitely differ on basic interpretations of verses dealing with Paul's life.

F. D. Nichol's book, *Ellen G. White and Her Critics*, was published in 1951. It gives statistics for how much material from Conybeare and Howson was included in *Sketches*. Direct quotations of words, phrases, and clauses, along with close paraphrases, amount to 7% of Mrs. White's book being taken from 4% of Conybeare's book. Another book utilized in this way was one by Farrar. 4% of her book came from 2% of his book. If we throw in loose paraphrases for good measure, we have a total of 15.35% of her book being taken from these two sources (pp. 424-426). This is a far cry from being "plagiarized in its entirety."

Script writer Lorri MacGregor sent this author alleged documentation to support this long-ago debunked lawsuit myth. It consisted of the *1919 Bible Conference Minutes* published in volume 10, number 1, of *Spectrum*. *Spectrum* is a theologically liberal journal which does not take the position that the Bible, the infallible Word of God, is the final authority in matters of faith and practice. This has led through the years to its publishing of articles endorsing evolution and denying the substitutionary atonement of Christ.

In these minutes discovered in the 1970's, General Conference president A. G. Daniells says that he compared *Sketches* with Conybeare, "and we read word for word, page after page, and no quotations, no credit, and really I did not know the difference until I began to compare them."

Obviously, he didn't know what he was talking about. The books are not the same "word for word, page after page."

A number of major factual errors like this one, coupled with the fact that the minutes were only recently discovered, raises the question of whether they are a forgery. It appears, however, that they are indeed genuine, and that sometimes Daniells would shoot from the hip, without being particular about accuracy. At times he would grossly exaggerate.

The *documentation package* is supposed to prove this charge under "Point 55." Rather than proof being given, a citation appears from page 27 of *The White Lie* which claims that Conybeare and Howson's book is "similar" to Mrs. White's book. Thus once again the *documentation package* proves the falsity of the video's charges, for if the books are "similar," they cannot be identical, and thus *Sketches* was not "plagiarized in its entirety."

#104: It resulted in a lawsuit. This myth was debunked at least by 1951 in F. D. Nichol's book.

First of all, Conybeare and Howson's book was from Britain. Since there was no copyright protection in the US for British works written prior to July 1, 1891, it was in the public domain. There thus was no legal basis for such a lawsuit.

Second, even if their book had been written after 1891, copyright protection still did not yet cover the making of derivative works. Conybeare and Howson would have had to prove in a court of law that Mrs. White's book was a plagiarized work, not a derivative work. They would have been hard pressed to do so.

The Thomas Y. Crowell Company of New York, a US publisher of Conybeare's book, wrote in 1924:

> We publish Conybeare's LIFE AND EPISTLES OF THE APOSTLE PAUL but this is not a copyrighted book and we would have no legal grounds for action against your book and we do not think that we have ever raised any objection or made any claim such as you speak of.—Nichol, p. 456.

Thomas Y. Crowell was just one publisher of Conybeare's book in America. By law they could freely publish the book without sending any royalties back to Britain, and never get sued, for it just was not a copyrighted work. Since they themselves were publishing the book in its entirety without needing to get permission, they well knew that there could be no lawsuit.

D. M. Canright, an extremely bitter former Adventist, included the lawsuit myth in his 1919 book, *Life of Mrs. E. G. White*. According to Nichol's research, this is the first time the myth appeared in print, the very year of the above mentioned Bible Conference. According to the *1919 Bible Conference Minutes*, A. G. Daniells did mention the lawsuit story as if it were a fact. All this shows is that Daniells likely read Canright's book and thought that the myth was factual. Yet Canright offered no proof whatsoever of the charge, and *there was no possibility that it could have been true* (Nichol, p. 438).

Sketches was published in 1883. Canright's first book against Adventism and Mrs. White, *Seventh-day Adventism Renounced*, came out in 1889. It contained three short paragraphs about plagiarism, but never mentioned a lawsuit. Over the next 25 years, it went through 14 editions, but the lawsuit myth was never included (*Ibid.*, p. 429). All this indicates that nobody had yet dreamed up this particular fable.

#105: It was quickly taken out of print. *Sketches* was published in 1883. The *Signs of the Times* promoted it through most of 1885. As late as 1887, editions of *The Great Controversy* sold by colporteurs to the general public contained direct advertisements for the book.

American editions of *The Great Controversy* mentioned *Sketches* on the title page. Editions in England, homeland of Conybeare and Howson, mentioned *Sketches* on the title page as late as 1907. Nichol put it well: "What a strange way to 'suppress' a book!" (pp. 443-446).

#106, #107, #108, & #109: "Despite the irrefutable evidence the Seventh-day Adventist Church chose to fight back against these charges with a book titled *The White Truth*. In it, their main line of defense was that since there were no copyright laws at the time, Ellen White hadn't actually broken the law, which of course side stepped the issue."—Narrator.

#106: The evidence is irrefutable. A careful reading of #100-#105 shows that the evidence is anything but irrefutable.

#107: The book's main line of defense concerned copyright laws. This is not true. The question of what the law was like back then was only one of a number of defenses presented in the book, not the main one.

The White Truth has six chapters composed of ninety-eight pages. The chapter titles are

1. The Truth About Sources
2. The Truth About Plagiarism
3. The Truth About Prophets
4. The Truth About Authority
5. The Truth About Inspiration and Revelation
6. The Truth About Lies.

In the chapter, "The Truth About Plagiarism," the question of what the law was like back then occupies less than 4 pages out of 16. Unless there is some brief mention elsewhere in the book about legal matters, we have only 4 pages out of 98 dedicated specifically to the question of nineteenth century copyright laws.

#108: It said that there were no copyright laws back then. This too is untrue. On page 32 is a description of a conversation with a judge who said that the first copyright law was passed in 1790. Thus *The White Truth* says clearly that there were copyright laws in America 37 years *before* Mrs. White was born.

But once again, these American copyright laws did not protect British books until 1891, and did not prohibit derivative works until 1909.

#109: This sidestepped the issue. No it didn't, as the video itself makes clear.

There are two issues being addressed: 1) Was Mrs. White "guilty" of "stealing," of "plagiarism"? 2) Did she get her inspiration from others instead of from God?

Was she "guilty"? Before we can have a trial and reach a verdict, we have to find out what the laws were like back then. If her critics would quit using such words as "guilty" and "stolen," what the laws were could be ignored. Since they choose to use such words, the matter must be investigated. It therefore is not sidestepping the issue that they themselves have chosen.

Did she get her inspiration from others instead of from God? We must conclude that, according to the Bible, inspired writers can borrow wording and document structure from other writers without making their own writings less than inspired (see #101). A portion of *The White Truth* is dedicated to dealing with this issue as well, so there was no sidestepping here either.

Additionally, *The White Truth* presents a number of other arguments besides these two, which the reader is invited to read for himself.

#110 & #111: "Yet the Seventh-day Adventist hierarchy has been unable to respond to the challenge to prove that even 20% of her writings were original."—Narrator.

#110: They're unable to respond even after twenty years. The truth is that the "hierarchy" responded 31 years before Mr. Rea's book was even published.

As brought out under #103, F. D. Nichol's 1951 book stated that, including loose paraphrasing, 15.35% of *Sketches from the Life of Paul*, a book which was "plagiarized in its entirety," was taken from two other books. That means that around 84.65% was Mrs. White's own work.

How about other books by Mrs. White that were not "plagiarized in" their "entirety"? Obviously, they should have an even higher percentage of original material.

A lot of this video's problems could have been avoided if its researchers had simply read F. D. Nichol's book *Ellen G. White and Her Critics.*

#111: Prove that 20% of her writings are original. Does this kind of challenge even make sense? How could one ever prove such a thing? You would have to have infinite knowledge of every book that Mrs. White could possibly have read, and would have to compare these books to every word she ever wrote.

A much easier task would be for the critics to prove that 80% of her writings were not her own. Yet that would be such a time-consuming task, they would not likely attempt it.

Another way to put it is, Would it be more appropriate to say, "Prove that 20% of the Gospel of Luke is original," or more appropriate to say, "Prove that 80% of the Gospel of Luke is not original." The latter approach would be more appropriate, because the former would be impossible to prove.

Here's a different sort of challenge for Jeremiah Films: Prove that 20% of the information contained in this video is both accurate and relevant. Try to respond within twenty years. Since it's going on three years since this writer contacted you, you still have seventeen to go.

#112: "Equally as shaky were the visions she claimed to have from God."—Narrator.

#112: Her visions were shaky. One thing the video does not touch with a ten-foot pole, and understandably so, is what would happen during her visions. There was unquestionably something supernatural about them. The 1868 book *Life Incidents* described it this way:

1. She is utterly unconscious of everything transpiring around her, as has been proved by the most rigid tests, but views herself as removed from this world, and in the presence of heavenly beings.

2. She does not breathe. During the entire period of her continuance in vision, which has at different times ranged from fifteen minutes to three hours, there is no breath, as has been repeatedly proved by pressing upon the chest, and by closing the mouth and nostrils.

3. Immediately on entering vision, her muscles become rigid, and joints fixed, so far as any external force can influence them. At the same time her movements and gestures, which are frequent, are free and graceful, and cannot be hindered nor controlled by the strongest person.

4. On coming out of vision, whether in the daytime or a well-lighted room at night, all is total darkness. Her power to distinguish even the most brilliant objects, held within a few inches of the eyes, returns but gradually, sometimes not being fully established for three hours. This has continued for the past twenty years; yet her eyesight is not in the least impaired, few persons having better than she now possesses.—p. 272.

Regarding "closing the mouth and nostrils," it might be added that Daniel T. Bourdeau himself performed this test for ten minutes on June 28, 1857. He had up to that point been "an unbeliever in the visions," but not any longer. More than thirty years later he declared, " 'Since witnessing this wonderful phenomenon, I have not once been inclined to doubt the divine origin of her visions.' "—*General Conference Daily Bulletin*, Jan. 31 and Feb. 1, 1893, p. 60.

John Loughborough, an early Seventh-day Adventist who was a bit of a historian, stated:

At my house on Champion street, in this city, in the autumn of 1863 she had a vision. A brother was present, a stone mason. While she was in vision, kneeling, as her arms moved about seemingly in an easy manner, Elder White said to the man, "Brother, that looks like an easy motion, and as though you could readily bend her arm. You can try it if you wish. This brother placed his knee in the bend of her arm, took hold of her extended hand with both his hands, and settled back with all his might. It made no impression. He said to Elder White, "I would as soon think of bending an iron bar as that arm." He had hardly spoken these words before her arm moved around the other way. As he tried to resist the pressure, he was slid along upon the floor. . . .

In the third vision of Miss Harmon, which was given in her father's house in Portland, she arose in vision, her eyes looking upward, took from the bureau one of the great family Bibles published in 1822 by Teale, Boston. (This Bible measured 18 x 11 x 4 inches, and weighs a little over eighteen pounds.) Opening this great book upon her left arm, extended at right angles from her body, she held it in that position for half an hour. With her right hand she turned from text to text, repeating the same to which her finger was pointing, yet her eyes meantime looking upward and away from the book. One or another of those present looked at every text quoted, and found that she was correctly repeating the scripture to which she pointed.—*Ibid.*, Mar. 18, 1891, p. 145.

What was really remarkable about the Bible-holding incident, which occurred more than once, is that a strong man cannot hold that kind of weight in that manner for that length of time. Try it and see.

What would be the purpose of such manifestations? Loughborough provides an answer:

> That God who wrought his wonders in Egypt did it that the people to whom he was going to speak his law might know that he who spoke to them, was none other than the God that made heaven and earth. So we should expect if he should reveal himself by vision to his people, there should be with the introduction of such manifestations such demonstrations as would arrest the attention of the people. That a feeble girl, seventeen years of age, should simply say, "I have had a vision," would not be sufficient. Should we not expect the Lord to work in such a manner as would cause the people to say, "I will turn aside and see what this is." . . .

> Some in these days, who have never seen Mrs. White in vision, undertake to explain it as disease, hysterics, or something of that kind. The fact is, the vision itself is a miracle. The voice proceeding from the burning bush was miraculous. What shall we call a voice quoting scripture, proceeding from a breathless body, but a miracle?—*Ibid.*

At the General Conference session two years later, Loughborough was back, this time with the testimonies of others. We already referred to his citation of Dr. M. G. Kellogg under #44 and that of Daniel Bourdeau here. Besides these, he cited that of the A. F. Fowlers, C. S. Glover, and W. R. and Eliza Carpenter regarding a vision in Waldron's Hall at Hillsdale, Michigan, in February, 1857. On that occasion, Mrs. White was examined by a Dr. Lord, who then said, "Her heart beats, but there is no breath. There is life, but no action of the lungs; I cannot account for this condition."—*Ibid.*, Jan. 31 and Feb. 1, 1893, p. 60.

And then there was the testimony of F. C. Castle regarding another examination by a physician in the summer of 1853 in Stowe, Vermont:

> "A lighted candle was held close to her eyes, which were wide open; not a muscle of the eye moved. He then examined her in regard to her pulse and also in regard to her breathing, and there was no respiration. The result was that he was satisfied that it could not be accounted for on natural or scientific principles."—*Ibid.*

The January 1861 vision predicting the Civil War (see #38) was the occasion of yet another examination that was a bit unusual:

> There was present a Doctor Brown, a hale, strong man physically, a spirit medium. He had said that her visions were the same as spirit mediumship, and that if she had one where he was, he could bring her out of it in one minute. . . . before he had half completed his examination, he turned deathly pale, and shook like an aspen leaf. Elder White said, "Will the Doctor report her condition?" He replied, "She does not breathe," and rapidly made his way to the door. Those at the door who knew of his boasting said, "Go back, and do as you said you would; bring that woman out of the vision." In great agitation he grasped the knob of the door, but was not permitted to open it until inquiry was made by those near the door, "Doctor, what is it?" He replied, *"God only knows; let me out of this house!"*

> It was evident that the spirit that influenced him as a medium was no more at rest in the presence of the power that controlled Sister White in vision, than were the demoniacs in the days of the Saviour, who inquired, "Art thou come hither to torment us before the time?"—*Ibid.*; cf. *Great Second Advent Movement*, pp. 204-211.

The video would like us to believe that Mrs. White's visions were only human. That, however, is not plausible.

Health Counsel, Wigs, and the Reform Dress

#113: "Dan Snyder followed in his father's footsteps by becoming a Seventh-day Adventist pastor. His examination of Ellen G. White's teachings caused him to eventually leave Adventism and enter the Christian ministry."—Narrator.

#113: The Adventist ministry is not a Christian ministry. This begs the question, for what solid evidence has been presented that would show us that Seventh-day Adventists are not Christians?

Besides, under #232 this same Dan Snyder says, "The last three years have been the most spiritually rewarding of my thirty-one years as a Christian."

Thus he informs us that he was a Christian for twenty-eight years while still a Seventh-day Adventist. And during part of those twenty-eight years, Mr. Snyder was also a Seventh-day Adventist minister. So by Mr. Snyder's own testimony, the Adventist ministry must be a Christian ministry.

#114, #115, & #116: "Researchers examining the early documents containing Ellen G. White's advice on diet and health are usually in for a rude awakening. We must concede that she was, after all, a Victorian lady, with very reserved ideas on the opposite sex. Most of her health advice had to do with bringing into submission the male sexual appetites, which she considered excessive."—Dan Snyder.

#114: In the early documents, most of her health advice had to do with . . . . This is a gross exaggeration. Consider the following statistics.

The picture on the video at this point is of *Health, or How to Live.* The six articles by Mrs. White appearing in this pamphlet are now found in book two of *Selected Messages,* pages 411-479. These articles were first published in 1864, the year after her famous health reform vision. In 1865 in *Spiritual Gifts* volume 4a, a chapter entitled "Health" appeared on pages 120-151.

A computerized search in these two early documents was conducted for:

self-(abuse or pollut*) or (secret or solitary)-(indulgence* or vice*) or immoral* or moral* or marri* or passion* or sensu* or vice* or sex* or lust*

If you aren't sure why some of these terms were searched for, it may become clearer to you under #117.

In the *Health, or How to Live* articles, statements dealing with morality, some very brief, appear on 11 to 14 pages out of 69. These statements, brief or otherwise, can be categorized thusly:

- 1 about the "moral pollution" before the Flood
- 3 dealing with the present immoral state of society
- 4 about the physical and mental results of immorality
- 4 regarding the causes of immorality
- 2 on the Christian duty to be morally upright
- 1 on the necessity of thinking about the upbringing of children before bringing them into the world

Some statements fall in more than one of these categories, and three pages contain statements that are vague: Were they talking about liquor or immorality?

In *Spiritual Gifts* volume 4a, statements touching on morality appear on 5 pages out of 32. Of these there were:

- 2 dealing with before the Flood and Sodom and Gomorrah
- 3 about the present immoral state of society
- 2 dealing with the physical and mental results of

immorality
- 1 about the causes of immorality
- 1 on the Christian duty to be morally upright

So in these two early documents on diet and health comprising 101 pages, but 16 to 19 pages had any reference somewhere on the page to issues of moral purity. That's 16% to 19%.

In 1864, Mrs. White's 30-page pamphlet, *Appeal to Mothers*, was published. It dealt almost exclusively with the subject of morality, though it also deals with some practical points relating to religious instruction and child rearing. Since it should probably be called an early document on morality instead of diet and health, it probably should be left out of the discussion, but we'll throw it in anyway.

27 of its 30 pages had some mention of morality issues somewhere on the page. Throwing it into our previous statistics, we now have 43 to 46 out of 131 pages dealing with moral purity, or 33% to 35% of the total number of pages.

If we adjust the percentage to account for the fact that *Appeal to Mothers* had fewer words on the page than the other documents, we end up with but 28% to 30%.

So that's what we come up with even when we skew the numbers in favor of the argument by 1) counting a whole page when only part of a page deals with moral purity, and 2) throwing in a book that's really on morality rather than on health and diet. "Most of her health advice"?

#115: Most of her health advice had to deal with . . . . In the previous number we dealt with Mrs.

White's *early* documents. But Mr. Snyder's statement could be understood to refer to *all* her health advice, an idea that is even more ludicrous.

Out of the 622-page *Counsels on Health*, a minor portion talks about morality, modesty, etc. The average born-again Christian would appreciate most, if not all, of what she wrote in this portion.

Whatever portion of her book *Ministry of Healing* that deals with this subject is extremely minute.

#116: . . . had to deal with excessive male urges. Technically, it is not the male sexual appetites that are excessive per se, but the indulgence of them. Would any born-again Christian disagree that there is all too much promiscuity today?

Anyone who has read what Mrs. White wrote on the subject will notice that she doesn't just talk about men. She also spends a good bit of time talking about women, even describing death-bed confessions by ladies who admitted that their own sinful, immoral practices were the cause of their dying (e.g. *Appeal to Mothers*, p. 12). But most of her health advice did not deal with this topic, whether regarding men or women.

Some might wonder what prompted James White to issue the pamphlet *Solemn Appeal*, which is quoted so much by the video. The immoral practices of a Seventh-day Adventist minister named Nathan Fuller had recently come to light, in which practices he had involved some of the members of his congregation (Arthur White, vol. 2, p. 287). If you had been a church leader back then, you just might have been concerned about moral purity too.

The following material does not appear in all copies of the video. To their credit, someone must have realized how preposterous this material was, since it was omitted from the second edition.

Who actually decided to omit it is a puzzle. The script writer defended its inclusion in a 1999 conversation with this writer, and the *documentation package* she sent "substantiated" its "accuracy." She emphatically stated that this writer was the first to complain about the video. Also, a lady at Jeremiah Films was surprised to hear that Mrs. White didn't write the statements quoted below, and that their context clearly indicated such. And both these conversations took place when the second edition was already out!

Another puzzle is why, when they were editing the second edition, they didn't omit the rest of the erroneous material. Yet that would essentially require starting from scratch at great expense. So the existing product was re-edited and shortened by about five minutes. Yet no one seems to have bothered to change the advertising, for it is still advertised as being fifty minutes long.

#117 & #118: "She singled out the practice of masturbation which she called secret vice or solitary vice as the basis for almost every disease."—Dan Snyder.
"Mrs. White felt she had been given special light on the subject of masturbation. Along with her ideas her husband James also quoted others with similar views and published them in *A Solemn Appeal*. 'There is hardly an end to the diseases caused by solitary vice; dyspepsia, spinal

complaint, headache, epilepsy, impaired eyesight, palpitations of the heart, pain in the side, bleeding at the lungs, spasms of the heart and lungs, diabetes, incontinence of the urine... rheumatism, affected perspiration, consumption, asthma...' A Solemn Appeal p. 12."—Narrator.

#117: She felt she had been given special light. The *documentation package* supports this one under "Point 58" with a statement by her grandson, Arthur White: ". . . a subject on which she had been given special light . . . ." Thus the *documentation package* proves that her grandson felt she had been given special light, but it provides no evidence that Mrs. White herself felt this way.

Which part of what she really did teach on the subject was "special light"? Much of what she wrote on the topic was already common knowledge in the medical circles of that time. This is readily apparent when one identifies the originators of the quotes that follow.

#118: This is the list of diseases she gave. The average viewer will think that she wrote the selection just quoted, though she did not.

Notice how the narrator said that James White also quoted others in the book *Solemn Appeal*, but then there is no clear identification of which things Mrs. White wrote and which things she didn't write. The average viewer can't distinguish which were her specific teachings and which were someone else's. This writer listened intently when viewing the video for the first time, and came away with the idea that the video said Mrs. White wrote these things.

From #119 and #122-#125 we can conclude that the video intended to connect these statements to Mrs. White rather than to her husband James.

The quotation as it appears on the video is not accurate. It combines a quotation from a Mrs. Gove, a "celebrated physiological lecturess," with a reference to the views of Dr. Deslandes, neither of whom were Seventh-day Adventists. The video adds words to the quotation that do not appear in *Solemn Appeal*, and deletes words and quotation marks without using an ellipsis. That this is true is apparent from "Point 59" of the *documentation package*.

So James White's *Solemn Appeal* included material from his wife, Mrs. Gove, and Dr. Deslandes, but that wasn't all. Also cited were Sylvester Graham (from which graham flour and graham crackers are named); Rev. E. M. P. Wells, teacher in the school of moral discipline in Boston; William C. Woodbridge, a well-known educator; Dr. Woodward, celebrated superintendent of the Massachusetts State Lunatic Hospital; Todd; Dr. Goupil; Dr. Dwight; Prof. O. S. Fowler; Margaret Prior; Dr. Combe; Dr. E. P. Miller; Dr. Alcott; Dr. Snow of Boston; Dr. J. A. Brown of Providence; Adam Clarke, the Wesleyan Commenta-

tor; and Dr. Trall.

How prevalent were such ideas back then? Prevalent enough that they even appeared in *Clarke's Commentary*, a Bible commentary extremely popular among Methodists. Here's what Adam Clarke identified as the health problems caused by "secret vice":

1. "speedily exhaust the vital principle and energy"
2. "the muscles become flaccid and feeble"
3. "the tone and natural action of the nerves relaxed and impeded"
4. "the understanding confused"
5. "the memory oblivious"
6. "the judgment perverted"
7. "the will indeterminate and wholly without energy to resist"
8. "the eyes appear languishing and without expression"
9. "the countenance vacant"
10. "the appetite ceases for the stomach is incapable of performing its proper office"
11. "nutrition fails"
12. "tremors, fears, and terrors are generated"
13. "a mind often debilitated even to a state of idiotism" (vol. 1, p. 417)

Now Dr. Clarke, are you sure about all this?

Reader, this is no caricature, nor are the colourings overcharged in this shocking picture. Worse woes than my pen can relate I have witnessed in those addicted to this fascinating, unnatural, and most destructive of crimes. If thou hast entered into this snare, flee from the destruction both of body and soul that awaits thee! God alone can save thee.—*Ibid.*

Undoubtedly, Mrs. White agreed with a bit of what these physicians, professors, lecturers, preachers, and scholars taught, but we cannot assume that she and her husband agreed with everything. James White sometimes printed an article without agreeing with absolutely everything the article said. And what else would you expect him to do? The Whites were broad-minded people, able to recognize and appreciate the good in material even though it wasn't 100% correct.

One thing Mrs. White did agree on was the effect that this practice has on mental health. The doctors above who worked with mental patients found that a high percentage of such patients, both men and women, were addicted to this vile habit.

A scientific basis for this is documented in

"Appendix A" of *Testimonies on Sexual Behavior, Adultery, and Divorce*. Two medical authorities pointed out, in 1978 and 1981, that those engaging in such a practice could easily become deficient in zinc. This in turn could lead to insanity since zinc is necessary for proper brain function (pp. 269, 270).

(Speaking of insanity, does it not seem insane in this day and age of safe sex and AIDS that a "Christian" video would criticize someone's stance on the need of moral purity?)

Back in 1870, Mrs. White wrote a pamphlet called *Appeal to the Battle Creek Church*, which was later adapted a little and then published in volume two of *Testimonies for the Church*. Besides referring a number of times to the reprehensible conduct of Nathan Fuller (see #116), she made these statements:

> Sexual excess will effectually destroy a love for devotional exercises, will take from the brain the substance needed to nourish the system, and will most effectively exhaust the vitality.—*Testimonies for the Church*, vol. 2, p. 477.

> The body is enervated, the brain weakened. The material deposited there to nourish the system is squandered. The drain upon the system is great.—*Ibid.*, p. 470.

This sounds like zinc, for there are large amounts of zinc in neurons, glial cells, and various structures of the hippocampus. Given the following facts from *Encyclopædia Britannica*, Mrs. White's statements are truly remarkable:

> Human zinc deficiency was not described until 1963, and it took an additional 10 years before it was confirmed and accepted that zinc is an important nutrient for humans.—"Nutrition: Recommended Intakes of Nutrients: Inorganic Elements."

> Features of zinc deficiency in humans have been protean: various combinations of loss of taste, retarded growth, delayed wound healing, baldness, pustular skin lesions, impotence in males, infertility in females, and reduced immunity to infections. —"Nutrition: Deficiency Diseases: Inorganic Elements."

Who told Mrs. White that there was a "substance" or "material" connected with the brain and with "the nourishment of the system"? Who told her this a century before it was confirmed and accepted that

zinc was an important nutrient for humans? Where did she *plagiarize* this from, pray tell?

Mrs. White connected "secret vice" with poor memory, stunted growth, lethargy, irritability, and depression (*Appeal to Mothers*, pp. 6, 7; *Testimonies for the Church*, vol. 2, p. 391). Since the practice does lower zinc levels, at least in men, and since zinc deficiency does result in poor memory, stunted growth, lethargy, irritability, and depression, her connection is valid. And given the need of zinc for the proper function of so many processes in the body, including the immune system, it isn't hard to see how zinc deficiency could result in greater susceptibility to many diseases.

Want evidence that zinc deficiency can cause these problems and more? Check out the "Current Bibliographies in Medicine 98-3" entitled "Zinc and Health" (http://www.nlm.nih.gov/cbm/zinc.html). Prepared by the U.S. government's National Institutes of Health, it lists 3619 citations of documents published from 1990 to 1998. These citations are broken down into seven categories, including:

- Zinc and the Gastrointestinal Tract
- Zinc and the Immune System . . .
- Zinc and Cellular Mechanisms
- Zinc and the Central Nervous System
- Zinc in Growth and Specific Disease Entities

The simple fact is that Mrs. White is still current, even if her statements are nearly 140 years old. Today's scientists are still playing catch up to what she wrote back then.

In 1864 she said that under certain conditions, "Cancerous humor, which would lay dormant in the system their life-time, is inflamed, and commences its eating, destructive work."—*Appeal to Mothers*, p. 27. Dormant cancer that can be activated? Why, J. Michael Bishop and Harold Varmus didn't publish their findings on "dormant viral oncogenes" until 1976, 112 years later! Their discoveries were deemed important enough that they won the Nobel Prize for Physiology or Medicine in 1989. It now appears that dormant genes utilized by viruses or activated by carcinogens play a roll in "all forms of cancer" ("Bishop, J(ohn) Michael," *Britannica® CD*). And Mrs. White hinted at this in 1864!

[The following does not appear in all copies of the video. See the note preceding #117-#118.]

#119: "Ellen White was also concerned about children, and the ever-present danger of secret vice. James White included this quote as a warning to parents. 'After having indulged in this habit for a time, the child loses its bright and happy looks; it becomes pale with a greenish tint...' A Solemn Appeal p. 91."—Narrator.

#119: Mrs. White said kids will get green skin. No, she did not. The book being shown at this point in the video is Mrs. White's *Appeal to Mothers*, and the narrator just said "Ellen White," leading the viewer to think that this statement was written by her. But the truth is simply that this quote is of E. P. Miller, M.D., physician of the Hygienic Institute in New York City, not Mrs. White. Dr. Miller was not a Seventh-day Adventist.

The *documentation package* gives but a photocopy of this quotation under #60. If Mrs. White had really written this, it would be on the CD-ROM of her published and released writings. The *documentation package* gets many of its quotes from computer printouts from this CD. But for the statements from *Solemn Appeal*, it has to resort to photocopies of the original book, since Mrs. White didn't write these particular statements.

Those born-again Christians who have concerns about the morality of their children might want to read what Mrs. White really did say on the subject. They just might find something helpful.

#120 & #121: "But her belief was that these sexual appetites could be controlled by diet. First she gave a list of foods to avoid. 'Mince pies, cakes, preserves, and highly seasoned meats, with gravies... create a feverish condition in the system and inflame the animal passions... dispense with animal foods, and use grains, vegetables, and fruits as articles of diet.' A Solemn Appeal pp. 65-66."—Dan Snyder.

#120: She said animal foods inflame the animal passions. This quotation is out of context. The impression is left that this quote says *all* animal foods inflame the animal passions. In reality, what it says is that *highly seasoned* meats, not *all* meats, inflame the passions.

The first ellipsis shouldn't be there. The second ellipsis represents an omission of eight and a half sentences. Here's the last part that was left out:

> In order to strengthen in them the moral perceptions, the love of spiritual things, we must regulate the manner of our living, dispense with animal food, and use grains, vegetables, and fruits, as articles of diet.

Thus while highly seasoned meats *inflame* the passions, a vegetarian diet would help to *strengthen* the moral perceptions.

What about the part about preserves and cakes? Mrs. White a number of times elsewhere referred to "rich cakes and preserves" not being best for us (e.g. *Spiritual Gifts*, vol. 4a, p. 130). Likewise, what she is talking about here is the connection between the "animal passions" and rich and highly seasoned foods. Today, many people who are not Adventists believe that avoiding rich foods is an important health practice. Your physician just may be one of them!

#121: Mrs. White felt that rich foods and highly seasoned foods act as aphrodisiacs. The problem with either verifying or disproving the accuracy of her counsel in this area is, "Despite long-standing literary and popular interest in internal aphrodisiacs, almost no scientific studies of them have been made." —"aphrodisiac," *Britannica*® *CD*. So she was making a pronouncement on a subject that medical science still has not researched.

As already noted under #118, this is not the only time she made such statements. Consider also this one from her 1905 book *Ministry of Healing*:

> Flesh was never the best food; but its use is now doubly objectionable, since disease in animals is so rapidly increasing. Those who use flesh foods little know what they are eating. Often if they could see the animals when living and know the quality of the meat they eat, they would turn from it with loathing. People are continually eating flesh that is filled with tuberculous and *cancerous germs*. Tuberculosis, *cancer*, and other fatal diseases *are thus communicated*.—p. 313, italics added.

This is really remarkable, considering the following:

> Rous, pronounced rows, Francis Peyton, pronounced PAY tuhn (1879-1970), an American medical researcher, proved that viruses cause some types of cancer. In 1910, Rous ground up a cancerous tumor from a chicken and filtered out everything larger than a virus. The resulting liquid produced cancer when injected into other chickens. For many years, scientists scoffed at Rous's discovery. These scientists believed cancer could not be caused by a virus because the disease is not contagious. In 1966, Rous shared the Nobel Prize for physiology or medicine for his work.—"Rous, Francis Peyton," *World Book Encyclopedia*.

In 1910 a maverick scientist proposed that cancer was caused by a virus and could be transmitted from chicken to chicken. He was subsequently derided by the scientific community for proposing such a ludicrous idea, and then waited fifty-six years before getting his Nobel Prize. Do you suppose that perhaps Mr. Rous "plagiarized" his novel idea from *Ministry of Healing*? Should Mrs. White be awarded a Nobel Prize posthumously?

Want to win a Nobel Prize?

1. Find a concept in her writings that sounds absurd.
2. Make sure it's something that can benefit humanity.
3. Find a way to prove it.
4. Get ridiculed for proposing such a ludicrous idea.

5. Wait awhile.
6. Collect your prize.

It's that simple.

To be fair, it would have been nice if the video had included one of a number of stories in which Mrs. White's health counsel predated the findings of science. As Leslie Martin says on the video, "We were taught as Adventists that we had a special message for the world with our health message, and that our prophetess Ellen White was years ahead of her time." Though she may not want to admit it now, what Mrs. Martin was taught is true.

#122: "Adherents were exhorted to 'Sip no more the beverage of China, no more the drinks of Java.' A Solemn Appeal p. 257."—Narrator.

#122: She said, "Sip no more." These are the words of Professor O. S. Fowler, not Mrs. White, from his section in *Solemn Appeal* that was eighty-seven pages long. He was not a Seventh-day Adventist.

The shorter second edition of the video omits the brief explanation that James White, not his wife, put together this book (see #117-#118). Thus it is inevitable that the viewer of the second edition will wrongly conclude that Mrs. White said this.

If the video wanted to criticize her views on tea and coffee, why didn't it quote what she really did say instead of what O. S. Fowler said?

She did take a stand against the use of drugs, including the caffeine found in tea and coffee. But then, your doctor may have told you to kick these habits as well. It isn't easy, is it? Drugs are hard to get off of, even the milder ones.

When you think about it, just about our entire nation is hooked on dope of some sort: caffeine, nicotine, alcohol, and the narcotics we usually think of. Just think how the world would be a better place if we took the money saved by not using these substances and spent it on helping people. And think of how much we would save on doctor bills: Lung cancer and emphysema would become rare. The frequency of liver ailments and heart disease would lessen. Without the blood vessel constricting effects of caffeine, high blood pressure would be more easily controlled or cured. Without the sugar that often accumulates doses of caffeine and theobromine, dental expenses would drop. All without nationalized healthcare or health insurance!

Sounds pretty good. But again, Mrs. White didn't write the words quoted on the video.

#123: "To bring under control the male sexual appetites, besides being vegetarians, it was advised by Ellen White that they not eat an evening meal at all."—Dan Snyder.

#123: She said to abstain from supper for this reason. Utterly false.

Under "Point 63" the *documentation package* offers as proof for this charge page 259 of *Solemn Appeal*, stating in the index that this is "EGW's advice to not eat an evening meal at all." Yet this is some of the lengthy advice of Professor Fowler, not Mrs. White.

As a good health practice, for reasons quite different than what Mr. Snyder gives, Mrs. White recommended two meals a day for most people, but not everyone. For those who either had to or chose to eat a third meal, supper should be light and eaten several hours before bed time (*Counsels on Diet and Foods*, p. 158). That way the stomach can also rest

through the night. This makes good common sense.

There were folk in her day who tried to make the recommendation of two meals mandatory upon all. Against this idea Mrs. White wrote, "The practice of eating but two meals a day is generally found a benefit to health; yet under some circumstances, persons may require a third meal."—*Ibid.*, p. 176. The next two pages come down on those who would force the two-meal-a-day plan on others. On page 178 she actually called for suppers to *begin* to be served at Avondale College in Australia.

Her position consistently was that most, not all, would do better on two meals a day, and that no one should be pushy about the matter.

What the video has done here and elsewhere is nothing new. Folk back in 1845 were doing the same:

> On the other hand, the nominal [first-day] Adventists charged me with fanaticism, and I was falsely, and by some wickedly, represented as being the leader of the fanaticism that I was actually laboring to correct.—*Early Writings*, p. 21.

By the way, when well-known medical doctor Sang Lee, newly converted to Christianity, was first given *Counsels on Diet and Foods*, he was immediately intrigued to find some of his modern ideas as an allergist in the book. He turned to the front of the book to find out where Mrs. White got her Ph.D. from, not knowing that she had only reached the third grade and had died in 1915.

Why don't you check out a copy?

[The following does not appear in all copies of the video. See the note preceding #117-#118.]

#124: "The book *A Solemn Appeal* also warned readers of the dangers of sleeping on feather beds '...sleeping on feather beds and feather pillows, in close, unventilated rooms... aids in inducing this vile practice of solitary vice...' A Solemn Appeal p. 96."—Narrator.

#124: She said not to sleep on feather beds. As with the quote under #119, this one comes from Dr. E. P. Miller, physician of the Hygienic Institute of New York City, not Mrs. White. His section in James White's *Solemn Appeal* was 21 pages long.

The seven words omitted at the middle ellipsis state clearly what Professor Fowler had in mind: ". . . is another cause of weakness and therefore . . . ." Since sleeping on feather beds in unventilated rooms causes weakness and poor health, wrong habits are less easily resisted.

Notice he said "sleeping on feather beds . . . in close, unventilated rooms." So sleeping on them in large, airy rooms isn't a problem.

It may sound strange today, but the idea that sleeping on feather beds in small, unventilated rooms was unhelathful was not an unheard of opinion back then. In 1856 a periodical listed seventeen "Ways of Committing Suicide" very slowly. Fourth on the list was "Sleeping on feather beds in seven by nine bedrooms" (*Review and Herald*, July 10, 1856, p. 83). Perhaps it had something to do with the bed accumulating moisture or mold.

At any rate, physicians who were not Adventists were still warning against feather beds decades after *Solemn Appeal* came off the press (*The People's Common Sense Medical Adviser*, pp. 279, 377, 378). James White apparently agreed in 1870 (*Solemn Appeal*, p. 270). In contrast, Mrs. White's writings never warned against using feather beds or pillows. She may never have agreed with the idea.

The video really ought to be criticizing the doctors of that age instead of Mrs. White, if they think there is a case to be made. But the criticizing of doctors who were never Adventists is not the purpose of the video.

[The following does not appear in all copies of the video. See the note preceding #117-#118.]

#125: "Interestingly enough, Ellen White on one occasion requested that her feather bed be sent to her without delay."—Dan Snyder.

#125: She hypocritically used a feather bed.
Apparently Mr. Snyder did not read well the previous quote from Dr. Miller. He said that feather beds were unhealthful in "close, unventilated rooms." Mrs. White never said she was going to use her feather bed in such a room, so she was not contradicting her own advice, advice that she never gave. Thus she was not being hypocritical.

Many Adventists do not know how Mrs. White's fourth son died in 1860:

> I have had a very afflicting experience in sleeping in damp beds. I slept with my infant two months old in a north bedroom [in someone else's house]. The bed had not been used for two weeks. A fire was kindled in the room, and this was considered all that was necessary. Next morning, I felt that I had taken cold. My babe seemed to be in great pain when moved. His face began to swell, and he was afflicted with erysipelas of the most aggravating form. My dear babe was a great sufferer for four weeks, and finally died, a martyr to the damp bed.—*Health Reformer*, Jan. 1, 1872; *Review and Herald*, Jan. 2, 1872.

Rest assured that Mrs. White, when she requested her feather bed to be sent in 1878 to where she was in Texas, planned on using it in a well-ventilated room. She knew by experience the importance of this as a measure for good health, even without connecting it to "secret vice."

By the way, even if this phony charge were true, what would it prove? What about the Bible writers?

Were any of them "hypocrites"? Does that mean we have to reject them as false prophets? We'll explore this issue more under #230.

[The following does not appear in all copies of the video. See the note preceding #117-#118.]

#126: "In the famous Battle Creek Sanitarium, while still under Adventist control, the so-called cure for secret vice was practiced. 'A sitz bath may be taken... at as low a temperature as can be tolerated without chilliness. Give at the same time a hot foot bath, and apply cool wet cloths to the head... . . .' A Solemn Appeal p. 271."—Narrator.

#126: This is the so-called cure. Thus hydrotherapy, a very potent treatment for a variety of ailments, is ridiculed.

This treatment isn't even the whole cure. It's only one part of five: "1. *Diet and Regimen*. . . . 2. *Sleeping*. . . . 3. *Bathing*. . . . 4. *Exercise*. . . . 5. *Social Surroundings*. . . ."—pp. 270-272.

The section this is found in has the heading, "Hygienic Treatment." What does this term mean? It refers to a particular school of medical thought. Today we have allopathic medicine, chiropractic medicine, and other modalities of treatment. Hygienic medicine was yet another one.

Hygienic physicians, such as Dr. E. P. Miller, avoided drug therapy with its side effects. Besides proper diet and exercise, they used simple treatments like hydrotherapy.

So what can hydrotherapy do? When used properly, it can relieve congestion, pain, fever, fatigue, and muscle spasms; increase white blood cell activity, antibody production, and toxin elimination; and either stimulate or sedate (Dail and Thomas, *Hydrotherapy, Simple Treatments for Common Ailments* 1, 6, 17, 40).

How effective can it be? Mrs. White advised a form of hydrotherapy for a malarial patient from Allegan, Michigan, who promptly recovered (*Manuscript Releases*, vol. 20, p. 279). Physicians at the General Conference sessions near the turn of the century reported the success they were having using hydrotherapy for a particular form of malaria. Their success was not attended with the side effects of drug therapy. Even in cases when quinine was unsuccessful, the hydrotherapy treatments worked (*General Conference Bulletin*, June 1, 1909, p. 236; June 6, p. 324; June 7, p. 357).

As drug resistance in microbes becomes more of a problem, it might be wise to research the effectiveness of hydrotherapy on yet other forms of malaria, as well as other diseases.

This writer knows of a physician who periodically has problems with bowel obstructions, due to scar tissue from previous surgery. She has treated herself with a particular form of hydrotherapy, and by so doing has recovered without surgery a number of times. Thus hydrotherapy rightly used is nothing to ridicule.

(Those who are not sure what "rightly used" means should consult a hygienic physician. This book is obviously not intended to diagnose disease or advise a specific medical treatment.)

The *documentation package* described "Point 66" in the index as "The Battle Creek cure for 'secret vice' used when EGW and Dr. Kellogg ran the sanitorium [*sic*]." The truth is that neither was running the sanitarium when *Solemn Appeal* was published in 1870. Kellogg was still a teenager, and didn't come on board the sanitarium staff until five or six years later. Mrs. White never ran any institution in the normal sense of the word. She only sat on one board, and that was of Madison College in Tennessee after the turn of the century.

The sanitarium was founded in 1866. Between its founding and the publication of *Solemn Appeal*, much of that time James and Ellen were living in northern Michigan, not in Battle Creek. They had moved there to facilitate James's recovery from the paralytic stroke he had had in 1865. During this same time period, attitudes in Battle Creek were such that Mrs. White found it difficult to do far less than run an entire institution (Arthur White, vol. 2, pp. 138, 168-289).

Page 268 of *Solemn Appeal* makes it clear that the advised course of treatment was being given by physicians who had treated "a large number of cases," the great majority of which must have been dealt with while Mrs. White was nowhere near Battle Creek. But for the video to have criticized the doctors of that time, whether Adventist or not, wouldn't have helped build its case against the ghost "behind the church."

[The following does not appear in all copies of the video. See the note preceding #117-#118.]

#127: [The picture used as the background for the previous quote, which shows a shivering, naked man sitting in a basin of ice water on top of an ice block. His feet are in a basin of boiling water which is on top of a camp fire.]

#127: The picture in the background illustrates the Battle Creek cure. The average viewer will likely miss this. An easy-to-see copy appears in the *documentation package* under "Point 66."

This picture is entirely out of place in a documentary film. Rather than informing the viewer of what was actually done, it is a caricature intended to ridicule the whole idea of hygienic hydrotherapy treatments.

The quote appearing on the video said that the sitz bath should be "at as low a temperature as can be tolerated *without chilliness.*" Obviously, since the man is visibly shivering, the treatment isn't being done properly.

The hot foot bath is not supposed to have the source of heat under the basin. Hot water is to be added by pouring. The proper way to do it is to have one's hand in the water as one is pouring it. Thus if it is too hot, the one adding the water will be able to tell before great discomfort is felt. And the hot foot bath may be contraindicated by diabetes.

WARNING: If anyone attempts to administer a hydrotherapy treatment as it is depicted on this video from Jeremiah Films, he or she could very well be sued by the injured party.

#128 & #129: "Women were not immune from Ellen G. White's health advice either, and she further controlled her female followers by issuing directives on their hairstyles and manner of dress. Speaking of wigs and other hair pieces she said, 'The artificial hair and pads covering the base of the brain, heat and excite the spinal nerves centering in the brain... in consequence... many have lost their reason and become hopelessly insane, by following this deforming fashion. Yet the slaves to fashion will continue to thus dress their heads, and suffer horrible disease and premature death...' The Health Reformer October 1, 1871."—Dan Snyder.

#128: She controlled her female followers with directives. Mrs. White did not issue "directives" on dress, nor did she try to control her "followers." Hear what she says regarding the reform dress, dealt with under #131 ff.:

> Some who adopted the reform were not content to show by example the advantages of the dress, giving, when asked, their reasons for adopting it, and letting the matter rest there. They sought to control others' conscience by their own. If they wore it, others must put it on. They forgot that none were to be compelled to wear the reform dress.
>
> It was not my duty to urge the subject upon my sisters. After presenting it before them as it had been shown me, I left them to their own conscience. . . .
>
> Some were greatly troubled because I did not make the dress a test question, and still others because I advised those who had unbelieving husbands or children not to adopt the reform dress, as it might lead to unhappiness that would counteract all the good to be derived from its use.—*Testimonies for the Church*, vol. 4, pp. 636, 637.

So others issued directives, but Mrs. White did not. Once again she has been charged with the very extremism she sought to counter.

#129: She was against wigs. Her statement has nothing to do with what we call wigs. There is not a single usage of the word "wig" or "wigs" in all her published and released writings.

Notice how the quote used by the video refers to something "deforming" that creates "heat." The context reveals even more clearly what she was talking about:

> Fashion *loads* the heads of women with artificial braids and pads, which do not add to their beauty, but give an *unnatural shape* to the head. The hair is *strained* and *forced* into unnatural positions, and it is *not possible* for the heads of these fashionable ladies *to be comfortable.* The artificial hair and pads covering the *base of the brain,* heat and excite the spinal nerves centering in the brain. The head should ever be kept cool. The heat caused by these artificials induces the blood to the brain. . . .
>
> The unnatural heat caused by these artificial *deformities* about the head, induces the blood to the brain, producing congestion, and causing the natural hair to fall off, producing *baldness.*—italics added.

The White Estate posted the following at their web site (www.whiteestate.org):

> In the context of today's comfortable wigs, critics

tend to ridicule this statement. But Mrs. White was referring to an entirely different product. The wigs she described were "monstrous bunches of curled hair, cotton, seagrass, wool, Spanish moss, and other multitudinous abominations." [*The Health Reformer*, July 1867.] One woman said that her chignon generated "an unnatural degree of heat in the back part of the head" and produced "a distracting headache just as long as it was worn."

Another *Health Reformer* article (quoting from the *Marshall Statesman* and the *Springfield Republican*) described the perils of wearing "jute switches"—wigs made from dark, fibrous bark. Apparently these switches were often infested with "jute bugs," small insects that burrowed under the scalp. One woman reported that her head became raw, and her hair began to fall out. Her entire scalp "was perforated with the burrowing parasites." "The lady . . . is represented as nearly crazy from the terrible suffering, and from the prospect of the horrible death which physicians do not seem able to avert." [*Ibid.*, January 1871.]

So Mrs. White was not condemning the use of a simple wig. But please, leave those jute switches alone. You might go crazy!

#130: [The picture used to illustrate the previous number, consisting of a skeleton looking through a window at a lady who is fixing her hair before a mirror.]

#130: This picture illustrates her concerns about wigs. The major problems with the picture, as can be seen from the context cited under #129, is that:

1. The picture does not show the lady's head *loaded*.
2. It does not show her head taking on an *unnatural shape*.
3. It does not show her wearing a wig which would make it *impossible* for her *to be comfortable*.
4. It does not show a wig that would cover the *base of the brain*.
5. It does not picture a style of wig that could be called a *deformity*.

For these reasons, this picture does not illustrate at all what Mrs. White was talking about.

#131, #132, #133, #134, #135, & #136: "Once the deadly peril of wearing wigs was dealt with, Ellen G. White tried to force a hot, uncomfortable, strange style of dress on her female followers. She claimed it was designed by God. It was in reality a pair of pants with a bulky, long dress over them."—Dan Snyder.

#131: After the wigs came the dress. False. The article Mr. Snyder cited under #129 was dated 1871. The "reform dress" was introduced more than six years earlier in 1865. Thus the dress came before the counsel on heavy hairpieces, not after.

#132: She tried to force a strange style of dress on her female followers. False. As pointed out under #128, she was against forcing the reform dress on anyone.

#133: The dress was hot. It was not hot. First of all, let's consider what ladies' dresses were like at the time:

As to the reasons for a need of reform in women's dress at that time, the New York *Independent* in 1913 painted a vivid picture:

"The chief points in the indictment of woman's dress of former times were that the figure was dissected like a wasp's, that the hips were overloaded with heavy skirts, and that the skirts dragged upon the ground and swept up the dirt.

"Nowadays the weight of a woman's clothing as a whole is only half or a third of what it used to be. Four dresses can be packed in the space formerly filled by one. In the one-piece dresses now in vogue the weight is borne from the shoulders, and the hips are relieved by reducing the skirts in weight, length, and number. The skirt no longer trails upon the street. . . .

"The women who, for conscientious reasons, refused to squeeze their waists, and in consequence suffered the scorn of their sex, now find themselves on the fashionable side. A thirty-two-inch waist is regarded as permissible, where formerly a twenty-inch waist was thought proper. A fashionably gowned woman of the present day can stoop to pick up a pin at her feet."—Arthur White, vol. 2, pp. 177, 178.

In contrast to the established fashion, Mrs. White's reform dress was lighter and shorter, and dispensed with the corset. Is it not interesting that the very improvements she advocated in the dress of women were eventually adopted by society?

One university professor has her students study

Mrs. White's position on dress reform, along with the silly criticisms she received. Hear what this professor has to say on the matter:

Since the 19th Century, the forces of dress reform won their sartorial battles with the impressively cumbersome, class ridden, unhealthy and (often) anesthetic styles of the Victorian era. Dress reform went mainstream after 1900, and now we just assume the rightness of clothing that is comfortable, easy to wash, easy to move in, and healthy for the wearer. . . . Reform dress often isn't "pretty," but if you time traveled the average college student to 1855, she'd be wearing it in a week, because it would be the only comfortable clothes she could buy. Moreover, if she thought anyone would be insisting that she should be in a corset and petticoats, she'd think it would be a religious person like White. It is a nice bit of enlightenment for modern feminists to see that what they imagine is a purely feminist statement (bloomers) was in fact a REFORM statement, very often pushed by religious reformers, and artistic and political folks, not just feminists.—Tara Maginnis, Ph.D., University of Alaska Fairbanks, May 5, 2002, personal email.

How much does Dr. Maginnis know about Adventism and Mrs. White? Is she biased? ". . . I'm not a member of this religion, know little about it and know next to nothing about White other than her stance on dress reform."—*Ibid.*

Back to temperature: Since it was so much lighter than what society was wearing, it couldn't have been hot. And yet at the same time, the wearer was not cold in the winter. While the trunk had fewer layers on it and was thus cooler, the extremities were not left exposed to the winter winds (*Health Reformer,* May 1, 1872).

#134: The dress was uncomfortable. How can not wearing corsets or long heavy skirts be uncomfortable?

Repeatedly over the years, Mrs. White called upon women to wear more comfortable clothing. Take for instance these quotes from 1864 and 1868:

Your girls should wear the waists of their dresses perfectly loose, and they should have a style of dress convenient, comfortable and modest.—*Selected Messages,* vol. 2, p. 471.

Christian Mother: Why not clothe your daughter as comfortably and as properly as you do your son? —*Health Reformer,* Sept. 1, 1868.

And these from 1905:

One of fashion's wasteful and mischievous devices is the skirt that sweeps the ground. Uncleanly,

uncomfortable, inconvenient, unhealthful—all this and more is true of the trailing skirt.—*Ministry of Healing,* p. 291.

No part of the body should at any time be made uncomfortable by clothing that compresses any organ or restricts its freedom of movement.—*Ibid.,* p. 382.

#135: The dress was bulky. It was anything but bulky. Rather, it was intended to replace the clothing of the day that really was bulky.

A wise grandmother counseled her granddaughter regarding a fashionable dress of that time:

"There is no beauty in the present style, and leaving aside the awkwardness of the design, one would suppose the shackling of the limbs and the oppressive heaviness of the dress, on so delicate a part of the body as the spine, would deter women from such fatuity."—quoted in *Health Reformer,* May 1, 1872.

The selection under #133 said that the style in 1913 had reduced the *number* of skirts. How ever many skirts the women of the 1870's were loading down their hips with, we do know this about Mrs. White's reform dress: "Our skirts are few and light, not taxing our strength with the burden of many and longer ones."—*Ibid.*

#136: The dress was long. If it was long, why was it called the "short dress"? The following quote is just one example of many where it was called "short." It also shows just how little forcing Mrs. White did:

Sisters who have opposing husbands have asked my advice in regard to their adopting the short dress contrary to the wishes of the husband. I advise them to wait. I do not consider the dress question of so vital importance as the Sabbath. Concerning the latter there can be no hesitation. But the opposition which many might receive should they adopt the dress reform would be more injurious to health than the dress would be beneficial. Several of these sisters have said to me: "My husband likes your dress; he says he has not one word of fault to find with it."—*Testimonies for the Church,* vol. 1, p. 522.

At that time, many spiritualists were adopting an even shorter dress that came "halfway from the hip to the knee" (p. 465). The public was outraged by such a novelty, and novel it was. Typically, women were wearing dresses so long that they swept the streets like a "mop" (*Health Reformer,* Aug. 1, 1868). The reform dress avoided both these extremes, thus being more healthful without outraging the public (*Testimonies for the Church,* vol. 1, pp. 457, 464, 465). How more balanced could Mrs. White have been?

#137, #138, & #139: "Faithful sisters struggled with the cumbersome dress, until Ellen White quietly stopped wearing hers some years later, with no explanation given."—Dan Snyder.

#137: Faithful sisters struggled. False. The dress was eventually dropped because:

1. Many "faithful" sisters wouldn't quit pushing the matter on people (see #128).
2. Other "faithful" sisters wouldn't quit complaining.
3. Other "faithful" sisters wouldn't use good taste in preparing the dress.

What was it about the reform dress that caused so much complaining? There were two principal reasons:

> "Oh! it looks so to see women with pants!" . . .
> It is true that this style of dress exposes the feet. And why should woman be ashamed of her well-clad feet any more than men are of theirs? It is of no use for her to try to conceal the fact that she has feet. This was a settled fact long before the use of trailing skirts.—*Health Reformer*, May 1, 1872.

So some didn't like the reform dress because then women would be wearing pants, something quite commonplace today. Also, they didn't like it because being able to see women's shoes was considered immodest. We've come a long ways since then. In fact, we've come too far, for there isn't a whole lot left unexposed in today's society.

And so the "faithful" sisters complained:

> Some who wore the dress sighed over it as a heavy burden. The language of their hearts was: "Anything but this. . . ." Murmuring and complaining were fast destroying vital godliness.—*Testimonies for the Church*, vol. 4, p. 637.

Then we have the "faithful" sisters who lacked good taste when making the dress:

> In some places there is great opposition to the short dress. But when I see some dresses worn by the sisters, I do not wonder that people are disgusted and condemn the dress. . . . There is certainly nothing in these dresses manifesting taste or order. Such a dress would not recommend itself to the good judgment of sensible-minded persons. In every sense of the word it is a deformed dress.—*Testimonies for the Church*, vol. 1, pp. 521, 522.

#138: The dress was cumbersome. No it was not. See #133-#136.

#139: Mrs. White gave no explanation for stopping wearing hers. To the contrary, she explained it well:

> In preparing my wardrobe, both long and short dresses were made. Of the former, there were one or two for travelling, and to appear in before those who are ignorant of our faith and of dress reform, whose minds are balancing in favor of the truth. We do not wish to bring before such hearers any question that is not vital, to divert their minds from the great and important subject, for Satan takes advantage of everything that can possibly be used to divert and distract minds.
> *I had explained all this fully.* But notwithstanding all this, my sisters were so weak they could not appreciate my motives, and were too glad of a pretext to lay aside the reform dress making my example their excuse. I had felt that, *for me*, discretion was highly essential while laboring in California, for the salvation of souls. With Paul, I could say I became all things to all if by any means I might save some. I did not do anything secretly. *I frankly gave my reasons.* But unsanctified hearts which had long galled and chafed under the cross of dress reform, now took occasion to make a bold push and throw off the reform dress. They have taken advantage of my necessity to misinterpret my words, my actions, and motives.
> My position upon health and dress reform is unchanged. I have been shown that God gave the dress reform to our sisters as a blessing, but some have turned it into a curse, making the dress question a subject of talk and of thought, while they neglected the internal work, the adorning of their souls by personal piety. Some have thought religion consisted in wearing the reform dress, while their spirits were unsubdued by grace. They were jealous and fault finding, watching and criticizing the dress of others, and in this neglected their own souls and lost their piety.
> If the dress reform is thus turned to a curse, God would remove it from us. God bestowed blessings upon ancient Israel and withdrew them again because those blessings were despised and became a cause of murmuring and complaint.—*Pamphlet 104*, pp. 10-12, italics added except "for me."

How could she have been more plain? She fully explained why she *temporarily* stopped wearing the reform dress. But as it is now, so it was then: Many wanted to misconstrue her motives and ignore her explanation.

#140: "Our prophetess Ellen G. White taught that we should be vegetarians, especially in consideration of the soon return of Jesus Christ, because if we were not vegetarian when Jesus came, we would not go to be with Him when he came to gather his people."—Leslie Martin.

#140: Mrs. White said non-vegetarians can't go to heaven. She never made such an extreme statement. In 1905 she wrote the following:

> Yet it might not be best to discard flesh food under all circumstances. In certain cases of illness and exhaustion — as when persons are dying of tuberculosis, or when incurable tumors are wasting the life forces — it may be thought best to use flesh food in small quantities. But great care should be taken to secure the flesh of healthy animals.—*Life and Health,* Sept. 1, 1905; *Bible Echo,* Nov. 13, 1905.

If she taught that those who aren't vegetarians when Jesus comes can't go to heaven, why would she say something like this so late in her life?

The *documentation package* under "Point 70," "substantiates" this charge with two statements. Let's look at the second one first:

> Grains and fruits prepared free from grease, and in as natural a condition as possible, should be the food for the tables of all who claim to be preparing for translation to heaven.—*Counsels on Diet and Foods,* p. 64.

While this statement most certainly says something, it doesn't say what Mrs. Martin said. Now let's look at the first one as it originally appeared in *Christian Temperance and Bible Hygiene*:

> Again and again I have been shown that God is trying to lead us back, step by step, to his original design,—that man should subsist upon the natural products of the earth. Among those who are waiting for the coming of the Lord, meat-eating will eventually be done away; flesh will cease to form a part of their diet.—p. 119.

Clearly, this is another one of Mrs. White's many predictions. Time will tell if this one too will prove true. It's not a condemnatory statement. It's a simple prediction of what God's people will be doing at the time of Christ's return.

That God's people will ultimately all be vegetarians is plain from Scripture:

> And there shall be no more death, neither sorrow, nor crying, neither shall there be any more pain: for the former things are passed away. (Rev. 21:4)
>
> The wolf and the lamb shall feed together, and the lion shall eat straw like the bullock: and dust shall be the serpent's meat. They shall not hurt nor destroy in all my holy mountain, saith the LORD. (Is. 65:25; cf. 11:7)

Anyone who isn't a vegetarian the day before Christ's return will be one the day after. In the new earth, even the lions will be.

The immediate context of the selection from *Christian Temperance and Bible Hygiene* will help us understand even better the biblical basis for Mrs. White's concepts on the matter. First of all, she mentions the original diet God gave Adam and Eve (p. 118). Indeed, according to the Genesis account, Adam and Eve were the very first vegetarians on the planet (Gen. 1:29; 3:18). Not until after the Flood did God permit the eating of flesh, after which man's life span drastically decreased (Gen. 9:3; 5:3-32; 11:10-32). Her point was that, in these last days, God is trying to lead us back to His original plan for mankind.

She also refers to the fact that God gave the Israelites a mostly vegetarian diet during their forty years in the wilderness. Six times a week manna was on the ground in the morning, a food made by angels (Ps. 78:24, 25). On only two occasions did God in a similarly miraculous fashion provide them with flesh. Regarding the second occasion Mrs. White writes: "They murmured at God's restrictions, and lusted after the fleshpots of Egypt. God let them have flesh, but it proved a curse to them."—*Christian Temperance and Bible Hygiene,* p. 119.

What was that second occasion? In Numbers 11 we find the Israelites being extremely rude, complaining about the food. So God declared:

> Sanctify yourselves against to morrow, and ye shall eat flesh: for ye have wept in the ears of the LORD, saying, Who shall give us flesh to eat? for it was well with us in Egypt: therefore the LORD will give you flesh, and ye shall eat. Ye shall not eat one day, nor two days, nor five days, neither ten days, nor twenty days; But even a whole month, until it come out at your nostrils, and it be loathsome unto you: because that ye have despised the LORD which is among you, and have wept before him, saying, Why came we forth out of Egypt? (vss. 18-20)

As Mrs. White wrote, "it proved a curse to them," for some didn't live long enough to eat the flesh for a whole month: "And while the flesh was yet between their teeth, ere it was chewed, the wrath of the LORD was kindled against the people, and the LORD smote the people with a very great plague" (vs. 33).

Now all this happened on their trip from Mt. Sinai to Kadeshbarnea. How far is it between the two? Just an "eleven days' journey" (Deut. 1:2).

At Kadesh they sent twelve spies into the land of Canaan. After forty days, ten came back and said, "We can't conquer the land." Two, Caleb and Joshua, came back and said, "God is able to deliver the land into our hand." The people went with the majority report, rebelled once again, and tried to stone Caleb and Joshua (Num. 13:17-14:10). As a result, they had to wander around in the wilderness till all that generation was dead.

Why would the Israelites have rebelled when they were on the very borders of the promised land? Psalm 106 gives us the secret: "They soon forgat his works; they waited not for his counsel: But lusted exceedingly in the wilderness, and tempted God in the desert. And he gave them their request; but sent leanness into their soul" (vss. 13-15).

Eating flesh for a whole month till it came out of their noses made their "souls" skinny. These effects were still wearing off when the spies returned and gave their report. If their souls had been fat in the Lord instead of lean, perhaps they would have gone forward in faith instead of sliding back in unbelief.

Flesh was not the best article of diet for the Israelites. It affected their dispositions to the point that they could not react properly when trials and tests came their way. Even so, God never told them, "If you don't stop eating flesh, you can't enter Canaan."

Let's take another look at the second of Mrs. White's two statements:

Grains and fruits prepared free from grease, and in as natural a condition as possible, should be the food for the tables of all who claim to be preparing for translation to heaven.—*Counsels on Diet and Foods*, p. 64.

Preparing for translation? Is there a preparatory work to be done?

Beloved, now are we the sons of God, and it doth not yet appear what we shall be: but we know that, when he shall appear, we shall be like him; for we shall see him as he is. And every man that hath this hope in him purifieth himself, even as he is pure. (1 Jn. 3:2, 3)

The First Epistle of John has a lot to say about overcoming sin. There is a work of preparation to be done, of giving all our sins to Jesus, and relying on Him for the power to overcome temptation. The eating of flesh does affect the disposition, and the hormones and chemicals in flesh do affect the body's processes in negative ways. Therefore, it is wise for those who are seeking to prepare for Christ's return to consider giving up eating flesh. It will only be a few days earlier than when we all will have to anyway.

Speaking of hormones and chemicals, man's original diet and what happened to the Israelites isn't the whole picture, according to Mrs. White:

Animals are frequently killed that have been driven quite a distance for the slaughter. Their blood has become heated. They are full of flesh, and have been deprived of healthy exercise, and when they have to travel far, they become surfeited, and exhausted, and in that condition are killed for market. Their blood is highly inflamed, and those who eat of their meat, eat poison.—*Selected Messages*, bk. 2, p. 418.

While the animals get to ride instead of walk these days, there still is the question of how the ones that go to market get selected:

Diseased animals are taken to the large cities and to the villages, and sold for food. Many of these poor creatures would have died of disease in a very short time if they had not been slaughtered; yet the carcasses of these diseased animals are prepared for the market, and people eat freely of this poisonous food.—*Medical Ministry*, p. 280.

As the apostle Paul said, "The love of money is the root of all evil" (1 Tim. 6:10). What we will do to save a buck and to make a buck. It's pathetic, isn't it?

Still another problem is the following: "A very serious objection to the practice of meat eating is found in the fact that disease is becoming more and more widespread among the animal creation." —*Manuscript Releases*, vol. 7, p. 421. The Bible basically predicts the same (Rom. 8:19-22; Is. 51:6). As we get closer to Christ's return, disease in animals will become more and more of a problem. How bad had it gotten in her day?

Cancers, tumors, diseases of the lungs, the liver, the kidneys, all exist among the animals that are used for food. Until late years we have never heard of anything approaching to the variety of diseases now apparent in the animal creation. It is stated that out of a herd of twenty cattle, the inspectors accepted only two; from another herd of one hundred, only twenty-five were accepted as having no apparent disease.—*Ibid.*

How much better is it today? According to Mrs. White, things were going to get worse, not better:

Let the people be taught how to prepare food without the use of milk or butter. Tell them that the time will soon come when there will be no safety in using eggs, milk, cream, or butter, because disease in animals is increasing in proportion to the increase of wickedness among men. The time is near when, because of the iniquity of the fallen race, the whole animal creation will groan under the diseases that curse our earth.—*Testimonies for the Church*, vol. 7, p. 135.

Really, it would get that bad? Because of man's wickedness?

Most folk have no clue what is being done for a profit today. When this writer asked a chicken farmer in Alabama around 1988 what was in the feed he was giving his chickens, the farmer replied that there was arsenic in it. It stimulated the appetites of the chickens to make them eat more and grow faster, giving higher profits in less time.

Another farmer said that his chicken litter got shipped out west to the cattle feed lots. "The cows eat it like candy," he said. It saves money, and the cows get more nourishment from the pre-digested corn than from straight grain. How in the world do cows eat chicken litter like candy? "They mix it with oats and molasses," the farmer said. That explained it.

Oh, but it probably wasn't just pre-digested corn.

The feet, feathers, and bills left over from the slaughtering process typically go to a plant that turns it all into chicken feed. Another way to cut costs. And all that ends up in the chicken-litter cattle feed.

It doesn't take too much intelligence to figure out that chickens aren't buzzards and cows aren't porkers. God didn't create them to eat such things. Are we not asking for trouble when we go so contrary to God's design just to make a buck?

Of course, some will disagree. But with that scary Mad Cow Disease around, it's a bit more difficult to be skeptical. Cows ate cows, and their brains turned into sponges. Can that happen to me if I eat the cows? "No way," said the British authorities, but they don't say that anymore.

So Mrs. White predicted that before the end, eating animal foods would become dangerous. To borrow some earlier wording from Sydney Cleveland, it either is or almost is "a matter of historical record that" this prophecy did "come true as she foretold."

Salvation, Grace, and Obedience

#141: "Ellen G. White stressed the keeping of the letter of the law along with many added rules to put one on the road to salvation."—Mark Martin.

#141: She said that before we can start on the road to salvation, we must keep the law. If this is true, which it is not, why did she say this?

Come with humble hearts, not thinking that you must do some good work to merit the favor of God, or that you must make yourself better before you can come to Christ. *You are powerless to do good,* and cannot better your condition. Apart from Christ we have no merit, no righteousness. Our sinfulness, our weakness, our human imperfection make it impossible that we should appear before God unless we are clothed in Christ's spotless righteousness. We are to be found in Him not having our own righteousness, but the righteousness which is in Christ. Then in the name that is above every name, the only name given among men whereby men can be saved, claim the promise of God, saying, "Lord, forgive my sin; I put my hands into Thy hand for help, and I must have it,

or perish. I now believe." The Saviour says to the repenting sinner, "No man cometh unto the Father, but by me" (John 14:6), "and him that cometh to me I will in no wise cast out" (John 6:37). "I am thy salvation" (Ps. 35:3).—*Selected Messages,* bk. 1, pp. 333, 334, italics added.

She well knew what the Bible teaches. We can't truly obey God until we have come to Christ (Gal. 5:17; Is. 64:6; Jer. 13:23). We "are powerless to do good." If we wait until we are keeping the law before we start on the road to salvation, we will never get on that road, for it is totally impossible to obey without Jesus in the heart.

As shown under #144 below, this statement of Mr. Martin is contradicted by the point he makes just two sentences and a quotation later.

#142 & #143: "She had no patience with Christians who dared to say 'I am saved.' 'We are never to rest in a satisfied condition... saying "I am saved"... they pervert the truth... They declare that we have only to believe on Jesus Christ and that faith is all sufficient; that the righteousness of Christ is to be the sinner's credentials... This class claim that Christ came to save sinners, and that he has saved them... But are they saved... No...' Signs of the Times February 8, 1897."—Mark Martin.

#142: She wrote this quote. Not really. The quotation is both out of context and altered.

Two quotes written seven years apart from two different periodicals from two different continents have been fused into one at the second ellipsis. The second quote is not from *Signs of the Times,* an American journal, but from *Bible Echo and Signs of the Times,* an Australian journal. Proof that all this is so can be found under "Point 71" in the *documentation package,* which reproduces both quotes.

The portions of the quotes that the video omitted reveal clearly what she was trying to say, something

quite different than Mr. Martin's allegation. We'll demonstrate this under the next number.

#143: She had no patience with those who believe in Jesus and say, "I am saved." To start with, let's fill in the first ellipsis in the quote from the first article, and the last two ellipses in the quote from the last article:

"We are never to rest in a satisfied condition, and cease to make advancement, saying, 'I am saved.' "
—*Review and Herald,* June 17, 1890.

But are they saved while transgressing the law of Jehovah?—No; for the garments of Christ's righteousness are not a cloak for iniquity.—*Bible Echo*, Feb. 25, 1897.

Will the reader please compare these two statements with what Mr. Martin said? Does his quoting of Mrs. White sound at all like what she really did say?

Before we go on, let's review a point from #66. If we want to avoid misconstruing Mrs. White's statements, we must recognize the definitions she was using. Typically, most folk who talk about when they were "saved" are referring to their justification and conversion. While this must be the definition Mr. Martin is using here, it isn't the one Mrs. White is using. She's referring more to the end of the Christian walk than its beginning:

> It is not he that putteth on the armor that can boast of the victory; for he has the battle to fight and the victory to win. It is he that endureth unto the end that shall be saved. The Lord says, "If any man draw back, my soul shall have no pleasure in him."—*Review and Herald*, June 17, 1890.

What was the problem with those in Mrs. White's day who, as Mr. Martin put it, "dared to say, 'I am saved' "? "As long as man is full of weakness,—for of himself he cannot save his soul,—he should never dare to say, 'I am saved.' "—*Ibid.* How interesting! Out of human pride they were in danger of trusting in self rather than Christ. In actuality, Mrs. White's concern was exactly opposite of what Mr. Martin alleges.

Human pride, ceasing to make advancement, forgetting that we are full of weakness, to these concerns we must add one more:

> But the doctrine is now largely taught that the gospel of Christ has made the law of God of none effect; that by "believing" we are released from the necessity of being doers of the word.—*Bible Echo*, Feb. 25, 1897.

Both articles expressed this same concern for the doctrine called "antinomianism," a term meaning "against law." There are those who believe that one can live like the devil and still go to heaven. One gentleman of this persuasion conversed a bit with this writer on the topic. He was emphatic that even if he murdered a thousand people in cold blood one at a time and never repented, he would still go to heaven, for he had at some point in the distant past believed in Christ.

Mrs. White just couldn't buy that, so she said that "such pervert the truth." Odds are, you probably agree with her.

#144 & #145: "The Adventist view of salvation is that Jesus made the down payment for our salvation at the cross, but once you've accepted his offer of salvation you've got to keep making up the monthly installments."—Mark Martin.

#144: Adventists believe that Jesus made the down payment for our salvation. Assuming that Adventists base their beliefs on Mrs. White, which they don't, Mr. Martin is contradicting himself.

Two sentences and a quotation ago he said, "Ellen G. White stressed the keeping of the letter of the law along with many added rules to put one on the road to salvation." So which is it? Did Jesus make the down payment? Or must we keep the law in order to put ourselves on the road to salvation? It can't be both. Either one or the other (or both) of Mr. Martin's statements is incorrect.

Jesus paid it *all*.

#145: But they believe we must make the monthly installments. Thus it is suggested that Adventists believe we partially earn our salvation. This is false.

First of all, and most importantly, such a position contradicts the Scriptures: "Are ye so foolish? having begun in the Spirit, are ye now made perfect by the flesh?" (Gal. 3:3).

Secondly, and less importantly, such a position contradicts Mrs. White: "The proud heart strives to earn salvation; but both our title to heaven and our fitness for it are found in the righteousness of Christ."—*Desire of Ages*, p. 300.

Title? Fitness? What does that mean?

> The righteousness by which we are justified is imputed; the righteousness by which we are sanctified is imparted. The first is our title to heaven, the second is our fitness for heaven.—*Review and Herald*, June 4, 1895.

So both our justification ("down payment") and our sanctification ("monthly installments") are found in the righteousness of Christ. We can earn neither.

#146, #147, & #148: "So not really relying upon the grace of God alone to save them, Adventists are striving to be rigidly obedient and this makes for an inflexible, guilt-ridden, legalistic lifestyle."—Mark Martin.

#146: Adventists do not rely upon the grace of God alone. This is not what Adventists believe, nor what Mrs. White taught:

> Only through the blood of the Crucified One is there cleansing from sin. His grace alone can enable us to resist and subdue the tendencies of our fallen nature.—*Ministry of Healing*, p. 428.
>
> . . . there is safety only in Christ. It is through His grace alone that Satan can be successfully repulsed. —*Testimonies for the Church* vol. 2, p. 409.
>
> His grace alone can quicken the lifeless faculties of the soul, and attract it to God, to holiness.—*Steps to Christ*, p. 18.
>
> Divine grace is needed at the beginning, divine grace at every step of advance, and divine grace alone can complete the work.—*Testimonies to Ministers*, p. 508.
>
> It was by self-surrender and confiding faith that Jacob gained what he had failed to gain by conflict in his own strength. God thus taught His servant that divine power and grace alone could give him the blessing he craved.—*God's Amazing Grace*, p. 279.

And the list could go on.

#147: They're striving to be rigidly obedient. Actually, there isn't as much striving as there ought to be. The average member will likely tell you that there is a bit of laxity in the Adventist Church today. And that trend seems to be growing.

#148: They're inflexible, guilt-ridden legalists. Probably every denomination has its legalists. This writer had one coming to a church he pastored back in the 1980's. She didn't seem guilt-ridden one bit, which was quite unfortunate given the situation. Repeatedly when confronted about her unchristlike behavior, she would list all the wonderful things she had done, as if good works could buy her a pardon for backbiting, gossip, and dishonesty.

It is probable that the average legalist feels no more guilt than the average person. Legalism is a way to get rid of guilt, not cause it.

> For I was alive without the law once: but when the commandment came, sin revived, and I died. And the commandment, which was ordained to life, I found to be unto death. For sin, taking occasion by the commandment, deceived me, and by it slew me. (Rom. 7:9-11)

The law tells us what God requires. When we realize that we fall short, we feel guilty. Then we have a choice to make regarding how we deal with that guilt.

Legalism is one way. The legalist thinks that his partial, imperfect, self-centered "obedience" can earn him salvation. As he deceives himself into thinking that he really is obeying God's commandments, guilt to a large degree goes away.

When an individual realizes what God requires and wants to obey, he soon finds out that he has a problem:

> For we know that the law is spiritual: but I am carnal, sold under sin. For that which I do I allow not: for what I would, that do I not; but what I hate, that do I. If then I do that which I would not, I consent unto the law that it is good. . . . For I know that in me (that is, in my flesh,) dwelleth no good thing: for to will is present with me; but how to perform that which is good I find not. For the good that I would I do not: but the evil which I would not, that I do. . . . For I delight in the law of God after the inward man: But I see another law in my members, warring against the law of my mind, and bringing me into captivity to the law of sin which is in my members. (Rom. 7:14-23)

This is a necessary experience to go through for the one who is seeking Christ. Such an experience reveals to us our great weakness apart from Christ. Then we know Whom we must rely upon for strength and power to live the Christian life:

> O wretched man that I am! who shall deliver me from the body of this death? I thank God through Jesus Christ our Lord. . . . There is therefore now no condemnation to them which are in Christ Jesus, who walk not after the flesh, but after the Spirit. For the law of the Spirit of life in Christ Jesus hath made me free from the law of sin and death. (Rom. 7:24, 25; 8:1, 2)

No condemnation to those who walk after the Spirit? And why might that be?

> That the righteousness of the law might be fulfilled in us, who walk not after the flesh, but after the Spirit. (Rom. 8:4)
>
> This I say then, Walk in the Spirit, and ye shall not fulfil the lust of the flesh. (Gal. 5:16)

The life of rebellion has been transformed into one of loving obedience. Isn't the gospel beautiful?

#149: "Despite modern Adventist attempts to soften law-keeping, Ellen White's teachings are unmistakable: 'No one is saved who is a transgressor of the law of God...' Advent Review and Sabbath Herald June 17, 1890."—Mark Martin.

#149: Mrs. White said, "No one is saved who is a transgressor." This statement was part of the first article referred to under #142. Let's add just a tad bit of context:

> If we are disobedient, our characters are out of harmony with God's moral rule of government, and it is stating a falsehood to say, "I am saved." No one is saved who is a transgressor of the law of God, which is the foundation of his government in heaven and in earth.

That's hard to argue with, given how the Bible defines salvation.

Jesus came to save us *from* our sins, not *in* our sins (Mat. 1:21). And what is sin? It's the transgression of the law (1 Jn. 3:4). In other words, part of salvation's work is to bring the sinner into repentance and obedience to all of God's commandments. Continued unrepentance for violations of God's law indicates that there is a sin that the individual refuses to be saved from. How then can one claim to be saved from sin while at the same time refusing to be saved from sin?

It is the clear teaching of the New Testament that we must repent of sin if we want to be saved. Mr. Martin could have just as well said, "Despite modern Adventist attempts to soften law-keeping, . . .

> . . . the apostle Paul's teachings are unmistakable: "Know ye not that the unrighteous shall not inherit the kingdom of God? Be not deceived: neither fornicators, nor idolaters, nor adulterers, nor effeminate, nor abusers of themselves with mankind, Nor thieves, nor covetous, nor drunkards, nor revilers, nor extortioners, shall inherit the kingdom of God." (1 Cor. 6:9, 10)

> . . . the apostle John's teachings are unmistakable: "And hereby we do know that we know him, if we keep his commandments. He that saith, I know him, and keepeth not his commandments, is a liar, and the truth is not in him." (1 Jn. 2:3, 4)

> . . . the apostle Peter's teachings are unmistakable: "And we are his witnesses of these things; and so is also the Holy Ghost, whom God hath given to them that obey him." (Acts 5:32)

> . . . the apostle Jude's teachings are unmistakable: "Behold, the Lord cometh with ten thousands of his saints, To execute judgment upon all, and to convince all that are ungodly among them of all their ungodly deeds which they have ungodly committed, and of all their hard speeches which ungodly sinners have spoken against him." (Jude 14, 15)

> . . . the apostle James's teachings are unmistakable: "For whosoever shall keep the whole law, and yet offend in one point, he is guilty of all. . . . So speak ye, and so do, as they that shall be judged by the law of liberty." (James 2:10, 11)

> . . . Jesus's teachings are unmistakable: "Think not that I am come to destroy the law, or the prophets: I am not come to destroy, but to fulfill. For verily I say unto you, Till heaven and earth pass, one jot or one tittle shall in no wise pass from the law, till all be fulfilled. Whosoever therefore shall break one of these least commandments, and shall teach men so, he shall be called the least in the kingdom of heaven: but whosoever shall do and teach them, the same shall be called great in the kingdom of heaven. For I say unto you, That except your righteousness shall exceed the righteousness of the scribes and Pharisees, ye shall in no case enter into the kingdom of heaven." (Mat. 5:17-20)

God forbid that any believer or preacher would say such things! Jesus came to save us "from our sins," and we must let Him do it!

#150 & #151: "Yet the Bible teaches that we are under a New Covenant and the Old Covenant is obsolete. Christ is the end of the law."—Mark Martin.

#150: We're under the New Covenant now. Though this is a popular antinomian argument, it doesn't make sense in the light of the *only* New Testament passage that describes the New Covenant:

> For if that first covenant had been faultless, then should no place have been sought for the second. For finding fault with them, he saith, Behold, the days come, saith the Lord, when I will make a new covenant with the house of Israel and with the house of Judah: . . . For this is the covenant that I will make with the house of Israel after those days, saith the Lord; I will put my laws into their mind, and write them in their hearts: and I will be to them a God, and they shall be to me a people. (Heb. 8:7-10)

First of all, this passage clearly says that the problem with the Old Covenant was the people, not the law. This harmonizes with how Romans 7:12 says that "the law is holy, and the commandment holy, and just, and good." There is nothing wrong with the law.

Secondly, the passage clearly says that the New Covenant is God's writing His laws in our hearts and minds. If we don't have to obey the law under the New Covenant, how then can the New Covenant be God's writing His law in us?

In looking for what the difference between the Old Covenant and New Covenant is, the following verses can be helpful:

> And all the people answered together, and said, All that the LORD hath spoken *we* will do. (Ex. 19:8)
> And Moses came and told the people all the words of the LORD, and all the judgments: and all the people answered with one voice, and said, All the words which the LORD hath said will *we* do. (Ex. 24:3)
> And he took the book of the covenant, and read in the audience of the people: and they said, All that the LORD hath said will *we* do, and be obedient. (Ex. 24:7)

They said they would obey, but since their promise didn't last forty days, they must have been trying to do it on their own. It is utterly impossible for us to write God's laws in our own hearts and minds. Only God can do that, for only He can convert the heart and bring us into repentance and obedience.

Therefore, a major difference between the Old and New Covenants must be who does the writing upon the heart. Under the Old, the people try to do it themselves, all in vain. Under the new, we let God do it.

Is the law of the New Covenant that's written in our hearts the Ten Commandments, or is it some other law? That's a fair question, and it deserves a fair answer.

"And the temple of God was opened in heaven, and there was seen in his temple the ark of his testament" (Rev. 11:19). Since "testament" is translated from the Greek word for "covenant," what we are seeing in this verse is the ark of God's covenant. But is it the ark of the Old Covenant or the New? Two points may be considered.

First, this verse is speaking of events that happen at the end of time. Since the Old Covenant is long since gone by the end of time, this ark must be the ark of the New Covenant.

Second, the sanctuary and its furniture that Moses made were but copies of the heavenly originals, and these originals belong to the New Covenant (Heb. 8:2, 5; 9:1). Since Revelation's ark is in a temple in heaven, not a temple on earth, it must therefore be the original ark, the ark of God's New Covenant.

But what was the purpose of the ark? Primarily, it served as a box to hold the Ten Commandments, the "tables of the covenant" (Deut. 9:9-11; 10:4). This is how it got its name. Thus Revelation's ark of God's New Covenant must likewise have "tables of the covenant" inside. Otherwise, the phrase "ark of his testament" is meaningless.

There is but one question left. Do the tables inside the ark of the Old Covenant and the tables inside the ark of the New Covenant read the same? Well, if the sanctuary that Moses made was but a copy of the heavenly, and if the ark he made was but a copy of the original in heaven, would not the earthly tables also be a copy of the originals in heaven? Of course!

#151: Christ is the end of the law. This too is a popular antinomian argument, taken from Romans 10:4. Yet it contradicts what Christ said:

> Think not that I am come to destroy the law, or the prophets: I am not come to destroy, but to fulfill. For verily I say unto you, Till heaven and earth pass, one jot or one tittle shall in no wise pass from the law, till all be fulfilled. (Mat. 5:17, 18)

It also makes Paul contradict himself in the very same book: "Do we then make void the law through faith? God forbid: yea, we establish the law" (Rom. 3:31).

So what does "Christ is the end of the law for righteousness to every one that believeth" mean? "Ye have heard of the patience of Job, and have seen the end of the Lord; that the Lord is very pitiful, and of tender mercy" (James 5:11). Apparently, "end" has more than one meaning, unless we want to say that the "Lord" has ended.

"End" in Romans 10:4 means "that which the law leads to." This makes the text parallel the thought of another passage of Paul: "Wherefore the law was our schoolmaster to bring us unto Christ, that we might be justified by faith. But after that faith is come, we are no longer under a schoolmaster" (Gal. 3:24, 25).

The law tells us what God requires and what sin is (Rom. 3:20; 7:7). When we realize our helplessness to atone for the past and to live in the present, we are drawn to Christ as our only hope. Christ is thus the "end" of the law because the law leads us to Christ.

Back to the ark of the covenant for a moment. "And after that I looked, and, behold, the temple of the tabernacle of the testimony in heaven was opened" (Rev. 15:5). Notice how the heavenly temple is described as the "tabernacle of testimony." Often in the Old Testament the tabernacle was called the tabernacle of testimony or witness. Why? Because the ark was inside, and it was called the ark of testimony or witness. And why was it called that? Because it contained the "tables of testimony" (Ex. 38:21; 25:16; 31:18; 32:15; 34:29). And why are the Ten Commandments called tables of testimony? Because they testify and tell us exactly what sin is, and how we are in dire need of a Savior.

The prophet Micah foretold the second coming (Mic. 1:3, 4). In that context, he had this to say to everyone in the end of time, whether Jew or Gentile: "Hear, all ye people; hearken, O earth, and all that therein is: and let the Lord GOD be witness against you, the Lord from his holy temple" (Mic. 1:2).

Will we let God testify to us about our sins through the Ten Commandments of His heavenly temple? Or shall we shut our ears to what God says through His Word, go on in our disobedience and sin, and be lost in the end? Dear reader, won't you choose to follow Christ wherever He leads?

#152: "The New Testament teaches that the law was given by God to be our tutor or teacher leading us to Christ. Listen to what Galatians 3:25 says. It says, 'We are no longer under a tutor.' " —Mark Martin.

#152: We're no longer under a schoolmaster or tutor. Is Mr. Martin implying that not being under the law means that we don't have to keep the law? Is he saying that those who obey the law are still under the law? Interpreting Paul's usage of the phrase "under the law" or "under a tutor" in such a way is highly inaccurate.

Certainly, Paul did not mean that we can continue to kill, hate, fornicate, lust, steal, covet, and lie and still go to heaven. The same book of Galatians says:

> Now the works of the flesh are manifest, which are these; Adultery, fornication, uncleanness, lasciviousness, Idolatry, witchcraft, hatred, variance, emulations, wrath, strife, seditions, heresies, Envyings, murders, drunkenness, revellings, and such like: of the which I tell you before, as I have also told you in time past, that they which do such things shall not inherit the kingdom of God. (Gal. 5:19-21)

Why can't people who do such things enter heaven? The next two verses answer this question: "But the fruit of the Spirit is love, joy, peace, longsuffering, gentleness, goodness, faith, Meekness, temperance: *against such there is no law*" (Gal. 5:22, 23). Clearly, what excludes the unrepentant murderer, fornicator, and thief from heaven in New Testament times is the law of God.

"But if ye be led of the Spirit, ye are not under the law" (Gal. 5:18). Why is this? Why is the believer not under the law?

> This I say then, Walk in the Spirit, and ye shall not fulfil the lust of the flesh. For the flesh lusteth against the Spirit, and the Spirit against the flesh: and these are contrary the one to the other: so that ye cannot do the things that ye would. (Gal. 5:16, 17)
>
> And they that are Christ's have crucified the flesh with the affections and lusts. If we live in the Spirit, let us also walk in the Spirit. (Gal. 5:24, 25)

Before continuing, let's summarize what these verses we've already looked at from Galatians are saying:

1. Unrepentant sinners can't go to heaven, because there is a law against that.
2. There is a war between the flesh and the Spirit, so that we in and of ourselves are powerless to do what is right.
3. If believers walk in the Spirit, they will not fulfill the lusts of the flesh.
4. Such believers who are not fulfilling the lusts of the flesh are not under the law.

It appears, then, that Paul is saying that the Spirit-filled believer is not under the law because he is truly keeping the law. Here is another way to arrive at the same conclusion:

1. "But before faith came, we were kept under the law, shut up unto the faith which should afterwards be revealed" (Gal. 3:23). So those who are under the law are not yet under faith.
2. "Whatsoever is not of faith is sin" (Rom. 14:23). Those who are not yet under faith must therefore still be under sin.
3. "Sin is the transgression of the law" (1 Jn. 3:4). Those who are still under sin must therefore be those who are transgressing the law.

Thus, those who are under the law must be those who are transgressing the law. In essence, to be under the law must mean to be under its condemnation. Consequently, it makes no sense whatsoever to say that a transgressor is not under the law, or that a law-abiding Christian is under the law. Someone who is truly keeping the law cannot be under the law, and someone who is breaking the law cannot but be under the law.

These conclusions harmonize with how the apostle

Paul equates being under sin's dominion with being under the law: "For sin shall not have dominion over you: for ye are not under the law, but under grace. What then? shall we sin, because we are not under the law, but under grace? God forbid" (Rom. 6:14, 15).

The law's purpose is to shut the mouth of both Jew and Gentile, and to make them both guilty before God: "Now we know that what things soever the law saith, it saith to them who are under the law: that every mouth may be stopped, and all the world may become guilty before God" (Rom. 3:19).

To conclude:

> Some time ago, when we were passing through Oswego, N. Y., we saw two stern officers, and with them two men were coupled, carrying in their hands large leaden balls. We did not come to the conclusion

that they had been keeping the law of the State of New York, but that they had been breaking it, and that they could not walk at liberty because they were transgressors of the law. We were trying to live in harmony with all the laws of the State of New York, and with the law of God; and we were walking at liberty,—we were not under the bondage of the law. If we live in harmony with the life of Christ, with the law of God, that law does not condemn us—we are not under the bondage of the law.—*Review and Herald*, Jan. 4, 1887.

There is full assurance of hope in believing every word of Christ, believing in Him, being united to Him by living faith. When this is his experience, the human being is no longer under the law, for the law no longer condemns his course of action.—*In Heavenly Places*, p. 144.

#153: "Christians are to grow in grace and keep God's commandments out of a love for Him, not under compulsion."—Mark Martin.

#153: Christians will keep God's commandments out of love. This statement is one of the most prominent contradictions in the video. How more self-destructive can this logic be? "We should not try to keep the law, but we will keep the law if we love God."

It can't be both ways. We have to pick one or the other: 1) Christians should keep the law of God and refrain from murder, adultery, theft, and lies. 2) Christians do not need to worry about that at all and can continue all the old perversions they used to do before they came to Christ.

If Mr. Martin's statement that Christians will keep the law because they love God is true, which it is, then whether they are indeed keeping the law or not is an indicator of how much they love Him. So adamantly refusing to keep a biblical command of God is evidence that we do not really love Him.

Why would Mr. Martin or anyone else contradict himself in this way? Actually, this kind of thing is all too common. It typically happens when someone is trying to avoid one of the Ten Commandments. The arguments against obedience are aimed at just one of the ten, while the statements in favor of obedience are concerning the other nine.

Which one of the ten do you think Mr. Martin might be trying to avoid? Is he trying to convince us that it is all right to kill, fornicate, steal, lie, covet, dishonor our parents, have other gods in place of God, bow down to images, or take God's name in vain? Or might he be trying to avoid the one that says to remember the Sabbath of the Lord to keep it

holy?

Christians will "keep God's commandments out of love." Mr. Martin's connection between obedience to God's law and love is biblically sound, supported by thirteen verses from the New Testament and eleven from the Old:

> If ye love me, keep my commandments. (John 14:15)
>
> He that hath my commandments, and keepeth them, he it is that loveth me. (John 14:21)
>
> If ye keep my commandments, ye shall abide in my love; even as I have kept my Father's commandments, and abide in his love. (John 15:10)
>
> Jesus said unto him, Thou shalt love the Lord thy God with all thy heart, and with all thy soul, and with all thy mind. This is the first and great commandment. And the second is like unto it, Thou shalt love thy neighbour as thyself. On these two commandments hang all the law and the prophets. (Mat. 22:37-40)
>
> Owe no man any thing, but to love one another: for he that loveth another hath fulfilled the law. (Rom. 13:8)
>
> Love worketh no ill to his neighbour: therefore love is the fulfilling of the law. (Rom. 13:10)
>
> For all the law is fulfilled in one word, even in this; Thou shalt love thy neighbour as thyself. (Gal. 5:14)
>
> By this we know that we love the children of God, when we love God, and keep his commandments. For this is the love of God, that we keep his commandments: and his commandments are not grievous. (1 Jn. 5:2, 3)

And this is love, that we walk after his commandments. (2 Jn. 6)

And shewing mercy unto thousands of them that love me, and keep my commandments. (Ex. 20:6; Deut. 5:10)

Know therefore that the LORD thy God, he is God, the faithful God, which keepeth covenant and mercy with them that love him and keep his commandments to a thousand generations. (Deut. 7:9)

Therefore thou shalt love the LORD thy God, and keep his charge, and his statutes, and his judgments, and his commandments, alway. (Deut. 11:1)

If ye shall hearken diligently unto my commandments which I command you this day, to love the LORD your God. (Deut. 11:13)

For if ye shall diligently keep all these commandments which I command you, to do them, to love the LORD your God. (Deut. 11:22)

If thou shalt keep all these commandments to do them, which I command thee this day, to love the LORD thy God. (Deut. 19:9)

In that I command thee this day to love the LORD thy God, to walk in his ways, and to keep his commandments and his statutes and his judgments. (Deut. 30:16)

But take diligent heed to do the commandment and the law, which Moses the servant of the LORD charged you, to love the LORD your God, and to walk in all his ways, and to keep his commandments. (Josh. 22:5)

O LORD God of heaven, the great and terrible God, that keepeth covenant and mercy for them that love him and observe his commandments. (Neh. 1:5)

O Lord, the great and dreadful God, keeping the covenant and mercy to them that love him, and to them that keep his commandments. (Dan. 9:4)

Whether in Old Testament or New Testament times, the obedience that God requires is an obedience that is motivated by love. Anything less is not really obedience at all.

We ought to briefly revisit one point. Remember how under #93 we saw that the New Testament teaches that no one has ever seen God the Father? Thus when we read about Abraham or Jacob or Manoah seeing God, it means that they saw Christ.

Then went up Moses, and Aaron, Nadab, and Abihu, and seventy of the elders of Israel: And they saw the God of Israel: and there was under his feet as it were a paved work of a sapphire stone, and as it were the body of heaven in his clearness. And upon the nobles of the children of Israel he laid not his hand: also they saw God, and did eat and drink. (Ex. 24:9-11)

So this must have been Christ as well who met with these folk on Mt. Sinai.

This answers for us the following question: When Jesus said, "If ye love me, keep *My* commandments" (John 14:15), do *His* "commandments" include the Ten?

#154: "In fact being under the law leads to sin. 1 Corinthians 15:56 says, 'The strength of sin is the law.' "—Mark Martin.

#154: Being under the law leads to sin. Mr. Martin appears to be saying that obeying the law leads to sin. This is a rather strange conclusion, for how can obeying the law lead to breaking the law?

What shall we say then? Is the law sin? God forbid. Nay, I had not known sin, but by the law: for I had not known lust, except the law had said, Thou shalt not covet. (Rom. 7:7)

Therefore by the deeds of the law there shall no flesh be justified in his sight: for by the law is the knowledge of sin. (Rom. 3:20)

According to the New Testament, while the law cannot save us, it does define what sin is. As we saw under #152, "under the law" means "under the condemnation of the law." These simple Bible facts make it clear that, rather than being under the law leading to sin, sin is what puts us under the law.

The text cited, 1 Corinthians 15:56, is an interesting one. What does it mean? Consider the thoughts on this very verse found in these well-known commentaries written by scholars who were not Seventh-day Adventists:

[N]ot that the law of God is sinful, or encourages sin: it forbids it under the severest penalty; but was there no law there would be no sin, nor imputation of it; sin is a transgression of the law: moreover, the strength of sin, its evil nature, and all the dreadful aggravations of it, and sad consequences upon it, are discovered and made known by the law; and also the strength of it is drawn out by it, through the corruption of human nature; which is irritated and provoked the more to sin, through the law's prohibition of it; and this is not the fault of the law, but is owing to the vitiosity of nature; which the more it is forbidden anything, the more desirous it is of it; to which may be added, that sin is the more exceeding sinful, being committed against a known law, and that of the great lawgiver, who is able to save and to destroy; whose legislative power and authority are slighted and trampled upon by it, which makes the transgression the more heinous; it is the law which binds sin upon a man's conscience, accuses him of it, pronounces him guilty, curses, condemns, and adjudges him to death for it.—*Gill's Expositor and the Body of Divinity.*

The strength of sin. Its power over the mind; its terrific and dreadful energy; and especially its power to produce alarm in the hour of death.

Is the law. The pure and holy law of God. This idea Paul has illustrated at length in Rom. 7:9-13, and he probably made the statement here in order to meet the Jews, and to show that the law of God had no power to take away the fear of death; and that, therefore, there was need of the gospel, and that this alone could do it. The Jews maintained that a man might be justified and saved by obedience to the law. Paul here shows that it is the law which gives its chief rigour to sin, and that it does not tend to subdue or destroy it; and that power is seen most strikingly in the pangs and horrors of a guilty conscience on the bed of death. There was need, therefore, of the gospel, which alone could remove the cause of these horrors, by taking away sin, and thus leaving the pardoned man to die in peace. —*Barnes' New Testament Notes.*

Without the law sin is not perceived or imputed (Rom. 3:20; 4:15; 5:13). The law makes sin the more grievous by making God's will the clearer. (Rom. 7:8-10).—*Jamieson, Faussett, and Brown.*

The law, broken, is sin, and when this law is consciously broken the conscience is wounded. When a moral law is broken, moral death follows. If there was no law of any kind, there would be no sin, no wounded consciences, no moral death. See Rom. 7:7.—*Peoples New Testament Notes.*

#155: "In contrast, being under grace leads to holiness. I love what Titus 2 verses 11 and 12 says. 'For the grace of God has appeared, bringing salvation to all men. It instructs us to deny ungodliness and worldly desires and to live sensibly, righteously and godly in the present age.' " —Mark Martin.

#155: Grace leads to holiness and righteousness. This too, similar to #153, is contradictory and self-destructive to Mr. Martin's principal argument. If we do not have to worry about keeping the law under the gospel of grace, why would that grace lead to holiness?

The Old Testament connects *holiness* with commandment keeping:

That ye may remember, and do all my commandments, and be holy unto your God. (Num. 15:40)

The LORD shall establish thee an holy people unto himself, as he hath sworn unto thee, if thou shalt keep the commandments of the LORD thy God, and walk in his ways. (Deut. 28:9)

Both the New Testament and the Old Testament connect *righteousness* with commandment keeping:

And they were both righteous before God, walking in all the commandments and ordinances of the Lord blameless. (Luke 1:6)

That the righteousness of the law might be fulfilled in us, who walk not after the flesh, but after the Spirit. (Rom. 8:4)

For it had been better for them not to have known the way of righteousness, than, after they have known it, to turn from the holy commandment delivered unto them. (2 Pet. 2:21)

And it shall be our righteousness, if we observe to do all these commandments before the LORD our God, as he hath commanded us. (Deut. 6:25)

O that thou hadst hearkened to my commandments! then had thy peace been as a river, and thy righteousness as the waves of the sea: Thy seed also had been as the sand, and the offspring of thy bowels like the gravel thereof; his name should not have been cut off nor destroyed from before me. (Is. 48:18, 19)

Hearken unto me, ye that know righteousness, the people in whose heart is my law; fear ye not the reproach of men, neither be ye afraid of their revilings. (Is. 51:7)

Did you notice the last two texts? These clearly connected commandment keeping with the fulfillment of God's covenant with Abraham and the New Covenant. Isaiah 48 referred to God's promise to Abraham that his seed would be as numerous as the sand of the sea (Gen. 22:17). Isaiah 51 referred to the New Covenant promise that God's law will be written in our hearts (Heb. 10:16; Jer. 31:33). Thus once again we see that the righteousness of Christ offered through the Abrahamic covenant, the New Covenant of grace, is vitally connected to the commandments of God.

According to Paul, God accounts a Gentile to be a Jew if he keeps the righteousness of the law: "Therefore if the uncircumcision keep the righteousness of the law, shall not his uncircumcision be counted for circumcision?" (Rom. 2:26). This is not to say that righteousness comes by the law, for this idea the New Testament emphatically denies (Gal. 2:21). Rather, the gospel of grace leads one into obedience to all of God's commandments. To quote Mrs. White,

[John Wesley] continued his strict and self-denying life, not now as the *ground*, but the *result* of faith; not the *root*, but the *fruit* of holiness. The grace of God in Christ is the foundation of the Christian's hope, and that grace will be manifested in obedience. Wesley's life was devoted to the preaching of the great truths which he had received—justification through faith in the atoning blood of Christ, and the renewing power of the Holy Spirit upon the heart, bringing forth fruit in a life conformed to the example of Christ.—*Great Controversy*, p. 256.

For Mr. Martin to say that the grace of God leads to holiness while seeking to avoid obedience to the fourth commandment is extremely contradictory. This is because the Sabbath in Scripture is a sign of sanctification and holiness:

Verily my sabbaths ye shall keep: for it is a sign between me and you throughout your generations; that ye may know that I am the LORD that doth sanctify you. (Ex. 31:13)

Moreover also I gave them my sabbaths, to be a sign between me and them, that they might know that I am the LORD that sanctify them. (Ezek. 20:12)

"Sanctification" and "holiness" come from the same root words in both Old Testament Hebrew and New Testament Greek. Thus, when the Bible says that the Sabbath is a sign of sanctification, it is also saying that it is a sign of holiness. So if the grace of God does in fact lead to holiness, which it does, surely it will lead to obedience to the fourth commandment as well as to the other nine!

Salvation, Cont.; Conditional Immortality

#156, #157, & #158: "Salvation by grace through faith alone is the heart of the gospel. But the Adventist doctrine of the 1844 investigative judgment colors all their major doctrines. It was because of this false teaching also known as the pre-advent judgment, which amounts to nothing more than a judgment of works which determines salvation, that the unbiblical doctrine of soul sleep was introduced. Obviously, you couldn't have believers going to heaven when they died before their lives were supposedly judged. What if they hadn't been good enough? They'd have to leave heaven, right?"—Mark Martin.

#156: A pre-advent judgment of works is incompatible with the gospel of grace. This statement contradicts Holy Scripture.

> And I saw another angel fly in the midst of heaven, having the everlasting gospel to preach unto them that dwell on the earth, and to every nation, and kindred, and tongue, and people, Saying with a loud voice, Fear God, and give glory to him; for the hour of his judgment is come: and worship him that made heaven, and earth, and the sea, and the fountains of waters. (Rev. 14:6, 7)

The Greek is a little more emphatic. "Is come" is in the aorist tense, the equivalent of our past tense. Thus we have an angel who in his preaching of the gospel is declaring to all the world that, "The judgment has already begun."

The next event portrayed is the second coming:

> And I looked, and behold a white cloud, and upon the cloud one sat like unto the Son of man, having on his head a golden crown, and in his hand a sharp sickle. And another angel came out of the temple, crying with a loud voice to him that sat on the cloud, Thrust in thy sickle, and reap: for the time is come for thee to reap; for the harvest of the earth is ripe. And he that sat on the cloud thrust in his sickle on the earth; and the earth was reaped. (Rev. 14:14-16)

Thus before the second coming we have as part of the gospel a message that the judgment has already commenced. If the gospel of grace cannot include such a pre-advent judgment, then Paul's gospel of grace is different than the gospel this angel is preaching. Yet that is impossible:

> But though we, or an angel from heaven, preach any other gospel unto you than that which we have preached unto you, let him be accursed. As we said before, so say I now again, If any man preach any other gospel unto you than that ye have received, let him be accursed. (Gal. 1:8, 9)

So the true gospel of grace must be compatible with a pre-advent judgment. But is that pre-advent judgment a judgment of works? As we saw under #62, it most definitely is.

> For God shall bring every work into judgment, with every secret thing, whether it be good, or whether it be evil. (Eccl. 12:14)
> But I say unto you, That every idle word that men shall speak, they shall give account thereof in the day of judgment. For by thy words thou shalt be justified, and by thy words thou shalt be condemned. (Mat. 12:36, 37)
> Therefore judge nothing before the time, until the Lord come, who both will bring to light the hidden things of darkness, and will make manifest the counsels of the hearts. (1 Cor. 4:5)

So the pre-advent judgment doesn't stop at just works. Our words, yes, even the thoughts of our hearts will be considered. But will this judgment "determine salvation"? The answer depends on what you mean by salvation. Do you mean conversion, forgiveness, and justification? Or do you mean actually arriving in heaven (see #66 and #143)?

Adventists have taught for over a century that conversion and justification must take place before an individual is judged in the judgment announced in Revelation 14:

In the typical service only those who had come before God with confession and repentance, and whose sins, through the blood of the sin offering, were transferred to the sanctuary, had a part in the service of the Day of Atonement. So in the great day of final atonement and investigative judgment the only cases considered are those of the professed people of God. The judgment of the wicked is a distinct and separate work, and takes place at a later period. "Judgment must begin at the house of God: and if it first begin at us, what shall the end be of them that obey not the gospel?" 1 Peter 4:17.—*Great Controversy*, p. 480.

Therefore Adventists do not believe that the judgment determines salvation when the term is defined as conversion or justification. However, they do believe that the judgment determines who will arrive in heaven. This idea Jesus clearly taught in Matthew 12:36, 37.

Why does Jesus say that our words will "determine our salvation"? Mr. Martin's own statements under #153 and #155 reveal the answer: Our words and our actions show whether or not we love Jesus, and whether or not we have allowed the gospel of grace to take root in our lives. If there is no fruit, the root either never grew or must have died.

Our words and actions also reveal whether we have really accepted the terms of the New Covenant, whether we have allowed Jesus to write His law in our hearts and minds (Heb. 8:10). The pre-advent judgment merely reveals who is really a New Covenant, New Testament Christian, and who is not.

The *documentation package* lists in its index as "Point 72" the charge that Adventists believe that "Believers must keep the Law to be saved, and will be judged by their works." When one turns to "Point 72," one finds the ninth paragraph of an article in the August 28, 1894, issue of the *Review and Herald*. Of the 39 lines of this paragraph, 30 are direct quotes of Bible verses in quotation marks. That leaves only 9 lines actually written by Mrs. White, lines which to some degree are allusions to and paraphrases of both the Scriptures quoted and other Scriptures not quoted. *Every Scripture quoted or alluded to is found in the New Testament!* So this charge against Adventists must be really a charge against the teachings of the New Testament! The evidence is in the *documentation package* for all to see.

#157: Soul sleep was introduced because of the investigative judgment. This is simply untrue, as brought out under #59.

The teaching that only God is immortal (1 Tim. 6:15, 16), that the dead will receive their reward at the resurrection instead of before, and that the dead

"know not anything" (Eccl. 9:5, 6) was introduced among Millerites before 1844. Mrs. White's family accepted it then, as the context for the statement under "Point 33" in the *documentation package* clearly shows.

The video makes a major point of the investigative judgment doctrine being developed after 1844. That makes the doctrine of "soul sleep" older than the doctrine of the investigative judgment, not vice versa.

#158: The doctrine of soul sleep is unbiblical. During the Reformation, many individuals went back to the Scriptures as the only authority for faith and practice. Men like John Wycliffe, William Tyndale, Martin Luther, and a host of others, including many Anglicans and Anabaptists, while studying the Bible became convicted that the dead are asleep (see #92). If the doctrine of soul sleep, also known as conditional immortality, is so unbiblical, pray tell where did all these men of God come up with the idea from?

Actually, Mr. Martin is inadvertently making a powerful argument, drawn from the Holy Scriptures, for the doctrine of soul sleep. Jesus said, "And, behold, I come quickly; and my reward is with me, to give every man according as his work shall be" (Rev. 22:12). He passes out His rewards at the second coming, not before.

> And the nations were angry, and thy wrath is come, and the time of the dead, that they should be judged, and that thou shouldest give reward unto thy servants the prophets, and to the saints, and them that fear thy name, small and great; and shouldest destroy them which destroy the earth. (Rev. 11:18)

Thus the judgment precedes the giving out of rewards at the second coming. What are the dead doing until then, and where?

The doctrine of the immortality of the soul calls into question certain key biblical teachings. To use Mr. Martin's illustration, if the dead already have their reward, why do we need a judgment?

"I go to prepare a place for you. And if I go and prepare a place for you, I will come again, and receive you unto myself; that where I am, there ye may be also" (John 14:1-3). If the dead in Christ are already with Jesus, why does He need to return to get them? Why do we need a second coming?

There is but one text in the New Testament that says what to preach at funerals (1 Th. 4:18). In that passage Paul points the bereaved to the hope of the resurrection. That is when they will live again. But if our loved ones are already in heaven, why do we need a resurrection?

Under "Point 78" in the *documentation package* is a

tract from MacGregor Ministries dealing with hell. The parable of the rich man and Lazarus is cited (Luke 16:19-31), which is a popular text among those who believe that our souls are innately immortal.

Yet this parable, if it really does bolster the idea that our souls are immortal, would also teach us that our souls have eyes, tongues, chests, and fingers. If our soul is immortal, and if our soul has all the parts that our body does, why do we need a resurrection?

Now for the most serious question of all: "For God so loved the world, that he gave his only begotten Son, that whosoever believeth in him should not perish, but have everlasting life" (John 3:16). If it is true that we cannot die and are already immortal, then why do we need to believe on Jesus in order to have eternal life? We already have it!

On the other hand, if we must accept Jesus as our Savior in order to have eternal life, we therefore are not naturally, innately immortal. So which is it? Must we accept Christ in order to have eternal life, or are our souls already immortal?

In conclusion, while "soul sleep" is far from being unbiblical, the doctrine of innate immortality calls into question the gospel, the resurrection, the second coming, and the judgment.

#159: "So the Adventists teach that when a person dies, he or she goes into the grave, into non-existence. But this teaching flies in the face of the Scriptures which clearly state that 'to be absent from the body is to be at home with the Lord.' 2 Corinthians 5:8. And when a believer dies he departs and is with Christ. Philippians 1:23."—Mark Martin.

#159: Conditional immortality flies in the face of two Scriptures. Actually, it doesn't, unless we want to say that the Bible contradicts itself.

While conditional immortality *seems* to fly in the face of two Scriptures, innate immortality, the idea that there is something in us that will not and cannot die, that not even God can kill, flies in the face of 265 verses found in 158 chapters taken from 35 books of the Bible (see "Immortality: Conditional or Innate?" at http://www.pickle-publishing.com/papers).

To illustrate the problem we are faced with, let us look at one concept that Mr. Martin is trying to drive home, one with which we agree, that we are saved by faith and not by works. Yet this, it would seem, "flies in the face" of a passage from James:

But wilt thou know, O vain man, that faith without works is dead? Was not Abraham our father justified by works, when he had offered Isaac his son upon the altar? . . . Ye see then how that by works a man is justified, and not by faith only. Likewise also was not Rahab the harlot justified by works, when she had received the messengers, and had sent them out another way? For as the body without the spirit is dead, so faith without works is dead also. (James 2:20-26)

Yet Paul clearly says in Galatians 2:16 that we are justified by faith apart from works of the law. Does the Bible contradict itself, or is there a way to harmonize the two passages? Every Bible-believing Christian should agree that there must be a way to harmonize James with Paul, and of course there is.

Mr. Martin has referred to two texts: 2 Corinthians 5:8 and Philippians 1:23. These must be harmonized with the 265 verses that seem to say something different. Since it is easier to harmonize two verses with 265 rather than 265 with two, let us look at the two first.

The context of 2 Corinthians 5:8 gives us an idea of what Paul is talking about:

For we know that if our earthly house of this tabernacle were dissolved, we have a building of God, an house not made with hands, eternal in the heavens. For in this we groan, earnestly desiring to be clothed upon with our house which is from heaven: If so be that being clothed we shall not be found naked. For we that are in this tabernacle do groan, being burdened: not for that we would be unclothed, but clothed upon, that mortality might be swallowed up of life. (2 Cor. 5:1-4)

Paul in these verses longs for the day when he will receive a glorified body, an event Christians typically identify with the resurrection at the second coming. He clearly does not want to be a disembodied spirit, for he does not want to be "naked." Rather, he wants to be clothed upon with the new body he calls a "house." Now for the next verses:

Now he that hath wrought us for the selfsame thing is God, who also hath given unto us the earnest of the Spirit. Therefore we are always confident, knowing that, whilst we are at home in the body, we are absent from the Lord: (For we walk by faith, not by sight:) We are confident, I say, and willing rather to be absent from the body, and to be present with the Lord. Wherefore we labour, that, whether present or absent, we may be accepted of him. (2 Cor. 5:5-9)

When the time comes for us to be absent from our present body and receive our new body, we will literally be present with the Lord. There is nothing necessarily incompatible here with the idea that the dead await the resurrection in their graves.

Let us look now at the context of Philippians 1:23.

> For to me to live is Christ, and to die is gain. But if I live in the flesh, this is the fruit of my labour: yet what I shall choose I wot not. For I am in a strait betwixt two, having a desire to depart, and to be with Christ; which is far better: Nevertheless to abide in the flesh is more needful for you. (Php. 1:21-24)

This passage does appear to put Paul with Christ at death. However, two points should be noted about both of these passages: 1) Neither passage says that those who have died are not really dead. 2) Neither passage says that the dead are conscious. Thus neither passage really contradicts the following crystal clear verses:

> The dead praise not the LORD, neither any that go down into silence. (Ps. 115:17)
>
> Put not your trust in princes, nor in the son of man, in whom there is no help. His breath goeth forth, he returneth to his earth; in that very day his thoughts perish. (Ps. 146:3, 4)
>
> For the living know that they shall die: but the dead know not any thing, neither have they any more a reward; for the memory of them is forgotten. Also their love, and their hatred, and their envy, is now perished; neither have they any more a portion for ever in any thing that is done under the sun. . . .
>
> Whatsoever thy hand findeth to do, do it with thy might; for there is no work, nor device, nor knowledge, nor wisdom, in the grave, whither thou goest. (Eccl. 9:5, 6, 10)

Thus the Bible teaches that the dead do not praise God, cannot think, and do not know anything. The fact is that neither 2 Corinthians 5:8 nor Philippians 1:23 contradicts these simple, plain, Bible truths.

Another basic problem with the doctrine of innate immortality is the way the Bible uses the Greek and Hebrew words for "soul" and "spirit." There are 157 verses using these words in ways that just don't fit (see "What Is the Soul and Spirit?" posted at http://www.pickle-publishing.com/papers). For example, when the second plague is poured out, "every living soul died in the sea" (Rev. 16:3). If souls are immortal and can't die, why are these souls dying? And why is it said that whales and fish are "souls"?

265 verses and 157 verses. Some passages are used in both documents, but between the two, there are a total of 411 different verses cited.

The *documentation package* under "Point 77" merely gives photocopies of the two verses Mr. Martin cited. It makes no attempt at all to explain any of the 411 other Bible verses that indicate that man does not have innate immortality.

#160: "Another thing that people might not be aware of is that Seventh-day Adventists do not teach the biblical doctrine of hell."—Mark Martin.

#160: They don't teach the biblical doctrine of hell. Actually, they do, and always have.

Adventists, unlike Jehovah's Witnesses, believe in taking the Bible literally when it says that hell will be a fire.

> For, behold, the day cometh, that shall burn as an oven; and all the proud, yea, and all that do wickedly, shall be stubble: and the day that cometh shall burn them up, saith the LORD of hosts, that it shall leave them neither root nor branch. . . . And ye shall tread down the wicked; for they shall be ashes under the soles of your feet in the day that I shall do this, saith the LORD of hosts. (Mal. 4:1-3)

They take this passage just as it reads. There will be a fire that burns up the wicked.

> For evildoers shall be cut off: but those that wait upon the LORD, they shall inherit the earth. For yet a little while, and the wicked shall not be: yea, thou shalt diligently consider his place, and it shall not be. But the meek shall inherit the earth . . . .
>
> But the wicked shall perish, and the enemies of the LORD shall be as the fat of lambs: they shall consume; into smoke shall they consume away. (Ps. 37:9-11, 20)

So while the redeemed will inherit the earth, the wicked will consume into smoke.

"For God so loved the world, that he gave his only begotten Son, that whosoever believeth in him should not perish, but have everlasting life" (John 3:16). Those who *believe* in Christ have *eternal life.* Those who do not will *perish* in hell's fire.

> Forasmuch then as the children are partakers of flesh and blood, he also himself likewise took part of the same; that through death he might destroy him that had the power of death, that is, the devil. (Heb. 2:14)

And how will Jesus destroy the devil? Regarding the end of Satan, the "covering cherub" that had been in "Eden," Ezekiel says:

> Therefore will I bring forth a fire from the midst of thee, it shall devour thee, and I will bring thee to ashes upon the earth in the sight of all them that

behold thee. . . . thou shalt be a terror, and never shalt thou be any more. (Ezek. 28:18, 19)

Seventh-day Adventists do indeed believe these simple Bible verses. The question is, does Mr. Martin?

When it's all over, "God shall wipe away all tears from their eyes; and there shall be no more death, neither sorrow, nor crying, neither shall there be any more pain: for the former things are passed away" (Rev. 20:4).

If the wicked did have eternal life in hell fire, even though they never accepted Christ, and if they were never burned up, though the Bible says they will be, how could this verse be true? Sorrow, crying, and pain would continue forever instead of being "no more."

The verses just cited are but a small sampling. Of the 265 verses in the paper, "Immortality: Conditional or Innate?," 148 verses from 88 chapters from 27 biblical books deal with hell. Check it out for yourself at http://www.pickle-publishing.com/papers.

Under "Point 78" and "Point 78a" in the *documentation package* is a tract by MacGregor Ministries on hell. In its first paragraphs it indicates that Adventists do not think that hell is hot. This of course is not true. Adventists believe that hell will be so hot, it will burn up the entire earth, just like the Bible says:

> But the day of the Lord will come as a thief in the night; in the which the heavens shall pass away with a great noise, and the elements shall melt with fervent heat, the earth also and the works that are therein shall be burned up. (2 Pet. 3:10)

The MacGregor Ministries tract makes no attempt to deal with any of the 148 verses of Scripture that declare that "the wages of sin is death" rather than eternal life in hell. It does however make this statement: "When we really believe the word of God as it is written, and don't try to 'figuratize' or 'spiritualize' it away as the cults do . . . ." Thus, by MacGregor Ministries' own admission, Seventh-day Adventism is not a cult. Adventists do not spiritualize the Word of God away when it says that Satan and the wicked will be "consumed," "destroyed," "turned into ashes," "perish," and "never be any more."

On the other hand, since MacGregor Ministries does not take these simple Bible verses literally, is it calling itself a cult? If so, such a conclusion is unwarranted. Just because MacGregor Ministries spiritualizes away what the Bible says about hell, that in itself doesn't make it a cult.

Speaking of hell, what sin is the only one mentioned in all three of Revelation's lists describing those who will end up in the lake of fire?

> But . . . all liars, shall have their part in the lake which burneth with fire and brimstone: which is the second death. (Rev. 21:7, 8)
>
> And there shall in no wise enter into [the New Jerusalem] any thing that defileth, neither whatsoever worketh abomination, or maketh a lie: but they which are written in the Lamb's book of life. (Rev. 21:27)
>
> For without are dogs, and sorcerers, and whoremongers, and murderers, and idolaters, and whosoever loveth and maketh a lie. (Rev. 22:15)

Since lying is the only sin included in all three lists, it would be well for the contributors to the video to consider the following: It is indisputable that this video, whether intentionally or not, contains a number of false statements. In light of the fact that lying can exclude people from the blessings of eternal life and send them to hell, why not play it safe? The best course is to repent, confess, and make things right as far as possible. The Lord is merciful and He will pardon, for Jesus died and shed His blood for us. We have the sure promise of His Word that every sin repented of will be forgiven.

The Sabbath of the Fourth Commandment

#161: "One of the primary distinctives of Seventh-day Adventism is the keeping of the Saturday Sabbath. To keep the seventh day is seen as a mark of true loyalty to God."—Mark Martin.

#161: It's seen as a mark of true loyalty to God. The narrator goes so far as to call this view "severe" under #179. Yet according to Mr. Martin's earlier statements, it has to be true.

"Christians are to grow in grace and keep God's commandments out of a love for Him . . ." (#153). "In contrast, being under grace leads to holiness" (#155). By Mr. Martin's own reasoning, if a person adamantly refuses to keep one of God's commandments, he doesn't really love God and is therefore not being loyal to Him. Such a one is also rejecting the holiness that results from being under grace. And this is all the more true since the Sabbath is the Bible sign of holiness (see #155).

The fourth commandment differs from the others in a very important way, and this makes it especially a mark of loyalty.

> For when the Gentiles, which have not the law, do by nature the things contained in the law, these, having not the law, are a law unto themselves: Which shew the work of the law written in their hearts, their conscience also bearing witness, and their thoughts the mean while accusing or else excusing one another. (Rom. 2:14, 15)

Everyone has a conscience that tells him what is right and wrong, whether he follows it or not. Jew and Gentile, Christian and heathen, all have a sense that murder, theft, and adultery are wrong. The awareness that such things are evil seems built into man's very nature. For this reason, in some theological circles, precepts like the sixth, seventh, and eighth commandments are called "natural law."

Commandments that are not built into the conscience, those that you have to be told about, are called "positive law." This is why the Sabbath commandment has been called by Catholic writers a "most positive command." While an awareness of the need for periodic rest is built into us, an awareness of which day to rest upon is not. Thus it is something we have to be told, not something we naturally know.

So which would be a greater mark of loyalty and love to God? Obeying a precept you naturally know is right, like honoring your parents? Or obeying a precept you don't naturally know is right, something you only know about because the God of heaven requested it, like keeping His Sabbath holy?

It's kind of strange. You can talk about most any of the commandments, and people will not argue with you. They will heartily agree, and rant and rave about the decay of morals in today's society. But once you mention the fourth commandment, they will start talking about how the law was nailed to the cross, how we are now under grace, and how we must not be legalists. Inconsistent, isn't it?

#162 & #163: "The idea of the seventh-day Sabbath was not original to Ellen White though. It was in fact initiated by a Seventh Day Baptist contact and Joseph Bates who subsequently talked James and Ellen White into the idea in 1846. Ellen obliged by conveniently having a vision and this introduced the teaching to her followers. 'I saw that the Holy Sabbath is, and will be, the separating wall between the true Israel of God and unbelievers.' Early Writings p. 85."—Mark Martin.

#162: She obliged by conveniently having a vision. The viewer is left with the impression that

somehow Mrs. White pretended to have a vision. However, as indicated under #44 and #112, her visions had a definitely supernatural element. They could not be faked. There was no way that Mrs. White could just decide that she was not going to breathe for an extended period.

#163: Her vision introduced the Sabbath to her followers. The vision referred to did not occur until April 3, 1847 (*Life Sketches*, pp. 100, 101). It did not introduce the Sabbath, for the Sabbath was already well introduced by that date.

The "Seventh Day Baptist contact," Rachel Oakes Preston, shared the Sabbath truth with Methodist minister Frederick Wheeler in 1844. He and many of his congregation in Washington, New Hampshire, began keeping the Sabbath by the end of that year.

T. M. Preble had been a Freewill Baptist preacher in Nashua, New Hampshire. In February 1845 he wrote an article endorsing the Sabbath, which was read by Joseph Bates. Bates then accepted the Sabbath truth and wrote his own tract about it in 1846.

"In the autumn of 1846," James and Ellen White "began to observe the Bible Sabbath, and to teach and defend it" (*Testimonies for the Church*, vol. 1, p. 75). This was roughly six months before the vision that "introduced the teaching to her followers."

The vision did not result in the Sabbath being significantly more accepted among Millerites. To the contrary, Mrs. White's acceptance of the Sabbath in 1846 resulted in her being rejected by many of her Millerite friends. She had fewer "followers" afterwards than before:

> The light upon the fourth commandment, which was new and unpopular and generally rejected by our Adventist brethren and sisters, we had accepted. . . . opposition unexpectedly came upon us from those with whom we had been united in the faith and glorious hope of the second advent of our Saviour. . . . there were those with whom we had taken sweet counsel together who denounced the third angel's message as heresy.—*Manuscript Releases*, vol. 4, p. 402.

Imagine treating the "absolute authority figure" (see #21) like this!

"Point 80 & 80a" are described in the *documentation package*'s index as "Saturday Sabbath teaching originated with a 7th day Baptist and Joseph Bates in 1846." Yet when one turns to this section, Rachel Oakes, Joseph Bates, and 1846 aren't even mentioned. Instead, events of 1848 and 1849 are described.

If this video is ever redone, it would be best to involve someone who knows a bit more about Adventism's history and doctrines.

#164: "In the early years when the Sabbath observance was kept, it always began at 6 pm Fridays. It was before sunset in the summer and after sunset in the winter. This went on for over nine years. Since the Bible says that the Sabbath was to be kept from sunset to sunset, a division arose. The matter was studied and presented to the Adventist conference in 1855. Finally they voted to keep the Sabbath from sundown Friday to sundown Saturday."—Mark Martin.

#164: The Bible says the Sabbath is to be kept from sunset to sunset. Mr. Martin thus suggests that the early Seventh-day Adventists were ignoring what is plainly stated in the Bible. It isn't that simple, for the Bible doesn't *say* to keep the Sabbath from *sunset* to *sunset*.

So what does the Bible say? "From even unto even, shall ye celebrate your sabbath" (Lev. 23:32). Okay, so when is evening? "Jesus answered, Are there not twelve hours in the day?" (John 11:9).

Based on this last text, and his experience in astronomy and as a sea captain, Joseph Bates was certain that evening began at 6 pm. It was only after careful Bible study, initially done by John N. Andrews at the request of James White, that it was seen that evening really begins at sunset.

Jesus on a particular Sabbath was preaching in the synagogue at Capernaum. He cast a devil out of a man in the congregation, and then went home to Peter's house and healed Peter's mother-in-law. There were a lot of sick folk in town, but no one came by to be healed until after sunset: "And at even, when the sun did set, they brought unto him all that were diseased, and them that were possessed with devils" (Mark 1:32).

The Jewish leaders of that time felt that it was wrong to be healed on the Sabbath. The people therefore waited until after the Sabbath was over before bringing their sick to Jesus. They waited until evening, "when the sun did set."

Thus while no single Bible verse teaches that the Sabbath begins and ends at sunset, by putting a few verses together we can see what is the truth of the matter. We can also see that there really is no reason to criticize anyone over the issue.

#165, #166, & #167: "There was still dissent however among Adventist followers. Mrs. White decided to have another vision to settle the matter. A delegate to the conference reported that 'After the conference, November 20th, the vision was given, establishing those undecided on the sunset time.' "—Narrator.

#165: She decided to have another vision. As shown under #44 and #112, for Mrs. White to decide to have another vision was an absolute impossibility.

#166: There still being dissent, her vision was intended to settle the matter. Actually, according to one account, the dissent came from only two people, Joseph Bates and Mrs. White:

> Now with the position of sunset time so amply supported by Scripture evidence, all the congregation, which included the church's leaders, readily accepted the light and were prepared to shift their practice. All, that is, but two—Joseph Bates and Mrs. White. —Arthur White, vol. 1, p. 323.

Perhaps there were a few others, but the implication of the accusation is clear: Mrs. White "decided" to have a vision to "settle the matter" among the undecided: herself! Does not this seem a bit odd?

We'll comment a little further about the source of the narrator's quotation under #167. For now, consider the fact that other portions of this very same source declare that the vision of November 20, 1855, never mentioned "sunset" at all:

> "3. We were present at the Conference referred to above, and also when the vision was given after the close of that Conference, and heard Sr. W. soon after coming out of vision, relate what she had seen. We are therefore prepared to testify that sunset-time was not once mentioned in the vision; but the words given to her in the previous vision were repeated, namely, 'From even to even shall ye celebrate your Sabbath;' and these words were now added: 'Take the word of God, read it, understand, and ye cannot err.

Read carefully, and ye shall there find *what* even is and *when* it is.' In the first vision we were directed to the word of God by the words 'From even to even;' but on astronomical grounds, it was then decided that even was six o'clock. In the second, exactly the same words were used, and we were more especially directed to the word of God, which when examined conclusively establishes sunset time. This settled the matter with Bro. B. and a few others, and general harmony has since prevailed on the question."—Uriah Smith, *Visions of Mrs. E. G. White*, p. 91.

If Mrs. White "decided" to have a vision to convince dissenters to begin the Sabbath at sunset, why didn't the vision she "decided" to have say to begin the Sabbath at sunset?

#167: This is what a delegate reported. This quotation from Uriah Smith is taken from his book *The Visions of Mrs. E. G. White*, which was written and published in 1866 and 1868. The 1866 edition was a reply to 39 quibbles, and the 1868 edition replied to another 13. In the 1868 edition, the five-page section dealing with when to keep the Sabbath was entitled, "Objection 32. - Time to Commence the Sabbath."

Why would the narrator ever want to quote from Smith's book, given the fact that it disproves every one of these accusations? Since the sentence the narrator quoted is the third-to-last sentence of the section, certainly some of the contributors to the video must have read Smith's explanations. They must therefore also know that these charges are entirely bogus (see #166, #168, #169, #174).

#168 & #169: "Far from the convenient vision establishing the matter, the Adventists continued to ask questions. Why could they not believe Mrs. White's original visions concerning the 6 pm Sabbath?"—Mark Martin.

#168: Adventists continued to ask questions. Yet the book that the narrator just quoted from plainly says that those asking such questions were enemies of Seventh-day Adventism, not friends:

> "But there are persons who seek to injure us as a people—and this class we hope to help by this article—who report and publish to the world that Mrs. White did profess to be shown that the time to commence the Sabbath was six o'clock, and that at a later period

she was shown that sunset was the true time."—Smith, p. 89.

And who might these critics have been? Such persons and the publications they produced fell into two different groups. The publishers of *Messenger of Truth*, *Hope of Israel*, and *The Advent and Sabbath Advocate* were individuals who left the Seventh-day Adventist movement, while the publishers of *Voice of the West* and the *World's Crisis* were never Seventh-day Adventists. Both groups grasped at anything they could find, whether factual or not, to criticize Seventh-day Adventists about.

One short-time writer for the *Messenger* was E. R. Seaman. This is what he had to say less than one year after the vision of November 20, 1855:

In the aggregate, I consider all my writing for the late "Messenger" to have been actuated by a false and wrong spirit, notwithstanding some truths might have been stated. My first retrograde from the true remnant was caused by taking the simple truth concerning the commencement of the Sabbath at sunset, which I was informed (erroneously) was established by a vision to be at 6 o'clock, independent of sun time. This error caused me to write what I did; having also, imbibed some of the war spirit. I am satisfied that this has done much injury. I am fully persuaded also that I have sympathized with those that were crooked and wrong at heart, to my hurt, and I cannot conceive why I have been permitted to go thus far, unless it be peradventure to fully open my eyes, and I hope, the eyes of others also that have likewise been deceived.

There are those spoken of in the Scriptures of truth, that walk disorderly, self-willed, having not the Spirit, who despise government: with such I desire not to walk.

As some exceptions have been taken to my last letter [in the *Review* of July 24, 1856], I would say I did not then fully regard the counsel and the testimony of the one the Lord has seen fit to reveal himself to, as I do now; and I can say for the help of any, that as far as myself and family are concerned, nothing has been given us but good, sound and kind instruction. I think I never said to the contrary. But I supposed one permanent discrepancy enough to cause doubts of the whole. But it is human to err, and better to exchange error for truth, let it be never so late.—*Review and Herald*, Oct. 30, 1856, p. 207.

#169: Mrs. White's original visions said to keep the Sabbath from 6 pm to 6 pm. They never did. In fact, none of the visions under discussion ever said when to keep the Sabbath, other than from "even to even." As the book from which the narrator quoted says:

Here the objector finds another contradiction in the visions, by asserting that they once taught that the Sabbath should commence at six o'clock p.m.; and

that the time was subsequently changed by vision to sunset. This we meet with an unqualified denial. The visions never taught that the Sabbath should commence at six o'clock . . . .

"1. Mrs. White has in two visions been shown something in regard to the time of the commencement of the Sabbath. The first was as early as 1847, at Topsham, Me. In the vision she was shown that to commence the Sabbath at sunrise was wrong. She then heard an angel repeat these words, 'From even unto even shall ye celebrate your Sabbaths.' Bro [Bates] was present and succeeded in satisfying all present that 'even' was six o'clock. Mark this: The vision at Topsham did not teach the six o'clock time. It only corrected sunrise time. I never received the idea that the six o'clock time was sustained by the visions . . . .

"Some have the impression that six o'clock time has been taught among us by the direct manifestation of the Holy Spirit. This is a mistake; 'From even unto even' was the teaching from which six o'clock time has been inferred."—Smith, pp. 88-90.

The *documentation package* gives no evidence to prove that any of Mrs. White's visions taught to keep the Sabbath from 6 pm to 6 pm. It does, however, make reference to an incident involving speaking in tongues and a clock face that made many believe that the Sabbath should be kept from 6 pm to 6 pm ("Point 82" and "Point 82a"). Smith's book dealt with this too:

"It is also stated that in vision she saw the dial-plate of a clock with one hand pointing to the 6, and other to 12, showing that six o'clock was the commencement and close of the Sabbath. . . .

"2. In regard to the clock-face, twenty competent witnesses are ready to testify that neither Mrs. W. nor her visions had anything to do with it whatever."—*Ibid.*, pp. 89-91.

The *documentation package* provides copies of two paragraphs from pages 199 and 200 of *Ellen G. White: The Early Years*. If one gets this book and reads the three short paragraphs *between these two*, one finds that it was E. L. H. Chamberlain, not Mrs. White, who spoke in tongues and drew the clock face on the floor with the chalk.

How did the compiler of the *documentation package* miss seeing this discrepancy?

#170, #171, #172, #173, & #174: "Why the change now nine years later? Had they not been in fact Sabbath breakers and not Sabbath keepers for the first nine years of the practice? It required another vision by Ellen White in which she promised to question the angel and get an explanation to cause the controversy to die down. 'I inquired why it had been thus, that at this late day we

must change the time of commencing the Sabbath. Said the angel, "Ye shall understand, but not yet, not yet..." ' Spiritual Gifts vol. 4[b] p. 3-4. Mrs. White died without ever giving the promised explanation from God."—Mark Martin.

#170: It required another vision. If it required another vision, why does Mr. Martin then proceed to quote from the same vision of November 20, 1855?

Mr. Martin quotes here from pages 3 and 4. The immediately preceding page, page 2, says: "November 20, 1855, while in prayer, the Spirit of the Lord suddenly and powerfully came upon me, and I was taken off in vision." That makes this vision the same as the one referred to by the narrator under #165-#167, meaning that *there was no other vision.*

#171: She promised in her vision to question the angel and get an explanation. Will the reader please notice what Mr. Martin quoted? She made no such promise in the vision. Rather, *the angel* promised that an explanation would come later.

#172: The angel said, "Not yet, not yet." Let's quote just a little more of this very passage. The second sentence after where Mr. Martin stopped says: "I saw that it was in the minds of some that the Lord had shown that the Sabbath commenced at six o'clock, when I had only seen that it commenced at 'even,' and it was inferred that even was at six."

If Mr. Martin had only read two more sentences, his questions would have been totally answered.

This quotation from *Spiritual Gifts* appears under "Point 85" in the *documentation package.* The last five lines of the paragraph are strangely missing. The last words before the cut-off lines are, "I saw that it was in the," the first seven words from the above sentence.

You might think this is evidence of dishonesty, and it does look quite incriminating. It appears that the compiler was trying to hide the truth from the reader. But actually, it could be just simple human error.

The *documentation package* provides 77 different extracts from the CD-ROM of Mrs. White's writings, 55 of which contain material that she really wrote. The compiler was using the Windows version of the software which provides two ways of printing out a desired selection. One can either print out the whole paragraph, or the current window being viewed, a default of 27 lines.

16 extracts went beyond a single window, and were included in their entirety in the *documentation package.* 4 others, including the one under discussion, were cut off at the end of the first window, omitting between 2 and 7 lines of material. Of these 4, only this one's missing lines represent context vital to the discussion.

So it is possible that the compiler neglected to read the last five lines and had the "window" "print range" setting checked. Yet even if this was a simple oversight, it really is inexcusable. Whenever one attacks something as sacred as someone's religious faith, it is wise to be certain of the facts first. And when ascertaining facts means reading only two more sentences or five more lines, finishing the paragraph becomes a Christian duty.

#173: She died without ever giving the promised explanation. The careful reader will note that the angel never said who would give the promised explanation. Mr. Martin thinks it had to be Mrs. White, but that's not what the passage said.

#174: The promised explanation was never given. Actually, the promised explanation appeared in Smith's book which the narrator quoted from (see #167):

> "2. Elder J.B., who was the first to teach the Sabbath in its importance, and faithfully labor to bring out a people from among the Adventists to observe it, was very decided upon the question, and respect for his years, and his godly life, might have been among the reasons why this point was not sooner investigated as thoroughly as some other points."—p. 89.

Seventh-day Adventists had relied on someone's opinion instead of searching out what the Bible actually taught on the matter. For this reason, they had to make a change after not quite keeping the Sabbath correctly for nine years.

This explanation was given publicly in the *Review and Herald* in 1868 (vol. 31 no. 11), and then reprinted in Smith's book of that year. This was a total of 47 years *before* Mrs. White's death.

The Seal of God and the Mark of the Beast

#175 & #176: "However the keeping of the Sabbath from sundown Friday to sundown Saturday came to be of prime importance in determining who would receive the seal of God and be saved and who wouldn't."—Mark Martin.

#175: After the change to sunset, the Sabbath "came to be" understood as the seal. In actuality, the idea that the Sabbath is the seal of God was in print over six years prior to the change of the time to keep the Sabbath: "The Sabbath then is a sign, or seal between GOD and his people forever."—*Present Truth*, July 1849, p. 3. Thus Mr. Martin has the timing reversed.

#176: They think it's of prime importance in determining who would be saved and who wouldn't. It should be pointed out that Mr. Martin is using the term "saved" differently than he did under #143. There he definitely meant justification, pardon, and conversion, while here he means glorification and entry into heaven (see also #66).

So is the impression the viewer is left with true? Have Seventh-day Adventists since 1855 felt that the question of the Sabbath determines everyone's entry into heaven? Not according to the very next quotation used on the video (see #177): "When the final test shall be brought to bear upon men . . . ." Unfortunately, the average viewer will not know enough about Adventist beliefs to rightly understand what this means. To put it simply, Adventists believe that this only becomes true at the very last moments of time when the mark of the beast is enforced. It isn't true today.

At least by 1852, Seventh-day Adventists were teaching far and wide that many Sunday keepers were children of God and would go to heaven, while many apparent Sabbath keepers would not. Sabbath keeping, therefore, was not considered the determining factor, and still is not. Consider the following which appeared in an issue of the *Review* in that year. Because the video makes such a major point of this subject, we quote it at length:

REMARKS IN KINDNESS.

We have received a letter from Bro. T----- of Broadalbin, N. Y., which we wish to notice, not only for the benefit of the writer, but others in a similar position.

T - I have no disposition to say anything disrespectful of the paper, or any of the writers. . . . If I rightly understand the Review, it teaches or judges thus: They that keep the seventh-day Sabbath have the Seal of the Living God. They that keep the first day as the Sabbath, and they that believe that the Sabbath is abolished, have the mark of the beast. I do not find that the Lord in his word judges thus. . . .

Reply - *We are far from believing that all Sabbath-keepers have the seal of the living God. The Jew that in his blindness rejects Jesus cannot have that seal, though he outwardly observes the fourth commandment. That there is to be a sign, distinguishing mark, or seal of God, that is to distinguish God's people in the time of trouble when the mark of the beast shall be enforced, is evident. And we are of the humble opinion that the despised Sabbath of the living God will be that very distinguishing sign. But let no one suppose that the "Review and Herald" teaches that those who embrace the Sabbath are now sealed and sure of heaven, for it teaches no such thing.*

In that hour of conflict, the time of trouble such as never was, when the mark of the beast shall be enforced, none will be able to stand, and bear the distinguishing sign or seal of God, only those who are sanctified through the whole truth, and washed from all sin, by the blood of Christ. May the Lord prepare Sabbath-keepers to stand in that time, and bear the seal of the living God. After they keep *all* the commandments, and repent before God of past transgression of his holy law, their only hope of salvation is through faith in the atoning blood of Jesus.

A man may outwardly observe all ten of the commandments of God, yet if he is not benefited by the atonement of Jesus it will profit him nothing. But the doctrine that one may live in constant violation of the law of the Father, and still be saved through faith in his Son, is a heresy that we fear, will sink souls in perdition. The Jew may be tenacious for the law of the Father, and reject the Son; the professed Christian may boast of his faith in the Son and reject the commandments of the Father, but will not both sink in perdition together if they remain in unbelief. O Lord, help thy people to see that "here are they that keep the commandments of God AND** have the faith of Jesus." God forbid that we should make void thy law through faith.

We do not teach that those "that keep the first day as a Sabbath, and they that believe the Sabbath is abolished, have the mark of the beast." We have shown that there is no divine authority for observing the first day of the week, as the Sabbath. We have also shown that it is an institution of Papacy. And we have given some of our reasons for believing that the observance of the first day of the week is to constitute the mark of the beast, when the line shall be drawn between the worshipers of the beast and image, and the worshipers, or servants of God.

Says the third angel, "If any man worship the beast and his image, and *receive* his mark," &c. This is a warning to those to whom the message is to be given not to receive the mark, consequently, they have not the mark now, in the sense it is yet to be received by the worshipers of the beast. *Christians who have conscientiously observed the first day of the week, in time past, whose minds were never called to investigate the Sabbath question, certainly did not* receive *the mark of the beast.* But after the true light on this subject shall be given, and that period of anguish when the mark of the beast shall be enforced shall have come, and the division made between the worshipers of God and the worshipers of the beast, *then* will be the danger of receiving the mark of the beast. In view of that decisive hour, the third angel gives his warning message, that we may be prepared to stand, and not receive the mark of the beast, instead of the seal of the living God. The burden, the loud cry of this message, is evidently future.

Our object is to give our views in the spirit of the gospel, and we know not why we should be charged with judging others, more than those who differ from us, and give their views of Bible truth. Some seem to forget that they differ from us as far as we do from them.

It is not our work to judge and pass sentence upon any one. Some rash spirits have greatly erred here. We wish to speak the truth in the spirit of Jesus, with all boldness, and let that do its work, on the heart. But when we do this, we are at once "judged" as having a lack of charity and of judging others. But we cannot stop here. Let others plead charity, and we will preach the truth. Charity ever "rejoiceth in the truth." See 1Cor.xiii,6.—[James White], *Review and Herald*, March 2, 1852, p. 100, italics added except for single words.

#177 & #178: " 'The Sabbath will be the great test of loyalty... When the final test shall be brought to bear upon men, then the line of distinction will be drawn between those who serve God and those who serve him not... the keeping of the true Sabbath... is an evidence of loyalty... one class... receive the mark of the beast, the other choosing the token of allegiance to divine authority, receive the seal of God.' The Great Controversy p. 605. So, failing to keep the Sabbath resulted in one receiving the mark of the beast and losing one's eternal life."—Mark Martin.

#177: This quote says that failing to keep the Sabbath "resulted" in receiving the mark of the beast. No, it does not. The ellipses in the quote represent missing context that prevents such a mistaken view of Seventh-day Adventist beliefs. The entire paragraph reads thusly:

The Sabbath will be the great test of loyalty, for it is the point of truth especially controverted. When the final test shall be brought to bear upon men, then the line of distinction will be drawn between those who serve God and those who serve Him not. While the observance of the false sabbath in compliance with the law of the state, contrary to the fourth commandment, will be an avowal of allegiance to a power that is in opposition to God, the keeping of the true Sabbath, in obedience to God's law, is an evidence of loyalty to the Creator. While one class, by accepting the sign of submission to earthly powers, receive the mark of the beast, the other choosing the token of allegiance to divine authority, receive the seal of God.

Since Sunday observance and Sabbath breaking are not presently enforced by state law, the choice to keep Sunday does not now constitute receiving the mark of the beast. This is only something that will occur at the very end of human history.

#178: They believe it "resulted" in receiving the mark of the beast. By choosing the past tense verb "resulted," Mr. Martin gives the false impression that Seventh-day Adventists believe Sunday keepers now have the mark of the beast. Nothing could be further from the truth, nor is any issue more clearly stated. And Mr. Martin, a former Adventist minister, is most certainly aware of this fact. If perchance the unlikely occurred, and he forgot this point of Adventist theology, the quote he just cited would have refreshed his memory.

Even though the choice to break the fourth commandment does not today result in receiving the mark of the beast, it would be wise to consider something else Mr. Martin said: "Christians are to grow in grace and keep God's commandments out of a love for Him . . ." (see #153). When the final test does comes, it will be much easier to choose the right if we have made a habit today of obeying God's commandments out of love. Don't you agree?

#179 & #180: "Today the view is equally severe. On page 167 of the Adventist publication *Twenty-Seven Fundamental Doctrines* **it says, 'When this issue is clearly brought before the world, those who reject God's memorial of creatorship, the Bible Sabbath... choosing to worship and honor Sunday, in the full knowledge that it is not God's appointed day of worship, will receive the mark of the beast. This mark is a mark of rebellion.' "—Narrator.**

#179: This view is severe. A rather strange conclusion. How can it be severe to believe that Christians ought to obey the commandments?

After all, the devil and his angels were kicked out of heaven for breaking the commandments of God. Adam and Eve were kicked out of the garden of Eden for breaking the commandments of God. How can God take us to heaven when we are knowingly living in unrepentance and disobedience to one of His commandments, and at the same time not take the devil to heaven too?

> Christians are to grow in grace and keep God's commandments out of a love for Him . . . . (Mark Martin under #153)
>
> If ye love me, keep my commandments. (Jesus in John 14:15)

So according to both Mr. Martin and Jesus, those who do not keep God's commandments reveal a lack of love toward God. Are these views of Mr. Martin and Jesus severe?

#180: This quote says it's a mark of rebellion. The whole topic has been grossly oversimplified.

While enough context was quoted to catch the thought of the statement, enough was left out so that the average viewer will not comprehend what is really being said. First of all, the final period in the quote should actually be an ellipsis, for the remaining 71% of the sentence was omitted. The portion omitted makes clear what the Seventh-day Adventist position really is.

Also omitted is any explanation regarding the identity of the beast. Who is the beast anyway? Once this question is answered, it is pretty easy to see that Sunday just might have something to do with the mark.

The context of the quotation, as found in the *documentation package* under "Point 87," follows:

> The beast described in Revelation 13:1-10 is the church-state union that dominated the Christian world for many centuries and was described by Paul as the "man of sin" (2 Thess. 2:2-4) and by Daniel as the "little horn" (Dan. 7:8, 20-25; 8:9-12 KJV). The image of the beast represents that form of apostate religion that will be developed when churches, having lost the true spirit of the Reformation, shall unite with the state to enforce their teachings on others. In uniting church and state they will have become a perfect image to the beast—the apostate church that persecuted for 1260 years. Hence the name *image of the beast.—Seventh-day Adventists Believe,* p. 167.

Let's pause for a moment. The first one that we know of to identify the little horn in this way was a Catholic Archbishop, Eberhard II of Salzburg, around 1240 AD (Froom, *Prophetic Faith*, vol. 1, pp. 796-806). Why would he want to identify the little horn as being the papal power, you ask? It isn't hard to understand if we remember some of the controversies of yesteryear.

One such controversy was whether the final authority in the church should be a single man accountable to no one, or a council of representatives from churches around the world. Another one was whether the pope should be just a spiritual leader, or a political ruler too.

What added fuel to the fire of these debates was the papal see's all-too-frequent political corruption, intrigue, and immorality. It's embarrassing to say it, but not a few popes had children, as even papal writers admit. Then there was simony, the selling of church offices, like that of cardinal, to whomever could pay.

The New Catholic Encyclopedia spends more time pointing out the abuses the pontiffs suppressed than the abuses they perpetrated, for obvious reasons. Still, it says that Innocent VIII was elected to be pope through "shameless bribery." After becoming pope, "to raise money, Innocent created numerous new posts, which he sold to the highest bidders."—"Innocent VIII, Pope." Regarding Pope Alexander VI, *New Catholic Encyclopedia* has this to say:

> Critical value is lacking in the pseudo-apologetic efforts made to deny Alexander's paternity of a number of children. The mothers of the first three children are unknown. . . . The other four children . . . were born of Vannozza Cattanei. . . . It has not been proved that Alexander VI was the father of Orsino Orsini or Laura Orsini (b. 1492), daughter of Giulia Farnese, who was the mistress of [Alexander] at the end of his cardinalate. . . . However, it is certain that Alexander VI was the father of Joan de Borja . . . . Also sufficiently proved was Alexander's paternity of Rodrigo de Borja . . . .—"Borgia."

Looks like we can't know for sure how many kids he had, but he had at least nine.

At any rate, Eberhard's views on the antichrist of Scripture struck a chord in many a Catholic's heart. Similar views were later adopted by Wycliffe, Luther, nearly all of the Protestant reformers, and the churches they founded. Even Abravanel, a Jewish expositor from Spain, identified the little horn this way in 1496 (Froom, vol. 2, pp. 55-57, 228, 229, 268).

Since the 1830's, the view that the beast and little horn are future instead of present has slowly gained ground, until today the standard views of old are largely forgotten.

Continuing with the quotation from *Seventh-day Adventists Believe*:

> The third angel's message proclaims the most solemn and fearful warning in the Bible. It reveals that those who submit to human authority in earth's final crisis will worship the beast and his image rather than God. During this final conflict, two distinct classes will develop. One class will advocate a gospel of human devisings and will worship the beast and his image, bringing upon themselves the most grievous judgments. The other class, in marked contrast, will live by the true gospel and "keep the commandments of God and the faith of Jesus" (Rev. 14:9, 12). The final issue involves true and false worship, the true and the false gospel. When this issue is clearly brought before the world, those who reject God's memorial of creatorship—the Bible Sabbath—choosing to worship and honor Sunday in the full knowledge that it is not God's appointed day of worship, will receive the "mark of the beast." This mark is a mark of rebellion; the beast claims its change of the day of worship shows its authority even over God's law.—*Seventh-day Adventists Believe*, p. 167.

Arriving at such conclusions is quite understandable, given the standard interpretation 150 years ago of the beast and the little horn being the papal power. Daniel 7:25 says that the little horn would "think to change *times* and *laws*." The only one of the Ten Commandments that has to do with time is the one about the Sabbath, and this is the only one that the papacy thinks it has changed.

Catholic writers have repeatedly used the change of the Sabbath as proof of Rome's absolute authority in spiritual matters. Some have even been so bold as to declare that Protestants are worshipping the authority of Rome by keeping Sunday. So it is only natural to connect worshipping the beast and receiving his mark with Sunday keeping, if one still holds to the standard view of prophecy taught for centuries from Protestant pulpits, and some Catholic pulpits as well.

Now let's utilize some of the phrases from the above quotation: Advocating a "gospel of human devisings," rejecting "God's memorial of creatorship," and "choosing to worship and honor Sunday in the full knowledge that it is not God's appointed day of worship," would not this constitute "rebellion"? All Bible-believing Christians should agree that the breaking of a command of God "in full knowledge" does indeed qualify as rebellion.

If this is severe, it isn't more so than what the apostle Paul wrote:

> For if we sin wilfully after that we have received the knowledge of the truth, there remaineth no more sacrifice for sins, But a certain fearful looking for of judgment and fiery indignation, which shall devour the adversaries. (Heb. 10:26, 27)

Oh, about those statements by Catholic writers. Perhaps you would like to read a few. The first ones below claim that the Church has changed one of the Ten Commandments, and that no basis for that change can be found in the Scriptures:

> Q. *Which day is the Sabbath day?*
> A. Saturday is the Sabbath day.
> Q. *Why do we observe Sunday instead of Saturday?*
> A. We observe Sunday instead of Saturday because the Catholic Church transferred the solemnity from Saturday to Sunday.—Peter Geiermann, *The Convert's Catechism of Catholic Doctrine*, p. 50.

> Q. What warrant have you for keeping the Sunday, preferable to the ancient Sabbath, which was the Saturday?
> A. We have for it the authority of the Catholic Church, and apostolical tradition.

Q. Does the Scripture anywhere command the Sunday to be kept for the Sabbath?

A. The Scripture commands us to hear the Church, St. Matt. xviii. 17. St. Luke x. 16, and to hold fast the traditions of the Apostles. 2 Thess. ii. 15. But the scripture does not in particular mention this change of the Sabbath.—Richard Challoner, *Catholic Christian Instructed*, p. 209.

The next ones use this change of the Sabbath as a proof, mark, or sign of Rome's authority:

Ques. — How prove you that the Church hath power to command feasts and holy days?

Ans. — By the very act of changing the Sabbath into Sunday, which the Protestants allow of; and therefore they fondly contradict themselves by keeping Sunday strictly, and breaking most other feasts commanded by the same Church.

Ques. — How prove you that?

Ans. — Because by keeping Sunday they acknowledge the Church's power to ordain feasts, and to command them under sin; and by not keeping the rest by her commanded, they again deny, in fact, the same power.—Henry Tuberville, *Abridgment of Christian Doctrine*, p. 58.

Q. Have you any other way of proving that the Church has power to institute festivals of precept?

A. Had she not such power, she could not have done that in which all modern religionists agree with her;—she could not have substituted the observance of Sunday, the first day of the week, for the observance of Saturday, the seventh day, a change for which there is no scriptural authority.—Stephen Keenan, *Doctrinal Catechism*, p. 174.

The Church is above the Bible; and this transference of Sabbath observance from Saturday to Sunday is proof positive of that fact.—London, Ontario, *Catholic Record*, Sept. 1, 1923, p. 4.

The next one claims that Sunday observance is an act of worship to the authority of Rome.

It was the Catholic Church which, by the authority of Jesus Christ, has transferred this rest to the Sunday in remembrance of the resurrection of our Lord. Thus the observance of Sunday by the Protestants is an homage they pay, in spite of themselves, to the authority of the Church.—Louis Gaston de Ségur, *Plain Talk about the Protestants of Today*, p. 225.

The next one criticizes the use of certain Bible verses in support of Sunday observance by some Protestants:

The word of God commandeth the seventh day to be the Sabbath of our Lord, and to be kept holy: you [Protestants] without any precept of scripture, change it to the first day of the week, only authorized by our traditions. Divers English Puritans oppose against this point, that the observation of the first day is proved out of scripture, where it is said the first day of the week. Acts xx,7; 1Cor.xvi,2; Rev.i,10. Have they not spun a fair thread in quoting these places? If we should produce no better for purgatory and prayers for the dead, invocation of the saints, and the like, they might have good cause indeed to laugh us to scorn; for where is it written that these were Sabbath days in which those meetings were kept? Or where is it ordained they should be always observed? Or, which is the sum of all, where is it decreed that the observation of the first day should abrogate or abolish the sanctifying of the seventh day, which God commanded everlastingly to be kept holy? Not one of those is expressed in the written word of God.—*An Antidote, or Treatise of Thirty Controversies.*

This is but a sampling. Many similar statements could be cited.

#181 & #182: "So, even today, Seventh-day Adventists have made salvation ultimately dependent on which day of the week one worships."—Mark Martin.

#181: They've made salvation ultimately dependent on which day . . . Since Seventh-day Adventists for the last century and a half have taught that there are Sunday keepers who are bound for heaven and Sabbath keepers who are bound for hell (see #176), how can this possibly be true?

#182: . . . of the week one worships. Notice Mr. Martin's use of the present tense for the word "worship" when talking about an event that he knows Adventists consistently place in the future (see #176 and #178).

#183 & #184: "Several New Testament Scriptures clearly identify the seal of God as a work of the Holy Spirit, not the keeping of a Sabbath day. For example Ephesians 4:30 plainly says, 'And do not grieve the Holy Spirit of God, by whom you were sealed for the day of redemption.' Mrs. White has no support at all for linking the seal of God with Sabbath keeping."—Mark Martin.

#183: Several New Testament Scriptures say that the seal is the work of the Holy Spirit, not the keeping of the Sabbath. It isn't that simple. Does Ephesians 4:30 say that the Holy Spirit is the seal, or does it say that the Holy Spirit is the one who applies the seal? This distinction is potentially crucial.

First of all, let's look at the passage upon which the whole discussion is based, where the end-time seal is likened to an object held in the hand rather than the Holy Spirit:

> And I saw another angel ascending from the east, having the seal of the living God: and he cried with a loud voice to the four angels, to whom it was given to hurt the earth and the sea, Saying, Hurt not the earth, neither the sea, nor the trees, till we have sealed the servants of our God in their foreheads. And I heard the number of them which were sealed: and there were sealed an hundred and forty and four thousand of all the tribes of the children of Israel. (Rev. 7:2-4)

Of course, this seal isn't merely the Sabbath, as made clear by James White under #176, as well as the following:

> Just as soon as the people of God are sealed in their foreheads—it is not any seal or mark that can be seen, but a settling into the truth, both intellectually and spiritually, so they cannot be moved . . . .—*Last Day Events*, pp. 219, 220.

To put it another way, the seal of God has something to do with sanctification, an idea supported by the following Scripture: "And I looked, and, lo, a Lamb stood on the mount Sion, and with him an hundred forty and four thousand, having his Father's name written in their foreheads" (Rev. 14:1). Those sealed have the Father's name in their foreheads. This signifies that they fully belong to God and reflect His righteous character. They are sanctified, and the Holy Spirit is the active agent in that process:

> But ye are washed, but ye are sanctified, but ye are justified in the name of the Lord Jesus, and by the Spirit of our God. (1 Cor. 6:11)
> Because God hath from the beginning chosen you to salvation through sanctification of the Spirit and belief of the truth: (2 Thess. 2:13)
> Elect according to the foreknowledge of God the Father, through sanctification of the Spirit, unto obedience and sprinkling of the blood of Jesus Christ. (1 Pet. 1:2)

While the Holy Spirit is the active agent in the work of sealing God's people, He Himself may not be the end-time seal. The last verse cited said that we are sanctified by the Spirit "unto obedience."

Obedience to what?

The seal of God is in opposition to the mark of the beast. In chapter 13 of Revelation we have a description both of the beast and of the enforcement of his mark. Next comes Revelation 14:1, already quoted, which mentions those who are sealed with the seal of God. Then comes the warning of the three angels, the last of which warns the world against taking the mark of the beast. All this is sandwiched between the following two verses:

> And the dragon was wroth with the woman, and went to make war with the remnant of her seed, which keep the commandments of God, and have the testimony of Jesus Christ. (Rev. 12:17)
> Here is the patience of the saints: here are they that keep the commandments of God, and the faith of Jesus. (Rev. 14:12)

These two verses suggest that the end-time struggle between the mark and the seal has something to do with God's commandments.

The seal is to go in the forehead. The mark may go in either the forehead or the hand. This is imagery taken from Deuteronomy where, after Moses repeats the Ten Commandments in chapter 5, he says, "And thou shalt bind them for a sign upon thine hand, and they shall be as frontlets between thine eyes" (Deut. 6:8). Since Moses said to put the Ten Commandments in the forehead and hand, this suggests that the seal has something to do with obedience to the Ten Commandments. Isaiah 8:16 indicates the same: "Bind up the testimony, seal the law among my disciples."

So God wants to place His law in our minds, which is the promise of the New Covenant, and the beast wants to place a counterfeit there instead. If the beast can't get us to believe his counterfeit with our minds, if he can't put the mark in our foreheads, then he is satisfied if he can get us to do it with our hands, to go along with the flow.

Now let's get a little more specific. A seal shows ownership or authority. It shows who the ruler is who gave the law in question, and typically contains both his name and his title. Looking through the Ten Commandments, we find that eight or nine of them might be given by just about any god on the planet. Various gods command their adherents to be good moral people, not killing, not stealing, and not committing adultery. But the fourth commandment is different from the rest. It identifies the God who gave this holy law:

> Remember the sabbath day, to keep it holy. Six days shalt thou labour, and do all thy work: But the seventh day is the sabbath of the LORD thy God: in it thou shalt not do any work, thou, nor thy son, nor thy daughter, thy manservant, nor thy maidservant,

nor thy cattle, nor thy stranger that is within thy gates: For in six days the LORD *made heaven and earth, the sea,* and all that in them is, and rested the seventh day: wherefore the LORD blessed the sabbath day, and hallowed it. (Ex. 20:8-11)

Only the God of heaven, the Living God, could make this claim of being the creator of all. The fourth commandment is thus the only one of the ten that contains His seal and identifies who the great Law Giver is.

Interestingly, the italicized words are quoted in the warning of the first angel of Revelation 14: "Saying with a loud voice, Fear God, and give glory to him; for the hour of his judgment is come: and worship him that *made heaven, and earth, and the sea,* and the fountains of waters" (Rev. 14:6, 7).

The fact that language found in Revelation's description of the seal-mark issue is taken from the fourth commandment is evidence that the seal has something to do specifically with the fourth commandment.

Consider what Paul said:

And he received the sign of circumcision, a seal of the righteousness of the faith which he had yet being uncircumcised: that he might be the father of all them that believe, though they be not circumcised; that righteousness might be imputed unto them also. (Rom. 4:11)

Here the words sign and seal are used interchangeably in reference to circumcision, which at that time symbolized righteousness by faith. The Sabbath has likewise been a sign of righteousness by faith, or sanctification (Ex. 31:13; Ezek. 20:12). God intended for the Sabbath to bring His people into a closer relationship with Himself: "And hallow my sabbaths; and they shall be a sign between me and you, that ye may know that I am the LORD your God" (Ezek. 20:20).

Even in New Testament times, the Sabbath is a sign of righteousness by faith, if we believe what the apostle Paul wrote:

For we which have believed do enter into rest . . . . For he spake in a certain place of the seventh day on this wise, And God did rest the seventh day from all his works. And in this place again, If they shall enter into my rest. . . . There remaineth therefore a rest [Greek: a keeping of a Sabbath] to the people of God. For he that is entered into his rest, he also hath ceased from his own works, as God did from his. (Heb. 4:3-10)

So just as in Old Testament times, the Sabbath is to be a sign today that the believer is ceasing from his own works, that he is seeking to be saved and sanctified by faith through the Holy Spirit. That makes the Sabbath a sign of salvation by faith, not salvation by works.

Consider also the fact that the papal power has claimed that the change of the Sabbath to Sunday is her mark of authority (see #180). Now if Eberhard, Luther, Calvin, Wesley, and all the rest were correct in who they said the antichrist of prophecy is, would not the seal of God have to contrast with the beast's mark in some way? If the beast claims that a day of worship is his mark, would not the seal also have to have something to do with a day of worship? Of course.

Besides the allusion to Deuteronomy 6:8, Revelation 13 contains another helpful allusion: "And he had power to give life unto the image of the beast, that the image of the beast should both speak, and cause that as many as would not worship the image of the beast should be killed" (Rev. 14:15). This refers to Daniel 3, where we have a law enforcing false worship *at a particular time:*

That at what time ye hear the sound of the cornet, flute, harp, sackbut, psaltery, dulcimer, and all kinds of musick, ye fall down and worship the golden image that Nebuchadnezzar the king hath set up. (Dan. 3:5)

Therefore at that time, when all the people heard the sound of the cornet, flute, harp, sackbut, psaltery, and all kinds of musick, all the people, the nations, and the languages, fell down and worshipped the golden image that Nebuchadnezzar the king had set up. (Dan. 3:7)

Thou, O king, hast made a decree, that every man that shall hear the sound of the cornet, flute, harp, sackbut, psaltery, and dulcimer, and all kinds of musick, shall fall down and worship the golden image. (Dan. 3:10)

Now if ye be ready that at what time ye hear the sound of the cornet, flute, harp, sackbut, psaltery, and dulcimer, ye fall down and worship the image which I have made; well: but if ye worship not, ye shall be cast the same hour into the midst of a burning fiery furnace; and who is that God that shall deliver you out of my hands? (Dan. 3:15)

The fact that Revelation 13 makes an allusion to this story implies that the seal-mark issue has to do not only with the commandments but also with the time of worship, the same idea suggested by Daniel 7:25. And the only one of the ten that has anything to do with the time of worship is the fourth.

Shall we look at just one more allusion from Revelation? "And he exerciseth all the power of the first beast before him, and causeth the earth and them which dwell therein to worship the first beast, whose deadly wound was healed" (Rev. 13:12). Notice how it says that he causes both the "earth" and its inhabitants to worship the first beast. How might the earth, the land, the ground, the dirt, the soil worship? We have a single passage in Scripture that identifies an act of worship on the part of the land, and it too should be considered in this discussion:

> Speak unto the children of Israel, and say unto them, When ye come into the land which I give you, then shall the land keep a sabbath unto the LORD. Six years thou shalt sow thy field, and six years thou shalt prune thy vineyard, and gather in the fruit thereof; But in the seventh year shall be a sabbath of rest unto the land, a sabbath for the LORD: thou shalt neither sow thy field, nor prune thy vineyard. (Lev. 25:2-4)

So the allusion to Deuteronomy 6 tells us that the seal-mark issue has something to do with the Ten Commandments, and the allusion to Daniel 3 tells us it has something to do with a legislated time of worship. This last allusion to Leviticus 25 completes the picture, telling us it must have something to do with a sabbath of some sort.

Lastly, consider what Ezekiel says:

> And he brought me into the inner court of the LORD'S house, and, behold, at the door of the temple of the LORD, between the porch and the altar, were about five and twenty men, with their backs toward the temple of the LORD, and their faces toward the east; and they worshipped the sun toward the east. . . . And the LORD said unto him, Go through the midst of the city, through the midst of Jerusalem, and set a mark upon the foreheads of the men that sigh and that cry for all the abominations that be done in the midst thereof. And to the others he said in mine hearing, Go ye after him through the city, and smite: let not your eye spare, neither have ye pity: Slay utterly old and young, both maids, and little children, and women: but come not near any man upon whom is the mark; and begin at my sanctuary. Then they began at the ancient men which were before the house. (Ezek. 8:16-9:6)

So the imagery of Revelation is also taken from here, where we have sun worshippers being slain by God after not receiving His sign in their foreheads.

Sun worship? What does that have to do with Sunday? It is an historical fact that the religion of sun worship infiltrated the Christian church in the early centuries, and it was this infiltration that gave us Sunday as a day of worship. At least, this is what a journal published by the largest church in the world has said, a church that existed at the time the infiltration was taking place:

> The church . . . took the pagan Sunday and made it the Christian Sunday. . . . Hence the church in these countries would seem to have said, "Keep that old, pagan name. It shall remain consecrated, sanctified." And thus the pagan Sunday, dedicated to Balder, became the Christian Sunday, dedicated to Jesus. The sun is a fitting emblem of Jesus. The Fathers often compared Jesus to the sun; as they compared Mary to the moon, the beautiful moon, the beautiful Mary, shedding her mild beneficent light in the darkness and night of this world . . . .—*Catholic World*, March 1894, p. 809.

This article's primary purpose was explaining how Easter used to be a pagan festival in honor of the sun, but how it was eventually Christianized. When this writer was in Hungary the fall of 1999, he visited some of the old cathedrals there and saw emblems of the sun above many of the altars. Evidence abounds that fragments of sun worship did indeed infiltrate the Christian church.

#184: Mrs. White has no support at all for linking the seal with the Sabbath. That this statement has no support at all can be seen from what appears immediately above.

And if that weren't enough, the papacy in recent years has called upon its followers to promote Sunday legislation in their respective countries (*Dies Domini*, May 31, 1998, sect. 65-67). What will it take before such efforts succeed? Why, it will take the pressure of the greatest nation on earth. And this is precisely what Adventists foretold, based solely on Bible study, long before America ever gained the position of world dominance that it has today (*The Great Controversy*, pp. 439-449).

In the 1880's some states in this nation used blue laws to harshly persecute those who kept the Bible Sabbath. At the same time, Sunday keepers who worked on Sunday were treated mildly (Alonzo Jones, *The Two Republics*, pp. 786-796).

Adventists have been predicting for a century and a half that the United States would lead the world in enforcing Sunday rest. Such a prediction is definitely not without historical precedent.

Sunday vs. the Lord's Day, and the Scapegoat

#185, #186, #187, #188, #189, & #190: "Christ's followers met on the Lord's Day resurrection day, for their worship and breaking of bread, not on the Jewish Sabbath."—Mark Martin.

#185: The Lord's Day is the resurrection day. Since the video apparently is trying to uplift the Bible as the authority for Christians, it may be assumed that Mr. Martin is using the Bible as his authority for this statement. Yet the Bible does not teach what he just said. The first time that an authentic, extant document equates the Lord's Day with the day of the resurrection is the last half of the second century (Samuele Bacchiocchi, *From Sabbath to Sunday*, p. 17). That's fifty years or more after the apostle John's death, and over a century after the death of our Lord.

What does the Bible say?

If thou turn away thy foot from the sabbath, from doing thy pleasure on my holy day; and call the sabbath a delight, the holy of the LORD, honourable; and shalt honour him, not doing thine own ways, nor finding thine own pleasure, nor speaking thine own words: (Is. 58:13)

So the Sabbath is the LORD's Day, but is that the Lord Jesus, or God the Father. Throughout these last chapters of Isaiah, sometimes it is clearly Jesus Himself that is speaking:

The LORD saw it, and it displeased him that there was no judgment. And he saw that there was no man, and wondered that there was no intercessor: therefore his arm brought salvation unto him; and his righteousness, it sustained him. (Is. 59:15, 16)

Wherefore art thou red in thine apparel, and thy garments like him that treadeth in the winefat? I have trodden the winepress alone; and of the people there was none with me: for I will tread them in mine anger, and trample them in my fury; and their blood shall be sprinkled upon my garments, and I will stain all my raiment. . . . And I looked, and there was none to help; and I wondered that there was none to uphold: therefore mine own arm brought salvation unto me; and my fury, it upheld me. (Is. 63:3-5)

Now compare this with the following description of Jesus in the book of Revelation: "And he was clothed with a vesture dipped in blood: and his name is called The Word of God. . . . and he treadeth the winepress of the fierceness and wrath of Almighty God" (Rev. 19:13-15).

So the "LORD" in Isaiah 59:15 must be Jesus. Then would not the "LORD" in Isaiah 58:13, just sixteen verses previous, also be Jesus? Therefore, the Sabbath must be the Lord Jesus' special day, according to His own words. And really, there is no biblical basis for calling any other day but the seventh-day Sabbath the Lord's Day.

So was this the day of the resurrection? Not at all. Christ rose on the first day of the week, not the seventh (Mark 16:9; Luke 24:1, 13, 20, 21). Even today we identify the day of the crucifixion with Good Friday and the day of the resurrection with Easter Sunday. The Lord's Day Sabbath was the day between the two (Luke 23:54-56).

The *documentation package* describes "Point 89 & 89a" in the index in this way: "Christ's followers met on the 'Lord's day' (Sunday--resurrection day) according to the Bible for their fellowship and communion. (On the Jewish Sabbath Christ preached in the synagogue.)"

Turning to "Point 89" and "Point 89a," one finds a two-page tract by MacGregor Ministries. Amidst its many assertions, this tract makes no attempt to prove from the Scriptures that the first day of the week rather than the seventh day is the Lord's Day.

#186: Christ's followers met regularly on the resurrection day for their worship. In all the New Testament, out of a grand total of eight references to the first day of the week, we have only one explicit mention of the disciples meeting on the first day of the week for worship. How can anyone then assume that this means they met regularly for worship on that day?

Let's consider the eight references. Five of them merely mention the fact that Jesus rose from the dead on the first day of the week (Mat. 28:1; Mark 16:2, 9; Luke 24:1; John 20:1). In the sixth reference, on the day of the resurrection, the disciples were "assembled for fear of the Jews," not for worship (John 20:19). We have but two references left to go.

In the seventh reference Paul wrote, "Upon the first day of the week let every one of you lay by him in store, as God hath prospered him, that there be no gatherings when I come" (1 Cor. 16:2). Nothing about worship services here. It tells each of the believers at Corinth to "lay by him" the offering he felt he could give when Paul next came through town. Everyone must have had some place in his house where he could "lay by him" the offering he wanted to set aside. If he had put his offering into the offering plate at church, it would no longer be "by him."

Thus, instead of being evidence in favor of regular Sunday church services, this text is evidence against such a practice. The believer was to determine on Sunday what he could give from his profits from the previous week. Why not calculate it on the Sabbath? Because he was resting on that day and was at church.

Now for the eighth and final reference:

And upon the first day of the week, when the disciples came together to break bread, Paul preached unto them, ready to depart on the morrow; and continued his speech until midnight. And there were many lights in the upper chamber, where they were gathered together. (Acts 20:7, 8)

This is the only New Testament reference to a meeting for worship on the first day of the week. Yet notice that it was the night of the first day of the week. Since the biblical days begin at sunset, as Mr. Martin emphatically told us under #164, this would have to be Saturday night rather than Sunday night. Thus Paul met with the disciples on the first day of the week, Saturday night, and he was ready to depart on the morrow, Sunday morning. In other words, he resumed his journey on Sunday morning instead of *going to church* (see Acts 20:13, 14).

It is therefore utterly impossible to make a biblical case for the early church keeping Sunday as a regular day of worship.

#187: They did not meet for worship on the Sabbath. The book of Acts tells us differently.

While there is only one explicit reference to the disciples meeting for worship on the first day of the week, there are a number of explicit references to their worshipping on the Sabbath. Take for example this one: "But when they departed from Perga, they came to Antioch in Pisidia, and went into the synagogue on the sabbath day, and sat down" (Acts 13:14).

No, they didn't just meet with Jews on the Sabbath, and Paul explicitly connected such Sabbath worship services with the grace of God:

And when the Jews were gone out of the synagogue, the Gentiles besought that these words might be preached to them the next sabbath. Now when the congregation was broken up, many of the Jews and religious proselytes followed Paul and Barnabas: who, speaking to them, persuaded them to continue in the grace of God. And the next sabbath day came almost the whole city together to hear the word of God. (Acts 13:42-44)

If Sunday was the regular day of worship, why didn't Paul say, "Come back tomorrow. I will be preaching on Sunday"? Why did the Gentiles have to wait until the following Sabbath to hear the Word of God preached? And if keeping the Sabbath is so legalistic, why did Paul say that the Sabbath keepers were "in the grace of God"?

Paul even worshipped upon the Sabbath when there was no Jewish synagogue in town: "And on the sabbath we went out of the city by a river side, where prayer was wont to be made; and we sat down, and spake unto the women which resorted thither" (Acts 16:13).

The only Bible writer who was a Gentile was Luke, who wrote the Gospel called by his name and the book of Acts. He must have felt Sabbath keeping was important, for notice how particular he was to tell us that both Jesus and Paul habitually worshipped upon the Sabbath, something no other Bible writer tells us:

And he came to Nazareth, where he had been brought up: and, as his custom was, he went into the synagogue on the sabbath day, and stood up for to read. (Luke 4:16)

And Paul, as his manner was, went in unto them, and three sabbath days reasoned with them out of the scriptures. (Acts 17:2)

And he reasoned in the synagogue every sabbath, and persuaded the Jews and the Greeks. (Acts 18:4)

So the statement that Christ's followers did not meet for worship on the Sabbath is simply not true.

#188: They usually broke bread on the resurrection day. There is no biblical basis for such a claim. True, they met to break bread on Saturday night according to Acts 20:7, but the Bible says they broke bread "daily":

And they continued stedfastly in the apostles' doctrine and fellowship, and in breaking of bread, and in prayers. . . . And they, continuing daily with one accord in the temple, and breaking bread from house to house, did eat their meat with gladness and singleness of heart. (Acts 2:42-46)

That being so, they could just as well break bread on Saturday morning, the seventh day of the week, as on Saturday night, the first day of the week.

#189: Christ's followers did not break bread on the Sabbath. As just noted above, the disciples broke bread daily. Since the Sabbath is one of the days of the week, the disciples must have broken bread on that day as well.

So on which day did they usually break bread? Though it's easy to assume that the answer is probably the biblical Lord's Day, the seventh day of the week, it should be noted that the Bible is silent on that question.

#190: The Sabbath is Jewish. Even if this were true, which it isn't, what would it prove? Our Savior is Jewish, and 64 of the 66 books of the Bible are too. If we must reject the Sabbath for such a reason, how can we remain Christians?

If the Sabbath is Jewish, why did Jesus say, "The sabbath was made for man, and not man for the sabbath" (Mark 2:27)? He didn't say that the Sabbath was made just for Jews. He said it was made for man.

Of Jesus it is said, "All things were made by him; and without him was not any thing made that was made" (John 1:3). Since He's the one who made the Sabbath for man, He ought to know what He's talking about.

Interestingly, the name Adam is also one of the Hebrew words for "man." Thus Jesus in Mark 2:27 is referring to the making of both the Sabbath and Adam in Genesis 2.

More than this, the Greek of Mark 2:27 says that the Sabbath was made for *"the man"*, not *"the man"*

for the Sabbath. Why did Jesus say "the man" instead of just "man"?

In the first eleven chapters of Genesis, the Hebrew word *adam* occurs 52 times, *always* in the singular, and is translated "Adam," "man," and "men." In 43 of these 52 times, *adam* occurs with the definite article "the." In 7 of the remaining 9, from Genesis 4:25 to 5:5, *adam* is used as a proper noun, and so the definite article is omitted. Only in 1:26 and 2:5 does the word *adam* appear neither as a proper noun nor with the definite article.

First the Hebrew phrase "the man" means either Adam or both Adam and Eve. Then, beginning with Genesis 6:1-7, the phrase begins to mean not just Adam but his descendants as well, or in other words, all mankind. Therefore, when Jesus said that He made the Sabbath for *"the man,"* He meant that He made it for Adam and all his descendants, since that is precisely what *"the man"* means. How then can anyone declare the Sabbath to be merely "Jewish"?

Paul uses similar language when talking about the woman: "Neither was the man created for the woman; but the woman for the man" (1 Cor. 11:9). If the Sabbath that was made for the man is really Jewish, then the woman that was made for the man is really Jewish as well. Essentially, that would mean that marriage is only for the Jew, not for the Gentile.

Adam took but two things out of the garden with him: the Sabbath and marriage. Both are under attack today. Even though the Lord blesses and sanctifies but one woman per man on wedding day, there are those who declare it doesn't matter what woman you keep. And though Jesus blessed and sanctified but one day for us, there are those who will say that you can keep any day you want.

#191: "Adventists further deviate in their salvation doctrine by teaching that Satan ultimately becomes the sin-bearer. They teach he bears away the sins of the world. 'As the priest in removing the sins from the sanctuary, confess them upon the head of the scapegoat, so Christ will place all these sins upon Satan, the originator and instigator of sin...' Great Controversy p. 485."—Mark Martin.

#191: Satan becomes the sin-bearer. Though the term "sin-bearer" appears in Mrs. White's published and released writings at least 186 times, she not once said that Satan is our "sin-bearer." She consistently taught that Christ is our "only sin-bearer":

> In His intercession as our advocate, Christ needs no man's virtue, no man's intercession. He is the only sin-bearer, the only sin-offering.—*Signs of the Times*, June 28, 1899.

How hard poor mortals strive to be sin-bearers for

themselves and for others! but the only sin-bearer is Jesus Christ. He alone can be my substitute and sin-bearer. The forerunner of Christ exclaimed, "Behold the Lamb of God, which taketh away the sin of the world."—*Review and Herald*, June 9, 1896.

> Proclaim remission of sins through Christ, the only Sin-bearer, the only Sin-pardoner. Proclaim the remission of sins through repentance toward God and faith in Christ, and God will ratify your testimony. —*The Voice in Speech and Song*, p. 340.

Now if Jesus is our "only sin-bearer," how can Satan be one too?

Mr. Martin's quote from *Great Controversy* appears in its entirety under "Point 90" in the *documentation package*, the only "proof" given for the charge. Notice carefully what even the part quoted in the video says: "As the priest in removing the sins from the sanctuary . . . ." Now if the high priest, representing Jesus Christ, removes the sins by carrying them *in his own person*, must he not be the sin-bearer?

Mr. Martin refers to what Seventh-day Adventists believe that the closing ceremonies of the services of the Day of Atonement represent. This has nothing to do with who the sin-bearer is. Consider carefully the following verses:

> And Aaron shall cast lots upon the two goats; one lot for the LORD, and the other lot for the scapegoat [the Hebrew reads "for Azazel"]. (Lev. 16:8)

> And when he hath made *an end of reconciling* the holy place, and the tabernacle of the congregation, and the altar, he shall bring the live goat: And Aaron shall lay both his hands upon the head of the live goat, and confess over him all the iniquities of the children of Israel, and all their transgressions in all their sins, putting them upon the head of the goat, and shall send him away by the hand of a fit man into the wilderness: And the goat shall bear upon him all their iniquities unto a land not inhabited: and he shall let go the goat in the wilderness. (Lev. 16:20-22)

Notice that the goat for Azazel has the sins put upon him only after the high priest has made an *end* of reconciling. Since the word for "reconciling" is the Hebrew word for "atoning," this means that the sins are only put upon him after the *end* of the atonement.

The high priest represents Jesus. Whom would Jesus put the sins of God's people upon *after* He has finished the atonement? Himself? If so, why would He need to have sins placed upon Himself after the atonement is finished?

If the only atonement that ever was or ever shall be occurred at the cross, why would Jesus place sins upon Himself *after* He had already died for sin?

The Adventist position that Azazel is Satan makes more sense and raises less questions: After the atonement is finished, Jesus our high priest, the great Sin-bearer, will place all our sins upon Azazel, Satan, since he is the cause and instigator of all sin.

Let's deal with several points one at a time. First of all, how do we know that Azazel is a name for Satan? We already saw that the book of 1 Enoch identifies Azazel as being a fallen angel. Consider also the following discussion by John N. Andrews, and his citation of scholars who were not Adventists:

Mr. [Charles] Beecher states two views respecting the meaning of this term Azazel, each of which he shows to be manifestly untrue. He then gives his own view, as follows:-

"The third opinion is, that Azazel is a proper name of Satan. In support of this, the following points are urged: The use of the preposition implies it. The same preposition is used on both lots, La Yehova, La Azazel; and if the one indicates a person, it seems natural the other should, especially considering the act of casting lots. If one is for Jehovah, the other would seem for some other person or being; not one for Jehovah, and the other for the goat itself.

"What goes to confirm this is, that the most ancient paraphrases and translations treat Azazel as a proper name. The Chaldee paraphrase and the targums of Onkelos and Jonathan would certainly have translated it if it was not a proper name, but they do not. The Septuagint, or oldest Greek version, renders it by *apopompaios*, a word applied by the Greeks to a malign deity, sometimes appeased by sacrifices.

"Another confirmation is found in the Book of Enoch, where the name Azalzel, evidently a corruption of Azazel, is given to one of the fallen angels, thus plainly showing what was the prevalent understanding of the Jews at that day.

"Still another evidence is found in the Arabic, where Azazel is employed as the name of the evil spirit.

"In addition to these, we have the evidence of the Jewish work, Zohar, and of the Cabalistic and Rabbinical writers. They tell us that the following proverb was current among the Jews: 'On the day of atonement, a gift to Sammael [a Jewish name for Satan].' . . .

"Another step in the evidence is when we find this same opinion passing from the Jewish to the early Christian church. Origen was the most learned of the Fathers, and on such a point as this, the meaning of a Hebrew word, his testimony is reliable. Says Origen: 'He who is called in the Septuagint *apopompaios* and in the Hebrew Azazel, is no other than the devil.'

"Lastly, a circumstance is mentioned of the Emperor Julian, the apostate, that confirms the argument. He brought as an objection against the Bible, that Moses commanded a sacrifice to the evil spirit. An objection he never could have thought of, had not Azazel been generally regarded as a proper name.

"In view, then, of the difficulties attending any other meaning, and the accumulated evidence in favor of this, Hengstenberg affirms with great confidence that Azazel cannot be anything else but another name for Satan. . . .

"The meaning of the term, viewed as a proper name, was stated in 1677, by Spencer, Dean of Ely, to be Powerful Apostate, or Mighty Receder."

Mr. Beecher, on the seventy-second page of his

work, states that Professor Bush considers Azazel to be a proper name of Satan.

Gesenius, the great Hebrew lexicographer, says:-

"Azazel, a word found only in the law respecting the day of atonement. Lev.16:8,10,26. . . . it seems to denote an evil demon dwelling in the desert and to be plac[at]ed with victims . . . . This name Azazel is also used by the Arabs for an evil demon."

Milton represents Azazel as one of the fallen angels, and the standard-bearer of Satan . . . . *Paradise Lost, book 1.*

The "Comprehensive Commentary" has the following important remarks:-

"Scape-goat. See different opinions in Bochart. Spencer, after the oldest opinions of the Hebrews and Christians, thinks Azazel is the name of the devil; and so Rosenmuller, whom see. The Syriac has Azzail, the angel (strong one) who revolted."

"Cassell's Illustrated Bible" speaks thus of the scape-goat:-

"We offer the following exposition as much more likely, and much more satisfactory: That Azazel is a personal denomination for the evil one."—J. N. Andrews, *The Judgment, Its Events and Their Order*, pp. 78-81.

Now for our next point. Leviticus 16:22 said that "the goat shall bear upon him all their iniquities unto a land not inhabited." If this goat is Satan, is he not a sin-bearer, even if the atonement is already over, since he is bearing sin? And what about when Andrews said:

> To show the reasonableness of that act which rolls back upon Satan the sins of the people of God, and also to define the nature of the act, let us carefully state the case. Every sin committed by men is instigated by Satan. This part of the transgression is the sin of Satan alone, and belongs solely to him, whether men repent or not. But consenting to the tempter, and obeying him, is the sin of the one tempted. This part of the transgression will, in the case of all who avail themselves of the work of our

High Priest, be placed upon the antitypical scape-goat, Satan, and he will have to bear the full punishment of all such sins.

One of the most important events, therefore, in the opening of the great day of judgment, is that of placing the sins of the overcomers upon the head of the great author of sin.—*Ibid.*, pp. 81, 82.

So what about it? If Satan bears "the full punishment" of certain sins after the atonement is over, does that not make him a sin-bearer? Not at all.

Every Bible-believing Christian knows that those who do not place their sins on the great Sin-bearer Jesus Christ will have to bear the full punishment of their own sins. Does then the unsaved person become his own sin-bearer? Of course not. Even though he has to bear the full punishment of his own sins, he does not become a sin-bearer.

The term "sin-bearer" carries the connotation of Savior, substitute, and mediator. This the unsaved can never be.

How Jesus can transfer sin to something after the atonement is finished is not the only thing Adventist theology explains. The first gospel promise said that Satan's head would be crushed under the feet of the "seed," which Paul identifies as both Christ and his followers (Gen. 3:15; Gal. 3:16, 29). Paul also says that "the God of peace shall bruise Satan under your feet shortly" (Rom. 16:20). While it is easy to see how Christ will crush Satan's head, what part do the redeemed have in all this? If after the atonement is over, Christ were to place their sins upon Satan, and Satan were to suffer punishment for those sins, then the redeemed would indeed have a part to play in the crushing of his head.

Placing sins upon the scapegoat after the atonement is over has nothing to do with our salvation. It has everything to do with the punishment of the great rebel who has caused so much misery on planet earth.

#192: "How different this is from the clear message of Scripture which says of Jesus that He Himself bore our sins in His body on the cross. The apostle John exclaimed, 'Behold the Lamb of God who takes away the sin of the world.' Truly salvation must be centered on Christ alone." —Mark Martin.

#192: Christ bore our sins on the cross, so Satan can't be our sin-bearer. The point is irrelevant, for Seventh-day Adventists believe wholeheartedly that Christ bore our sins on the cross, and that salvation is centered in Christ alone. It really is inappropriate to use a verse that says Christ bore our sins on the cross to prove that Satan cannot be the scapegoat after the atonement is finished (see #191).

According to Holy Scripture, the sins are placed on the goat for Azazel *by* the high priest *after* the atonement is finished. Therefore, Christ our high priest will place the sins on someone after salvation is completely over. If this be not Satan, then who is it?

Wrapping Up the Case

#193: "Today, Seventh-day Adventists strive to be included as mainline, evangelical, Protestant Christians, and therefore object very strongly to any hint that they may be teaching cultic doctrine."—Steve Cannon.

#193: They strive to be included as mainline, evangelical, Protestant Christians. Actually, there really isn't all that much striving. And why should there be, given Adventism's strong stance on the final authority of Scripture? That used to be one of the cornerstones of Protestantism, but it's been abandoned by many mainline churches.

Representatives of the largest church in the world have declared that Adventists definitely are Protestants, since they repudiate tradition in favor of what the Scriptures teach. Here's one such quote:

> The Protestant, claiming the Bible to be the only guide of faith, has no warrant for observing Sunday. In this matter the Seventh Day Adventist is the only consistent Protestant.—"The Question Box," *The Catholic Universe Bulletin*, Aug. 14, 1942, p. 4.

Seriously, why should "the only consistent Protestant" have to strive? Rather, the churches who are following tradition instead of the Scriptures are the ones who ought to be striving.

Other quotations from Catholic writers on the subject follow:

> People who think that the Scriptures should be the sole authority, should logically become 7th Day Adventists, and keep Saturday holy.—Saint Catherine Catholic Church, *Sentinel*, May 21, 1995.

> [Seventh-day Adventists] are the most fundamental of all the fundamentalist sects, holding to literal interpretation of the Bible . . . .—Kenneth Ryan, *What More Would You Like to Know About the Church*, p. 137.

> If the Bible is the only guide for the Christian, then the Seventh Day Adventist is right in observing the Saturday with the Jew.—Bertrand L. Conway, *The Question Box* (1903 ed.), p. 254.

> Cath.: Is the Bible the rule or guide of Protestants for observing Sunday?

> Prot.: No, I believe the "Seventh Day Adventists" are the only ones who know the Bible in the matter of Sabbath observance.—*The Bible, an Authority Only in Catholic Hands*, pp. 26, 27.

If you follow the Bible alone there can be no question that you are obliged to keep Saturday holy, since that is the day especially prescribed by Almighty God to be kept holy to the Lord. In keeping Sunday, non-Catholics are simply following the practice of the Catholic Church for 1800 years, a tradition, and not a Bible ordinance. What we would like to know is: Since they deny the authority of the Church, on what grounds can they base their faith of keeping Sunday. Those who keep Saturday, like the Seventh Day Adventists, unquestionably have them by the hip in this practice. And they cannot give them any sufficient answer which would satisfy an unprejudiced mind. With the Catholics there is no difficulty about the matter. For, since we deny that the Bible is the sole rule of faith, we can fall back upon the constant practice and tradition of the Church which, long before the reign of Constantine, even in the very days of the apostles themselves, were accustomed to keep the first day of the week instead of the last.—F. G. Lentz, *The Question Box*, pp. 98, 99.

The last quote put the change of the Sabbath back in the days of the apostles, or thereabouts. This is what tradition says happened, which is good enough for some, but there is no biblical or historical basis for such a claim.

At any rate, the major points these Catholic authors make is that:

1. The Bible says to keep Saturday.
2. The Bible doesn't say to keep Sunday.
3. Protestantism claims to go by the Bible alone.
4. Protestants who keep Sunday are being inconsistent.

5. Seventh-day Adventists as Protestants are being consistent by keeping Saturday.

So say representatives from the largest church in the world.

#194: "An Adventist pastor supplied the following five marks of a cult. You be the judge whether or not his denomination fits his own definition of a cult."—Narrator.

#194: An Adventist pastor supplied this. When one reads what this pastor wrote, the credibility of all the information in the video is called into question.

These five marks were part of a letter to the editor of the *Nelson Daily News* written by Pastor Dan Stapleton. His letter, which can be found in its entirety in the *documentation package* under "Point 92," was in answer to charges which Keith MacGregor made in a newspaper article. The letter contains this interesting statement:

> As for the accusations made by K. MacGregor against the Seventh-day Adventist Church and Ellen White, I'm sorry to see again his misrepresentations, historical inaccuracies, and false assessments in print. It was 14 years ago that I first read such things published by the "ministry" he represents and they are no more true now than they were then.

We have referred more than once to Lorri MacGregor, the script writer for this video. In the credits at the end of the video, her name tops the list of six who were responsible for the research. Keith MacGregor is her husband. The two of them were this video's co-producers, and they operate what is known as MacGregor Ministries, which is the publisher of the *documentation package.*

The reader likely will see the problem. The very *documentation package* that is supposed to substantiate the "facts" of the video actually provides documentation explaining why there are so many mistakes and misrepresentations in this video. As of 1997, the date of the article Pastor Stapleton referred to, the MacGregors had been doing this kind of thing *for 14 years.*

#195 & #196: " 'Point 1: Cults or false religions usually have a single powerful human leader who becomes the cult's "messiah." ' "—Narrator.
"Who can deny the total reliance of the group on the teachings of Ellen G. White. She may not be called their messiah, but is certainly their messenger of God, revered by all."—Steve Cannon.

#195: They totally rely on her teachings. As presented under #21, #23-#26, and #45, the Adventist Church uses the Scriptures as their ultimate and final authority. It proves its doctrines from the Bible, not Mrs. White.

Second to the Bible, Mrs. White is officially viewed by the church as having more authority than the average person. This, however, does not mean that there is a "total reliance" on her.

By the way, it is because of the respect shown to the counsel of Mrs. White that there is no single, powerful human leader at the helm of the Adventist Church. She advocated spreading the responsibilities around, not centering all power in a few (*Testimonies for the Church*, vol. 8, p. 236).

#196: She is revered by all. It simply isn't true, as Sydney Cleveland makes clear toward the end of the video under #231.

One of the sources referred to earlier by the video was Walter Rea's *The White Lie.* The situation is not as bad as he describes it, but consider carefully what he

has to say:

> Perhaps one of the strangest twists of the white lie is that in many respects few in or out of the Adventist Church seem to be greatly affected anyway by the specific details of Ellen and her instruction, counsels, and reproofs. . . . In actuality not a great many pay much attention to the church's "spirit of prophecy," no matter where Ellen's ideas came from. . . .
>
> There is not overwhelming evidence that the members of the Adventist Church follow the solemn nineteenth-century counsel of Ellen . . . . Neither Adventist ministers nor Adventist lay people practice or promote to any serious degree certain legalisms they claim came from God by the inspiration and authority of their prophet. . . .
>
> That Adventists really believe that all the instructions of Ellen's pen came from God has to be doubted — because they have chosen to ignore a great deal of that instruction.—pp. 250, 251.

Thus wrote two decades ago one of the primary sources for information for this video.

A minority of Seventh-day Adventists who are theologically liberal openly deny the authority of both the Bible and the writings of Mrs. White. Among many of those who do profess to believe in the authority of inspired writings, many things just aren't followed or are explained away. Some seek to put into practice the counsel offered, but it definitely isn't as unanimous as Mr. Cannon thinks. Mrs. White is not "revered by all."

The *documentation package* identifies this item as "Point 93," but when one turns to "Point 93," no citation relevant to this item can be seen.

#197 & #198: " 'Point 2: The cult leader's word, or teachings of the cult, become absolute truth, overshadowing the teachings of the Bible.' "—Narrator.

"No Seventh-day Adventist would dare deny that Ellen G. White's comments on a certain portion of Scripture, determine the group's acceptance or rejection of historical views held on those Scriptures. Her interpretations prevail and become Adventist doctrine. Even today her writings are considered to be of equal inspiration with Scripture."—Steve Cannon.

#197: Her comments overshadow the Bible's teachings. False, as already brought out under #21, #23-#26, and #45.

According to the *documentation package*'s index, this charge is "substantiated" under "Point 94." There we find quoted number seventeen of Adventism's twenty-seven fundamental beliefs:

> One of the gifts of the Holy Spirit is prophecy. This gift is an identifying mark of the remnant church and was manifested in the ministry of Ellen G. White. As the Lord's messenger, her writings are a continuing and authoritative source of truth which provide for the church comfort, guidance, instruction, and correction. They also make clear that the Bible is the standard by which all teaching and experience must be tested.

Thus, since Mrs. White's comments must be tested by the Bible, they cannot simultaneously overshadow the teachings of Scripture. Once again, the *documentation package* proves the utter falsity of the video's charge.

#198: Her comments determine the acceptance or rejection of historical views. Incredible! Mr. Cannon didn't say "acceptance or rejection of Scripture." He instead said "acceptance or rejection of historical views," which is another way of saying "tradition."

So, Adventists are being condemned because they reject what *tradition* teaches about the Bible. But, being Protestants, they have to reject tradition when it contradicts the Bible, for that is in essence what Protestantism is all about.

> What says the Bible, the blessed Bible?
>   This my only question be.
> The teachings of men so often mislead us.
>   What says the Bible to me.

If an individual who truly has the biblical gift of prophecy declares some *tradition* to be an error, how can that possibly be wrong?

#199, #200, #201, #202, & #203: " 'Point 3: Each cult uses pressure tactics to coerce members into submission.' "—Narrator.

"Ellen G. White knew how to pressure people into submission. First she would claim to receive a reproof from God for the person, which she would air publicly through her testimonies. Usually the person conformed under the pressure. 'I have uttered reproofs... because the Lord has given me words of reproof... for the church.' The Remnant Church; Its Organization, Authority, Unity, and Triumph p. 6."—Steve Cannon.

#199: She pressured people into submission. Remember how she, unlike others, refused to push the reform dress or not eating suppers on people (#123, #128, #132)? Where was the pressure?

Mrs. White set before her readers God's own example of how to treat people we do not agree with or who are erring:

> The government of God is not, as Satan would make it appear, founded upon a blind submission, an unreasoning control. It appeals to the intellect and the conscience. "Come now, and let us reason together" is the Creator's invitation to the beings He has made. Isaiah 1:18. God does not force the will of His creatures. He cannot accept an homage that is not

willingly and intelligently given. A mere forced submission would prevent all real development of mind or character; it would make man a mere automaton. Such is not the purpose of the Creator. . . . It remains for us to choose whether we will be set free from the bondage of sin, to share the glorious liberty of the sons of God.—*Steps to Christ*, pp. 43, 44.

She advocated the taking of these principles manifested in God's government into the home and the classroom:

To direct the child's development without hindering it by undue control should be the study of both parent and teacher. Too much management is as bad as too little. The effort to "break the will" of a child is a terrible mistake. Minds are constituted differently; while force may secure outward submission, the result with many children is a more determined rebellion of the heart. Even should the parent or teacher succeed in gaining the control he seeks, the outcome may be no less harmful to the child. The discipline of a human being who has reached the years of intelligence should differ from the training of a dumb animal. The beast is taught only submission to its master. For the beast, the master is mind, judgment, and will. This method, sometimes employed in the training of children, makes them little more than automatons. Mind, will, conscience, are under the control of another. It is not God's purpose that any mind should be thus dominated. Those who weaken or destroy individuality assume a responsibility that can result only in evil. While under authority, the children may appear like well-drilled soldiers; but when the control ceases, the character will be found to lack strength and steadfastness. Having never learned to govern himself, the youth recognizes no restraint except the requirement of parents or teacher. This removed, he knows not how to use his liberty, and often gives himself up to indulgence that proves his ruin.—*Education*, p. 288.

Would not the world be a better place if preachers, parents, teachers, and public officials sought to put into practice these simple principles Mrs. White advocated?

#200: She publicly aired reproofs. Obviously, Mr. Cannon must not be too acquainted with her writings. Most of the time, as the *documentation package* under "Point 95a" indicates, the person's name was *never* used when a personal testimony was made public.

Under "Point 95a" there are three "publicly aired reproofs." Of these, two were personal letters that were not published until the 1980's or 1990's, so they were never publicly aired.

The third "example" represents a selection from volume 3 of *Testimonies for the Church*. It talks about Brother B. Who is Brother B? Did his name begin with B? Not at all. Brother A is referred to two pages before and Brother C is referred to four pages after. Letters were assigned to replace the people's names in the order in which they appeared in the book.

The specific city or town where Brother B was from is stated to be ----- on pages 339 and 340, thus protecting the guilty as far as possible. In other words, even where he lived is kept a secret. Only those acquainted with both the man and his problem might be able to guess who Mrs. White was talking about.

Why would she "air publicly" the reproof if she left the name and address out?

I have given some personal communications in several numbers of my testimonies, and in some cases persons have been offended because I did not publish all such communications. On account of their number this would be hardly possible, and it would be improper from the fact that some of them relate to sins which need not, and should not, be made public.

But I have finally decided that many of these personal testimonies should be published, as they all contain more or less reproof and instruction which apply to hundreds or thousands of others in similar condition. These should have the light which God has seen fit to give which meets their cases. It is a wrong to shut it away from them by sending it to one person or to one place, where it is kept as a light under a bushel.—*Testimonies for the Church*, vol. 1, pp. 631, 632.

So not all were "aired," for that would have been improper, but many were, with the names and places usually deleted to protect the guilty. Usually? Well, there were some exceptions, and one such exception appears in the very same chapter:

In this testimony I speak freely of the case of Sister Hannah More, not from a willingness to grieve the Battle Creek church, but from a sense of duty. I love that church notwithstanding their faults. I know of no church that in acts of benevolence and general duty do so well. I present the frightful facts in this case to arouse our people everywhere to a sense of their duty.—*Ibid.*, p. 632.

Why this exception? What was the problem? As an unmarried missionary in Africa, Hannah More accepted the Sabbath truth and was consequently dropped from employment by her missionary society. She came to Battle Creek, Michigan, but no Adventist took an interest in her. Ms. More actively sought employment, for there were quite a few Adventist ministries there at the time, but no one wanted to hire this intelligent and devoted lady. She therefore lodged with friends in northern Michigan who were not of her faith. Unaccustomed to the winters of northern Michigan, Hannah More died that very winter.

Because of neglect, someone died! Do you think this might be reason enough to get more specific about people and places? Would you call this an unwarranted, cultic pressure tactic?

As the result of Mrs. White confronting this issue, the denomination started an association which had the primary responsibility of aiding widows and orphans. Praise the Lord! The possibility of future neglect causing such problems was therefore lessened.

Here is what she wrote about the public exposure of naughty students. The principles expressed in this quote would be applicable in other settings as well.

> Great care should be shown in regard to making public the errors of students. To make public exposure of wrong is harmful in every respect to the wrongdoer and has no beneficial influence upon the school. It never helps a student to humiliate him before his fellow students. This heals nothing, cures nothing, but makes a wound that mortifies.—*Counsels to Parents, Teachers, and Students*, p. 267.

Wise counsel, wouldn't you say? And she did her best to practice what she preached.

#201: Usually the person conformed. Since this matter has been quite oversimplified, let's add a few details regarding a problem Mrs. White had to address, and how she addressed it.

One of the "publicly aired reproofs" under "Point 95a" in the *documentation package*, the one not published until 1991, is a letter written in 1886. It was addressed to a very prominent Seventh-day Adventist leader named J. H. Waggoner who apparently did "conform." Yes, Mrs. White comes down pretty hard on this minister who was guilty of *adultery*:

> Had you, Elder Waggoner, an elder of the church, looked up, you would have seen yourself a spectacle to God and to the pure angels who veil their faces and turn away from your pollution of soul and body. My words seem tame as I pen them when I think of the wonderful truths we profess and the great light that shines upon us from the Word of God. The Judge of all the earth is standing before the door, and every case must pass in solemn review before Him. I inquire, How can anyone with this light shining upon them dare in thought or word to deny the Lord God who hath bought them? Make haste, my brother, to cleanse your hands. Jesus is still pleading as your Intercessor. Commence the work of forsaking your sins without delay. Do not rest till you find pardon,

for no soul can enter the paradise of God who has a single spot or stain in his character. Make thorough work for eternity.—*Manuscript Releases*, vol. 21, p. 387.

Now that we actually read it, it doesn't sound like she came down all that hard. After all, this gray-haired man wasn't just having an adulterous affair in secret. He had gotten to the point where he was even putting his head in his mistress's lap at public church gatherings (Letter 10, 1885, as quoted in *Testimonies on Sexual Behavior, Adultery, and Divorce*, p. 182, and *Manuscript Releases*, vol. 5, pp. 243, 245). Such grievous sins must be dealt with firmly. What else should the prophetess have said instead?

That incident at the public church gathering probably occurred on New Year's eve in 1882, though it may have occurred two years later (Arthur White, vol. 3, pp. 209, 288; cf. *Evangelism*, p. 315). On November 4 of 1885, she wrote a letter to Waggoner about that incident. Still he did not repent of his grievous conduct. So ten months later, she wrote the letter quoted above to plead with him further to cease his affair with another man's wife. This man, in the sunset of his life, was allowing too much time to go by before he made his peace with God. Yes, he finally did "conform," but he should have "conformed" much sooner.

#202: This was because of the pressure. Actually, Mrs. White was present at the gathering where J. H. Waggoner had his head in the lap of his mistress:

> The very things that transpired at the Piedmont Sabbath school reunion, I would not have [had] occur for thousands of dollars. You, a gray-haired man, lying at full length with your head in the lap of Georgie S. *Had I done my duty, I would have rebuked you there.* Many saw this and made remarks about it.—*Testimonies on Sexual Behavior, Adultery, and Divorce*, p. 182, italics added.

So she later felt that she had not rebuked Waggoner as duty required. At the time, at this public religious gathering, she *didn't say anything.* Pressure tactics?

While Waggoner finally did "conform" under the "pressure" of Mrs. White's earnest entreaties, along with the entreaties of his brethren, she never made his case known to the general Adventist public. Most today still don't know that this man had such a severe problem.

It is apparent from both this situation and others like it that Mrs. White didn't just write about the character of Christ. She ever sought to emulate His lovely character:

> Christ Himself did not suppress one word of truth, but He spoke it always in love. He exercised the

greatest tact, and thoughtful, kind attention in His intercourse with the people. He was never rude, never needlessly spoke a severe word, never gave needless pain to a sensitive soul. He did not censure human weakness. He fearlessly denounced hypocrisy, unbelief, and iniquity, but tears were in His voice as He uttered His scathing rebukes.—*Desire of Ages*, p. 353.

#203: This type of pressure is one of the marks of a cult. If such an idea be true, then the prophets of the Bible were just as cultic as Mrs. White. Consider what Nathan told David when he had committed adultery and murder:

And Nathan said to David, Thou art the man. Thus saith the LORD God of Israel, I anointed thee king over Israel, and I delivered thee out of the hand of Saul; And I gave thee thy master's house, and thy master's wives into thy bosom, and gave thee the house of Israel and of Judah; and if that had been too little, I would moreover have given unto thee such and such things. Wherefore hast thou despised the commandment of the LORD, to do evil in his sight? thou hast killed Uriah the Hittite with the sword, and hast taken his wife to be thy wife, and hast slain him with the sword of the children of Ammon. Now therefore the sword shall never depart from thine house; because thou hast despised me, and hast taken the wife of Uriah the Hittite to be thy wife. Thus saith the LORD, Behold, I will raise up evil against thee out of thine own house, and I will take thy wives before thine eyes, and give them unto thy neighbour, and he shall lie with thy wives in the sight of this sun. For thou didst it secretly: but I will do this thing before all Israel, and before the sun. And David said unto Nathan, I have sinned against the LORD. (2 Sam. 12:7-13)

Looks like David "conformed" under the "pressure." And let's not forget Elijah:

And Elijah the Tishbite, who was of the inhabitants of Gilead, said unto Ahab, As the LORD God of Israel liveth, before whom I stand, there shall not be dew nor rain these years, but according to my word. (2 Kings 17:1)

That was only the beginning of Elijah's "pressure tactics." In the New Testament we have more of the same from Peter:

But Peter said, Ananias, why hath Satan filled thine heart to lie to the Holy Ghost, and to keep back part of the price of the land? Whiles it remained, was it not thine own? and after it was sold, was it not in thine own power? why hast thou conceived this thing in thine heart? thou hast not lied unto men, but unto God. And Ananias hearing these words fell down, and gave up the ghost: and *great fear* came on all them that heard these things. And the young men arose, wound him up, and carried him out, and buried him. And it was about the space of three hours after, when his wife, not knowing what was done, came in. And Peter answered unto her, Tell me whether ye sold the land for so much? And she said, Yea, for so much. Then Peter said unto her, How is it that ye have agreed together to tempt the Spirit of the Lord? behold, the feet of them which have buried thy husband are at the door, and shall carry thee out. Then fell she down straightway at his feet, and yielded up the ghost: and the young men came in, and found her dead, and, carrying her forth, buried her by her husband. And *great fear* came upon all the church, and upon as many as heard these things. (Acts 5:1-12)

But Peter said unto him, Thy money perish with thee, because thou hast thought that the gift of God may be purchased with money. Thou hast neither part nor lot in this matter: for thy heart is not right in the sight of God. Repent therefore of this thy wickedness, and pray God, if perhaps the thought of thine heart may be forgiven thee. For I perceive that thou art in the gall of bitterness, and in the bond of iniquity. Then answered Simon, and said, Pray ye to the Lord for me, that none of these things which ye have spoken come upon me. (Acts 8:20-24)

To cite every example in the Bible of prophets and apostles using the same kind of "pressure tactics" that Mrs. White used, we would certainly have to reprint a large portion of the Scriptures.

#204 & #205: "The tactics may not be as blatant today, but believers are subject to pressure tactics today as well to conform to the group. Love, acceptance, and fellowship are very often withheld from anyone who questions the official teachings of the church."—Steve Cannon.

#204: Love, acceptance, and fellowship are *very often* withheld. Love is a word that can mean different things to different people. It might mean giving a lollipop to your kid, or it might mean giving

him some necessary discipline.

Essentially, Mr. Cannon is talking about church discipline here, a biblical teaching that Adventists definitely believe in. Sometimes discipline is the most loving thing to do.

Yet unlike Jehovah's Witnesses or the Amish, Adventists do not practice shunning. To them, church discipline does not mean that family members cannot associate with erring family members. It does not mean that erring ones cannot attend church services.

There are two forms of church discipline within the Seventh-day Adventist Church:

1. Vote of Censor. This is for a stated period of time. The erring one loses the church offices that he or she holds, and, during the period of censure, cannot have a voice or vote in the affairs of the church, cannot have a public part in the services of the church, and cannot transfer his or her membership to another church.

2. Disfellowship. This is when the person's name is actually removed from the membership roles of the church. He or she is then no longer a Seventh-day Adventist.

Chapter 14 of the *Seventh-day Adventist Church Manual*, which outlines these procedures, gets very specific about what a member can and cannot be disciplined for. After the erring one is disciplined, notice the attitude of kindness that must be displayed:

> *Notification to Persons Removed from Membership* —It is incumbent upon the church that removes a member from church membership to notify the individual in writing of the action that was reluctantly taken with the assurance of enduring spiritual interest and personal concern. This communication should, where possible, be delivered in person by the church pastor or by a church board designee. The erring member should be assured that the church will always hope that reaffiliation will take place and that one day there will be eternal fellowship together in the kingdom of God.—p. 189.

Thus churches are to be as kind as possible in their dealing with members who do such things as:

1. murder,
2. commit adultery,
3. steal,
4. habitually lie,
5. embezzle,
6. commit fraud,
7. take to alcohol or tobacco or narcotics,
8. commence a warfare against the church, or
9. deny the basic teachings of the Bible.

Back to Mr. Cannon's statement. He said that "acceptance, and fellowship are *very often* withheld from anyone who questions the official teachings of the church." Perhaps he doesn't really understand what is going on, for if he did, he would think it actually isn't done often enough!

Receiving the Word, by Samuel Koranteng-Pipim, documents what has been going on for a number of decades among an influential minority of Adventists who no longer take the Bible as it reads. Based on his book, and some of the liberal publications he cites, some of the views being expressed are these:

1. God is so kind, He will never punish sinners.
2. Jesus's death on the cross was not as our substitute; His blood did not have to be shed.
3. Evolution is how we got here, and there was no world-wide flood.
4. No one has the right to tell any couple not to engage in premarital sexual activities.
5. Scripture does not clearly condemn homosexual practices (pp. 159, 160, 172, 173, 109, 112, 184, 185, 107).

What do you think? Should people holding such views be just as accepted and enjoy just as much fellowship as those who still believe the Bible?

There are those who seek to liberalize the theology of the Seventh-day Adventist denomination. It would be much more appropriate if they started their own denomination rather than try to change one that has stood so strongly for the authority and inspiration of Scripture.

Receiving the Word documents it well. Additional evidence can be found in the journal *Spectrum*. The *documentation package* cites this journal under "Point 6" and "Point 14." The *Time* article under "Point 54" calls *Spectrum* an "independent journal for church liberals." Grab a copy and look through it, and you will likely see that a number of influential Adventists are openly propagating skepticism while still enjoying acceptance and fellowship. If the Adventist Church is so hard on those who question its teachings, why does *Spectrum* still exist?

#205: Withholding of acceptance and fellowship for questioning doctrine is a characteristic of a cult. Adventist members are not disfellowshipped for merely asking questions about doctrines. But attacking and going to war against, that ought to be a different matter.

Would Mr. Cannon call the apostle Paul a cult leader? Regarding what to do with a church member guilty of fornication, Paul wrote:

> In the name of our Lord Jesus Christ, when ye are gathered together, . . . deliver such an one unto Satan for the destruction of the flesh, . . . Know ye not that a little leaven leaveneth the whole lump? Purge out therefore the old leaven. . . . I have written unto you not to keep company, if any man that is called a brother be a fornicator, or covetous, or an idolater, or

a railer, or a drunkard, or an extortioner; with such an one no not to eat. . . . Therefore put away from among yourselves that wicked person. (1 Cor. 5:4-13)

Is Paul advocating a type of treatment toward those in apostasy that is cultic in nature? Or should behavioral problems be handled differently than doctrinal ones?

> Whosoever transgresseth, and abideth not in the doctrine of Christ, hath not God. He that abideth in the doctrine of Christ, he hath both the Father and the Son. If there come any unto you, and bring not this doctrine, receive him not into your house, neither bid him God speed: For he that biddeth him God speed is partaker of his evil deeds. (2 Jn. 9-11)

So John tells us that there are certain cases that the church must deal with, even cases involving doctrine. God forbid that anyone would call the apostle John a cult leader!

#206, #207, #208, #209, & #210: " 'Point 4: Each cult denies the central truth of the gospel that Jesus is the divine Son of God without beginning or ending. They deny that His death has provided salvation... for the entire human race. As a result, salvation is earned by adherence to the teachings of the cult rather than accepting Christ and following Him.' "—Narrator.

"We would point out that the group originally denied the deity of Jesus Christ. Today they believe Jesus Christ is eternal, but they are stuck with the old doctrine that Jesus is the Archangel Michael. They need to firmly establish one doctrine and discontinue the other. However, they cannot give up this doctrine which contradicts Hebrews 1:13 without having to acknowledge that Mrs. White made a mistake. Instead they try to accommodate both conflicting doctrines. This is an impossible situation."—Steve Cannon.

#206: They originally denied the deity of Christ. This is not true, as pointed out under #94.

James White was editor of the *Review and Herald*, and Joseph Bates and J. N. Andrews were on the publishing committee when a work by an English author was printed in the issue of October 18, 1853. It contained the following statement:

> Christians, keep not silence while your Lord is dishonored, and souls are perishing. Warn those who deny the divinity of the only Saviour, that they must perish everlastingly if they go on rejecting him, for it is fearful and blasphemous to reject him.—p. 116.

Mr. Cannon is really dealing with two separate issues: the deity of Christ and Christ being eternal. They aren't the same.

For example, consider the views of well-known Adventist preacher Ellet J. Waggoner (1855-1916) in his 1890 *Christ and His Righteousness*. Chapters two and four are entitled "Christ is God" and "Christ not a Created Being." He obviously believed in the divinity of Christ.

In chapter four he deals with some opinions that "actually deny His Divinity." One such is

> . . . the idea that Christ is a created being, who, through the good pleasure of God, was elevated to His present lofty position. No one who holds this view can possibly have any just conception of the exalted position which Christ really occupies.—pp. 19, 20.

Waggoner explains what Revelations 3:14 means when it says that Christ is the "Beginning of the creation of God":

> And so the statement that He is the beginning or head of the creation of God means that in Him creation had its beginning; that, as He Himself says, He is Alpha and Omega, the beginning and the end, the first and the last. Rev. 21:6; 22:13. He is the source whence all things have their origin.—p. 20.

Likewise, regarding the term "archangel," Waggoner says:

> This does not mean that He is the first of the angels, for He is not an angel but is above them. Heb. 1:4. It means that He is the chief or prince of the angels, just as an archbishop is the head of the bishops. Christ is the commander of the angels. See Rev. 19:11-14. He created the angels. Col. 1:16.—*Ibid.*

Waggoner also spends some time dealing with Colossians 1:15. "Neither should we imagine that Christ is a creature, because Paul calls Him (Col. 1:15) 'The First-born of every creature' for the very next verses show Him to be Creator and not a creature." —p. 21.

Then he begins to delve into that aspect of the orthodox Trinity doctrine known as the processions, which teaches that Christ proceeded forth from and was begotten of the Father (see #94):

> The Scriptures declare that Christ is "the only begotten son of God." He is begotten, not created. As

to when He was begotten, it is not for us to inquire, nor could our minds grasp it if we were told. The prophet Micah tells us all that we can know about it in these words, ". . . whose goings forth have been from of old, from the days of eternity." Micah 5:2, margin. There was a time when Christ proceeded forth and came from God, from the bosom of the Father (John 8:42; 1:18), but that time was so far back in the days of eternity that to finite comprehension it is practically without beginning.—pp. 21, 22.

Here is a man who says that Christ is God, is divine, and is not a created being, while at the same time he says that Christ is "practically without beginning." Was he contradicting himself? No, he wasn't. We are dealing with multiple issues here.

Notice how clearly Waggoner upheld the full deity of Christ:

> And since He is the only-begotten son of God, He is of the very substance and nature of God and possesses by birth all the attributes of God, for the Father was pleased that His Son should be the express image of His Person, the brightness of His glory, and filled with all the fullness of the Godhead. So He has "life in Himself." He possesses immortality in His own right and can confer immortality upon others.—p. 22.

Typically, the debate over whether Christ is divine or not is called the Arian controversy, dating back to the fourth century. After the initial stages, the difference between the two sides hinged on a single letter, the letter "i." The "orthodox" position was that Christ was *homoousios*. This Greek word means "of the same substance" or essence. The semi-Arian position was that Christ was *homoiousios*, of "like essence."

Since Waggoner said that Christ was "of the very substance and nature of God," he was on the orthodox side of the question. He was neither Arian nor semi-Arian. Presumably, Mr. Cannon is in agreement with most, if not all, of what Waggoner wrote in these selections.

Regarding Christ being eternal, Mrs. White wrote in 1878:

> The unworthiness, weakness, and inefficiency of their own efforts in contrast with those of the eternal Son of God, will render them humble, distrustful of self, and will lead them to rely upon Christ for strength and efficiency in their work.—*Review and Herald*, Aug. 8, 1878.

Even before this, the *Review* from 1854 to 1859 published five quotes and selections using the phrase "eternal Son" (Feb. 28, 1854, p. 43; Sept. 12, 1854, p. 33; April 15, 1858, p. 172; March 17, 1859, p. 131; April 21, 1859, p. 169). Searching through each issue

through 1863, we find that the only writer to argue against the usage of the phrase was J. M. Stephenson (Nov. 14, 1854, p. 105). Yet his views on some subjects were by no means typical of Seventh-day Adventists, leading to his departure about a year later.

Isaiah speaks of those who "make a man an offender for a word" (29:21). In the fourth century they made a man an offender for a single letter. Things got so bad that by 381 AD, the "orthodox" emperor had forbidden the Arians to worship publicly. Any building in which they met was seized and donated to the imperial treasury (*Theodosian Code*, bk. 16, title 5, statute 8).

That was only the beginning. Over the centuries that followed, love, acceptance, and fellowship were withheld from those who differed on this and many other issues. Millions died for their faith.

Let's be more tolerant lest our behavior be called cultic. Especially let's be tolerant of those whom we don't really disagree with anyway.

#207: They must discontinue the doctrine that Jesus is the archangel Michael. Sorry, Adventists must be true to Scripture (see #93).

Mr. Cannon, you just condemned Adventists under #198 for their "rejection of historical views held on those Scriptures." Why then criticize them for retaining the "historical view" that Michael is a name for the uncreated, fully divine Son of God (see #87)?

#208: This doctrine contradicts Hebrews 1:13. No, the Bible does not contradict itself. After all, if the Angel who claims to be God in the Old Testament is not Christ, than we have more than one God, and that cannot be.

Hebrews 1:13 makes it plain that Christ is not one of the angels of heaven, but we have to consider that Paul is using a specific definition for the word "angel" in that verse.

By one count, the Hebrew word for "angel" occurs in the Old Testament 214 times. Of these, 98 times it is translated "messenger" and 4 times "ambassadors." Nearly half of the occurrences of this Hebrew word in the Old Testament refer to human beings, not what we normally call angels. Therefore, in the biblical sense anyone who is a messenger can be called an "angel," and that includes Christ.

The context of Hebrews 1:13 makes it pretty plain that Paul is not referring to men or Christ by the term "angel." He thus is restricting his meaning to just the angelic beings of heaven.

Why the script writer thought that the Adventist understanding of Michael contradicts Hebrews 1:13 can be seen from the index to the *documentation package*. Under "Point 96" in the index is this revealing sentence: "Jesus cannot be eternally God and a created angel at the same time!" Seventh-day Adventism has never taught that Michael is a *created angel*. If He isn't, then the whole objection to Michael and Christ being the same divine person collapses.

#209: They can't discontinue it without acknowledging that Mrs. White made a mistake. That's putting it too simply. Adventists can't discontinue this doctrine without acknowledging that Charles Spurgeon, John Gill, Matthew Henry, the writer of the footnotes in the 1599 Geneva Bible, and a host of others made a mistake as well (see #87).

As the video informs us, Mr. Cannon is a regional director for Personal Freedom Outreach. His office happens to be in Glendale, Arizona, home to the video's executive producer, Mark Martin.

According to Personal Freedom Outreach's web site, Mr. Cannon "has an associate of arts degree in biblical studies from Antioch Baptist Bible College" (http://www.pfo.org/about.html). Why then would he make such a big deal of this issue? Charles Spurgeon and John Gill are some of the most well known Baptists of all time, and the Baptists sure aren't a cult.

#210: It is impossible to accommodate both doctrines. Why not? It's been done for centuries.

Notice what Jesus says regarding the resurrection:

> And hath given him authority to execute judgment also, because he is the Son of man. Marvel not at this: for the hour is coming, in the which all that are in the graves shall hear his voice, And shall come forth; they that have done good, unto the resurrection of life; and they that have done evil, unto the resurrection of damnation. (John 5:27-29)

So the voice of Jesus raises the dead. Yet the apostle Paul says that it is the voice of the archangel that does it: "For the Lord himself shall descend from heaven with a shout, with the voice of the archangel, and with the trump of God: and the dead in Christ shall rise first" (1 Th. 4:16). And Jude tells us who raised Moses: "Yet Michael the archangel, when contending with the devil he disputed about the body of Moses, durst not bring against him a railing accusation, but said, The Lord rebuke thee" (Jude 1:9). So who raises the dead? Jesus or Michael?

> But the prince of the kingdom of Persia withstood me one and twenty days: but, lo, Michael, one of the chief princes, came to help me; and I remained there with the kings of Persia. (Dan. 10:13)
>
> But I will shew thee that which is noted in the scripture of truth: and there is none that holdeth with

me in these things, but Michael your prince. (Dan. 10:21)

Notice how the old *King James* said, "I will shew *thee*," and, "Michael *your* prince." In this archaic English, "thee" and "thy" are singular, and "you" and "your" are plural. Thus "thee" must refer only to Daniel, and "your" must refer to either the Jews or all of God's people.

So the angel in Daniel 10:21 is saying that Michael is "the prince of the Jews." Why, that's an interesting title! The phrases "king of Israel" and "king of the Jews" are used in the gospels eighteen times to refer to Christ. Remember why He was condemned and crucified? The placard above His head on the cross said that His crime was that He was "the King of the Jews" (Mark 15:26).

The only references to Michael in the Old Testament are the three made by an angel in Daniel 10:13, 21; 12:1. A careful reading of chapter 10 suggests that Daniel at some point actually saw Michael, and that Michael must be Christ:

> Then I lifted up mine eyes, and looked, and behold a certain man clothed in linen, whose loins were girded with fine gold of Uphaz: . . . and his face as the appearance of lightning, and his eyes as lamps of fire, and his arms and his feet like in colour to polished brass, and the voice of his words like the voice of a multitude. (Dan. 10:5, 6)
>
> And in the midst of the seven candlesticks one like unto the Son of man, clothed with a garment down to the foot, and girt about the paps with a golden girdle. . . . and his eyes were as a flame of fire; And his feet like unto fine brass, . . . and his voice as the sound of many waters. . . . and his countenance was as the sun shineth in his strength. (Rev. 1:13-16)

One last quote may be considered:

> And at that time shall Michael stand up, the great prince which standeth for the children of thy people: and there shall be a time of trouble, such as never was since there was a nation even to that same time: and at that time thy people shall be delivered, every one that shall be found written in the book. (Dan. 12:1)

So Michael is the great prince who will "stand up" at the very end of time. Stand up? What does that mean?

> Four kingdoms shall stand up out of the nation, but not in his power. . . . a king of fierce countenance, and understanding dark sentences, shall stand up. (Dan. 8:22, 23)
>
> Behold, there shall stand up yet three kings in Persia . . . . And a mighty king shall stand up, that shall rule with great dominion, and do according to his will. (Dan. 11:2, 3)

But out of a branch of her roots shall one stand up in his estate. (Dan. 11:7)

Then shall stand up in his estate a raiser of taxes in the glory of the kingdom . . . . And in his estate shall stand up a vile person, to whom they shall not give the honour of the kingdom: but he shall come in peaceably, and obtain the kingdom by flatteries. (Dan. 11:20, 21)

Repeatedly, when Daniel says that a kingdom or king or prince "stands up," he's saying that they are beginning to reign. Thus, in the time of trouble, Michael the great prince begins to reign. Begins to reign?! I thought Christ was the one who did that (Rev. 11:15; Mat. 13:41; 16:28; 25:31; 2 Tim. 4:1)!

#211, #212, #213, & #214: "As to salvation by grace through faith in Christ alone, Adventists have added the investigative judgment, the keeping of the Sabbath, and obedience to the Ten Commandments and other Old Testament laws as requirements for salvation."—Narrator.

#211: Adventists have added the investigative judgment to salvation by grace through faith in Christ alone. Really? Then why did Paul say, "In the day when God shall judge the secrets of men by Jesus Christ according to my gospel" (Rom. 2:16)? If God will judge all by the gospel, it cannot be true that the judgment is *added* to the gospel. And as Revelation 14:6, 7 clearly shows, even a pre-advent judgment is part of the gospel.

In actuality, someone who denies the truth of these Scriptures is *deleting* the judgment from the gospel. Who authorized the contributors to this video to *delete* the judgment from salvation by grace through faith in Christ alone? The penalty for deleting anything is severe:

And if any man shall take away from the words of the book of this prophecy, God shall take away his part out of the book of life, and out of the holy city, and from the things which are written in this book. (Rev. 22:19)

#212: Adventists have added Sabbath keeping to salvation by grace through faith in Christ alone. Who gets quoted so much on these issues? Why it's the apostle Paul. And what did he teach?

The Gentiles besought that these words might be preached to them the next sabbath. Now when the congregation was broken up, many of the Jews and religious proselytes followed Paul and Barnabas: who, speaking to them, persuaded them to continue in the grace of God. (Acts 13:42, 43)

So Sabbath keeping is not at odds with salvation by grace. Besides, Paul made it pretty clear that he was not a Sabbath breaker:

Neither against the law of the Jews, neither against the temple, nor yet against Caesar, have I offended any thing at all. (Acts 25:8)

Men and brethren, though I have committed nothing against the people, or customs of our fathers, yet was I delivered prisoner from Jerusalem into the hands of the Romans. (Acts 28:17)

The worst rumor that the Judaizers could bring against Paul was that he had told Jews not to circumcise their children (Acts 21:21), a charge that was totally baseless. If he really had been teaching that the weekly Sabbath was incompatible with the gospel, then the Judaizers would have had some facts to relate rather than just baseless rumors. The absence of a record of a controversy over the Sabbath in the book of Acts tells us plainly that Paul always sought to keep holy the Lord's Day Sabbath.

Now if these considerations aren't enough, we also have that first angel of Revelation 14 quoting from the fourth commandment while preaching the everlasting gospel: "And worship him that made heaven, and earth, and the sea, and the fountains of waters" (Rev. 14:7).

Sabbath keeping is also a component of the New Covenant, for the New Covenant promise is:

For this is the covenant that I will make with the house of Israel after those days, saith the Lord; I will put my laws into their mind, and write them in their hearts: and I will be to them a God, and they shall be to me a people. (Heb. 8:10)

Speaking of covenants: "Brethren, I speak after the manner of men; Though it be but a man's covenant, yet if it be confirmed, no man disannulleth, or addeth thereto" (Gal. 3:15). When was the New Covenant ratified?

And for this cause he is the mediator of the new testament, that by means of death, for the redemption of the transgressions that were under the first testament, they which are called might receive the promise of eternal inheritance. For where a testament is, there must also of necessity be the death of the testator. For a testament is of force after men are dead: otherwise it is of no strength at all while the testator liveth. (Heb. 9:15-17)

Since the Greek word for "testament" (a will) is the same as the word for "covenant," it is quite apparent from this passage that the New Covenant could not be altered after Christ died. Therefore, the New Testament, the New Covenant, was ratified on Friday, the day of Christ's death.

That evening, what did Christ's followers do? "And they returned, and prepared spices and ointments; and rested the sabbath day according to the commandment" (Luke 23:56).

Christ's will states that the law is to be written in the hearts and minds of believers. If the Sabbath were to be deleted from that law, it would have to be deleted before Christ died. Since it was not, the fourth commandment must still be in force. Resurrection Sunday came three days too late.

Would the contributors to this video please consider that they are at risk of being charged with the crime of deleting from and altering a Man's will after His death? Such activities are highly illegal. Contact the heavenly court for full details.

#213: Adventists have added obedience to the Ten Commandments as requirements for salvation. If by "salvation" the narrator means justification or conversion, then it need only be pointed out that Adventists believe that obedience is impossible before salvation occurs. If the narrator means "glorification," then it is a simple fact that Adventists haven't *added* anything.

The gospel of Luke says:

And a certain ruler asked him, saying, Good Master, what shall I do to inherit eternal life? And Jesus said unto him, Why callest thou me good? none is good, save one, that is, God. Thou knowest the commandments, Do not commit adultery, Do not kill, Do not steal, Do not bear false witness, Honour thy father and thy mother. (Luke 18:18-20)

Jesus wasn't saying that we can work our way to heaven, but He was pointing out that sin must be put away.

For verily I say unto you, Till heaven and earth pass, one jot or one tittle shall in no wise pass from the law, till all be fulfilled. Whosoever therefore shall break one of these least commandments, and shall teach men so, he shall be called the least in the kingdom of heaven: but whosoever shall do and teach them, the same shall be called great in the kingdom of heaven. (Mat. 5:18, 19)

It is only through salvation by grace through faith in Christ alone that our lives can be brought back into harmony with God's holy law. But the point of these verses is that our lives *must* be brought back.

Paul cannot be clearer:

For in Christ Jesus neither circumcision availeth any thing, nor uncircumcision, but a new creature. (Gal. 6:15)

For in Jesus Christ neither circumcision availeth any thing, nor uncircumcision; but faith which worketh by love. (Gal. 5:6)

Circumcision is nothing, and uncircumcision is nothing, but the keeping of the commandments of God. (1 Cor. 7:19)

If we want to be in God's kingdom at last, we must become a new creature, we must have that faith that works by love, we must keep God's commandments.

The idea that people can continue to break the commandments of God and still go to heaven must be *another gospel.* It certainly wasn't the gospel Paul taught in the book of Galatians (Gal. 5:19-21). That book also says:

I marvel that ye are so soon removed from him that called you into the grace of Christ unto another gospel: Which is not another; but there be some that trouble you, and would pervert the gospel of Christ. (Gal. 1:6, 7)

Why did the contributors to the video *delete* commandment keeping from the gospel, thus producing a different gospel than the one that Jesus and Paul preached? Did they have a vision or dream, or did an angel come to tell them to do so? "But though we, or an angel from heaven, preach any other gospel unto you than that which we have preached unto you, let him be accursed" (Gal. 1:8).

#214: Adventists have added obedience to other Old Testament laws as requirements for salvation. Again, this is untrue. Adventists haven't *added* anything.

What Old Testament laws is the narrator talking about? Is he talking about abstaining from eating blood? Yet Acts 15 tells Christians that they must still abide by this Old Testament regulation:

For it seemed good to the Holy Ghost, and to us, to lay upon you no greater burden than these necessary things; That ye abstain from meats offered to idols, and from blood, and from things strangled, and from fornication: from which if ye keep yourselves, ye shall do well. Fare ye well. (Acts 15:28, 29)

Or is the narrator talking about abstaining from eating unclean animals? Yet Isaiah said that those living in the end of time just before Christ returns must abstain from eating such:

For, behold, the LORD will come with fire, and with his chariots like a whirlwind, to render his anger with fury, and his rebuke with flames of fire. For by fire and by his sword will the LORD plead with all flesh: and the slain of the LORD shall be many. They that sanctify themselves, and purify themselves in the gardens behind one tree in the midst, eating swine's flesh, and the abomination, and the mouse, shall be consumed together, saith the LORD. (Is. 66:15-17)

And the apostle Paul indicates that we should abstain from them as well:

> Wherefore come out from among them, and be ye separate, saith the Lord, and touch not the unclean thing; and I will receive you, And will be a Father unto you, and ye shall be my sons and daughters, saith the Lord Almighty. (2 Cor. 6:17, 18)

That's what we all want, isn't it? Don't you want God to be your Father? And let's not forget that, years after the cross, Peter testified: "I have never eaten any thing that is common or unclean" (Acts 10:14).

Or is the narrator talking about tithing? In the context of events that occur in New Testament times, Malachi says:

> Will a man rob God? Yet ye have robbed me. But ye say, Wherein have we robbed thee? In tithes and offerings. Ye are cursed with a curse: for ye have robbed me, even this whole nation. Bring ye all the tithes into the storehouse, that there may be meat in mine house, and prove me now herewith, saith the LORD of hosts, if I will not open you the windows of heaven, and pour you out a blessing, that there shall not be room enough to receive it. And I will rebuke the devourer for your sakes, and he shall not destroy the fruits of your ground; neither shall your vine cast her fruit before the time in the field, saith the LORD of hosts. (Mal. 3:8-11)

Many Bible-believing Christians of many denominations have been greatly blessed by simply taking God at His word. They have claimed this promise and have had their crops, their homes, and their lives preserved.

This writer is one of these. His house in Dobbins, California, was in the midst of a 5800-acre forest fire in 1997. The hard-plastic weather stripping around two of his windows melted from the intense heat of the fire as it raced to the top of the ridge where his house stood. A forty-foot or taller pine tree twenty feet from the house was torched all the way up. A cedar with foliage four feet from the roof was badly burned on its side away from the house. Though there was no defensible space between the house and the trees on the downhill side, the house stood totally untouched, other than the weather stripping. Eighty-three other houses did not fair so well. One nearby went down in ten minutes.

Paul indicates that as the preachers of the Old Testament were supported, even so were the preachers of the New Testament to be supported:

> Do ye not know that they which minister about holy things live of the things of the temple? and they which wait at the altar are partakers with the altar? Even so hath the Lord ordained that they which preach the gospel should live of the gospel. (1 Cor. 9:13, 14)

Another hint regarding the perpetuity of the three things mentioned above (abstaining from blood and unclean animals, and tithing), is that they are all precepts that existed before the Jews came to be:

1. Noah and all his descendants were forbidden to eat blood (Gen. 9:4).
2. Noah knew all about the clean-unclean animal distinctions (Gen. 7:2, 3).
3. Abraham paid tithes, and Jacob promised to (Gen. 14:20; 28:22).

A careful study of Acts 15 reveals some vital points. First, the issue that prompted the church council of Acts 15 was whether the Gentiles had to be circumcised before they could be saved (vss. 1, 5). Such a position in effect was saying that Gentiles had to become Jews, and thus that only Jews could be saved. Nowhere in the Old Testament are Gentiles ever told to be circumcised if they want to be saved. These Judaizers were thus trying to add to the Word of God.

Second, the council decided to ask the Gentiles to obey laws that had been binding upon them in Old Testament times (vss. 20, 29; cf. Lev. 17:13; 18:24, 25). So while they didn't have to obey laws that applied only to Jews in Old Testament times, they were still expected to heed the laws that had always applied to everyone.

Now since the Sabbath dates back to Adam, since both abstaining from blood and the clean-unclean animal distinctions date back at least to Noah, and since tithing dates back at least to Abraham, these must be precepts that applied to Gentiles back then. That being so, Acts 15 indicates that they still apply today.

Much more could be said on the subject, but suffice it to say that Adventists haven't added anything here either.

#215, #216, & #217: "In addition they believe the world's sins have been placed upon Satan rather than Christ, and that Christians must stand before God without Christ as their mediator.

'Those who are living upon the earth when the intercession of Christ shall cease in the sanctuary above are to stand in the sight of a holy God without a mediator.' Great Controversy p. 425."
—Narrator.

#215: They believe that sins have been placed upon Satan. No Adventist believes that sins have been placed upon Satan. This charge is a total fabrication.

As shown under #191, Adventists believe that sins will be placed upon Satan only *after* salvation is completely done. Since Christ has not yet returned, since the "redemption of our body" (Rom. 8:23) has not yet taken place, since probation has not yet closed, no sins have yet been placed upon Satan.

#216: And that means rather than Christ. Utterly false. Adventists have never taught that our sins are laid upon Satan instead of Christ. Christ is our only Sin-bearer (see #191).

#217: They believe we must stand without a mediator. Quite irrelevant, for as every Bible-believing Christian who has studied the matter knows, the mediatorial work of Christ must cease at some point. Will we need a mediator throughout the ceaseless ages of eternity? Of course not.

> He that is unjust, let him be unjust still: and he which is filthy, let him be filthy still: and he that is righteous, let him be righteous still: and he that is holy, let him be holy still. And, behold, I come quickly; and my reward is with me, to give every man according as his work shall be. (Rev. 22:11, 12)

According to Jesus's own words, therefore, His mediation will cease just before He comes. There will be no more switching sides. Sinners will be forever lost, and saints will be forever saved.

This is also indicated in the following passage:

> And another angel came and stood at the altar, having a golden censer; and there was given unto him much incense, that he should offer it with the prayers of all saints upon the golden altar which was before the throne. And the smoke of the incense, which came with the prayers of the saints, ascended up before God out of the angel's hand. And the angel took the censer, and filled it with fire of the altar, and cast it into the earth: and there were voices, and thunderings, and lightnings, and an earthquake. (Rev. 8:3-5)

Voices, thunderings, lightnings, and an earthquake are associated with the second coming of Christ in the book of Revelation (Rev. 16:18). The censer with the incense is a symbol of the intercession going on in heaven for us. The casting down of the censer must therefore represent the cessation of that intercessory work just before the return of Christ.

Though Adventists believe that this is something that becomes reality only in the last moments of time, the narrator gives no hint of this fact.

#218, #219, & #220: "Contrast this with the plain statement from the Bible in Hebrews chapter 7 verse 25 concerning Jesus Christ. 'Hence also, He is able to save forever those who draw near to God through Him, since He always lives to make intercession for them.' Truly the salvation for the Seventh-day Adventists, placing sin upon Satan, is not the salvation taught in the Bible."—Steve Cannon.

#218: This contradicts Hebrews 7:25. As should be readily apparent from #217, the use of this text is irrelevant to the point. Will this verse be still true ten million years after Christ returns? Of course not. There will be no need of salvation or intercession then, since sin will be no more. The saved of earth will enjoy total bliss throughout eternity without needing a mediator.

> And there shall be no more curse: but the throne of God and of the Lamb shall be in it; and his servants shall serve him: And they shall see his face; and his name shall be in their foreheads. (Rev. 22:3, 4)
> And [God] said [to Moses], Thou canst not see my

face: for there shall no man see me, and live. (Ex. 33:20)

What makes the difference? Why was Moses unable to see God's face in Old Testament times, but the redeemed throughout eternity will be able to? We cannot today approach a holy God except through our divine Mediator, because of our sinfulness. However, once sin is fully dealt with, this impediment will be removed, and we will be able to see the face of God. The clear implication is that when Revelation 22:3 and 4 are fulfilled, there will no longer be the need of a mediator.

Hebrews 7:25 is talking about the present. It has no

bearing whatsoever upon that time when those who are filthy will be filthy still, when those who are righteous will be righteous still.

#219: Seventh-day Adventists believe their salvation comes from placing sin upon Satan. Maybe Mr. Cannon is talking about the Church of Satan, but he cannot be talking about Seventh-day Adventists. The placing of sins upon Satan in the end

purchases salvation for no one. Yet it is a biblical fact that the one responsible for all sin will receive his just deserts (see #191).

#220: This isn't the salvation taught in the Bible. Since Seventh-day Adventists do not believe, and never have, that their salvation comes from placing sins upon Satan, this argument is clearly irrelevant.

#221 & #222: " 'Point 5: Cults often urge their converts to leave their families.' "—Narrator.

"At last we can find a point on which we can agree. Adventists do not urge their converts to leave their families. That means that out of the five points marking a group as a cult, four of them apply to Seventh-day Adventists. Many feel this is too cult-like for them."—Steve Cannon.

#221: Four of the five points apply to Seventh-day Adventists. As we have just seen, not one of the five points applies.

1. Has single, powerful human leader who becomes the group's "messiah." Adventists do not make Mrs. White out to be their "Messiah." She is not "revered by all." They do not have a "total reliance" upon her. The Bible is their final authority.

2. Leader's word or teachings of the group overshadow the teachings of the Bible. Adventism exalts the Bible above all.

3. Uses pressure tactics to coerce members into submission. Neither Mrs. White nor the Seventh-day Adventist Church uses cultic pressure tactics.

4. Denies that Jesus is the divine Son of God, and that his death has provided salvation; salvation earned by following the group's teachings rather than accepting Christ and following Him. The Seventh-day Adventist Church has consistently advocated the doctrine of the deity of Christ since its very beginnings. Adventists believe that salvation is provided through the death of Christ. They do not believe that anyone can be saved by works. Even those in Old Testament times were saved by grace through faith in Christ, not by works.

Roughly 115 years ago, many Adventists had strayed away from a solid emphasis on salvation by faith in Christ. The Lord then used Alonzo Jones, Ellet Waggoner, and Mrs. White to put the doctrine of justification by faith at the center of Adventist theology.

At least some of the contributors to the video must know about that bit of Adventist history. Too bad the video didn't mention it. Giving Mrs. White credit for at least one positive thing, like her support for the doctrine of righteousness by faith at the 1888 General

Conference session, would have made the video seem much less biased.

5. Urges converts to leave their families. As Mr. Cannon admits, Seventh-day Adventists do not fit this one.

#222: The makers of this video think that these five marks of a cult are important. Do they really?

There are so many denominations out there that are much bigger than the Seventh-day Adventist Church. Suppose a larger denomination could be found that fits these five points better. If Jeremiah Films, MacGregor Ministries, and the rest really feel these five marks are so important, then they should have already made a video about it before making this one.

Let's consider the five marks one more time.

1. Has single, powerful human leader who becomes the group's "messiah." Many denominations got started by a single, powerful human leader. Calvin, Wesley, and Luther are a few examples of men raised up by God to do a special work at a special time.

The pope happens to be a single leader too. And as the teaching goes, he's pretty powerful. The official dogma is that he has the power to forgive sins, can lock and unlock heaven, and is the representative of Jesus Christ on earth. You can't get much more powerful than that.

It's not wrong to have strong leaders. The problem is when the followers of those leaders follow them instead of God's Word.

2. Leader's word or teachings of the group overshadow the teachings of the Bible. A most unfortunate thing happened after the death of the reformers. As the pilgrims departed from Holland on their journey to America to find religious freedom and a new home, their pastor John Robinson had a few words to say, quoted for us in *Great Controversy*, pages 291, 292:

"... I charge you before God and His blessed angels to follow me no farther than I have followed Christ. If God should reveal anything to you by any other instrument of His, be as ready to receive it as ever you were to receive any truth of my ministry; for I am very confident the Lord hath more truth and light yet to break forth out of His holy word."—Martyn, vol. 5, p. 70.

"For my part, I cannot sufficiently bewail the condition of the reformed churches, who are come to a period in religion, and will go at present no farther than the instruments of their reformation. The Lutherans cannot be drawn to go beyond what Luther saw; ... and the Calvinists, you see, stick fast where they were left by that great man of God, who yet saw not all things. This is a misery much to be lamented; for though they were burning and shining lights in their time, yet they penetrated not into the whole counsel of God, but were they now living, would be as willing to embrace further light as that which they first received."—D. Neal, *History of the Puritans*, vol. 1, p. 269.

To be honest, even Seventh-day Adventists are in danger of doing the same. And it isn't just Protestants that are in danger of this. While the Bible says that we only have one mediator (1 Tim. 2:5), yet all too often Catholic Christians look to priests, saints, and Mary as mediators too. And, as John Paul II acknowledges, Jesus forbade the use of certain titles for the pope:

Have no fear when people call me the "Vicar of Christ," when they say to me "Holy Father," or "Your Holiness," or use titles similar to these, which seem even inimical to the Gospel. Christ himself declared: "Call no one on earth your father; you have but one Father in heaven...." (Mt 23:9-10).—*Crossing the Threshold of Hope*, p. 6.

All of us, whether Catholic or Baptist or Lutheran or Adventist, must exalt the Scriptures as being the final authority. The Bible's teachings must supersede every tradition, every human doctrine.

3. Uses pressure tactics to coerce members into submission. Sometimes when folk talk about persecution, they point the finger at the Medieval Church. It is true that somewhere between 50 and 150 million people were put to death during that time period at the behest of Rome. It is also true that the oppression did not cease with the end of the Middle Ages. One writer, loyal to the papacy till the end of his life, served as a spy and diplomat for three popes. He tells us the following:

Between 1823 (death of Pius VII) and 1846 (when Pius IX was elected), almost 200,000 citizens of the papal states were severely punished (death, life imprisonment, exile, galleys) for political offenses; another 1.5 million were subject to constant police surveillance and harassment.

There was a gallows permanently in the square of every town and city and village. Railways, meetings of more than three people, and all newspapers were forbidden. All books were censored. A special tribunal sat permanently in each place to try, condemn, and execute the accused. All trials were conducted in Latin. Ninety-nine percent of the accused did not understand the accusations against them. Every pope tore up the stream of petitions that came constantly asking for justice, for the franchise, for reform of the police and prison system. When revolts occurred in Bologna, in the Romagna, and elsewhere, they were put down with wholesale executions, sentences to lifelong hard labor in the state penitentiary, to exile, to torture.—Malachi Martin, *Decline and Fall of the Roman Church*, p. 254.

Yet Protestants have not been squeaky clean on this matter either. The established churches of Protestant countries all too often, in days gone by, repressed and persecuted the faiths that were in the minority. Such practices were then exported to America in the days of her infancy. Roger Williams, founder of Rhode Island, faced just such persecution from Protestants in Massachusetts. Though quite ill at the time, he fled into the wilderness in the depth of winter, and endured fourteen weeks of misery.

Today there are those who wish to take us back to those times by once again forcing people to keep religious observances:

Laws in America that mandated a day of rest from incessant commerce have been nullified as a violation of the separation of church and state. In modern America, shopping centers, malls, and stores of every description carry on their frantic pace **seven** days a week. As an outright insult to God and His plan, only those policies that can be shown to have a clearly secular purpose are recognized.—Pat Robertson, *The New World Order*, p. 236.

While it is an insult to God's plan to conduct commerce on His holy Sabbath, it is by no means an insult to not force people to keep Sunday.

Regarding the lack of enforcement of the first table of the Decalogue, including the Sunday substitute, another American writer lamented:

In other words, things that should be criminal because they represent an affront to the very foundations of society and of justice are declared legitimate.

—John Whitehead, *The Second American Revolution*, p. 80.

Then we have John Paul II calling for Sunday legislation as well in his 1998 apostolic letter, *Dies Domini*. Where are the voices of protest from Catholics and Protestants who believe in religious freedom? Is the only impediment to such agendas the pervasive secularism of our society? Or are there still some people of faith who believe that no one must be pressured to serve God?

4. Denies that Jesus is the divine Son of God, and that his death has provided salvation; salvation earned by following the group's teachings rather than accepting Christ and following Him. Regarding Christ's death providing salvation, consider the following insightful quotation from Conway's *The Question Box*:

> "In the economy of salvation the sinner is bound to give personal satisfaction; if he does not, his lot is damnation. Christ was not punished instead of the sinner, nor against His own will as sinners are punished; by the holiest of free acts He bore the penalties of sin in order to merit for the sinner a means of satisfying which lay beyond human power. His vicarious satisfaction is not the transfer of punishment from the unjust to the just, but the transfer of the merits of the just to the unjust."—1903 ed., p. 63.

Did Jesus die in our place, or must we pay our own debt? This quotation seems to say the latter. Similar ideas underlie the papal doctrine of indulgences. Indulgences are a way to get merit placed to your account through good works, thus lessening the "temporal punishment" you will receive for your sins.

And Protestants aren't clean on this one either. The various denominations have been ravaged by skepticism due to the infiltration of what is called higher criticism. This philosophy does not take the Bible to be the infallible Word of God, and has resulted in many preachers rejecting certain basic Bible truths. These rejected truths include the Bible teaching that Christ's death was a substitutionary atonement, that His shed blood purchased our pardon. In reaction to the rejection of such teachings by liberal Protestants, the fundamentalist movement began.

5. Urges converts to leave their families. While some have left family and friends to pursue a life of celibacy and exclusion, it doesn't seem like this one is too common.

There was an incident that hit the newspapers in 1855. A seven-year-old Jewish boy in Bologna in the Papal States was kidnapped by the authorities. The Jews of Bologna raised a considerable amount of money for the ransom of the boy, all to no avail. Piedmont, France, England, and America were outraged. Emperor Napoleon III insisted that the pope return the boy to his parents, but he refused. The boy was catechized and eventually became a priest (R. De Cesare, *The Last Days of Papal Rome*, pp. 176-179).

The Bible-believing Christian, regardless of his particular faith, will shun the doctrines and practices referred to above. And down through the years, many have.

Are these five marks really important? The hesitancy of denominations to accept anything their founders didn't teach, the religious right's desire to enforce religion, liberalism's departure from the Biblical teachings of salvation, the doctrines and persecutions of Rome: Have Jeremiah Films, Mark Martin, and the rest made any videos on these topics yet?

#223, #224, & #225: "During the 1950's, certain well-known evangelical Christian ministries approached the Seventh-day Adventist hierarchy in an effort to find out the true nature of their doctrinal beliefs. In a gesture similar to the Mormons, the Adventist leaders desiring the approval of the Christian community at large deceptively espoused the evangelical view of salvation by grace alone. While this temporarily pacified many Christian denominations, it wreaked havoc within Seventh-day Adventism. Many followers felt betrayed and began searching the teachings of Ellen White for themselves in an effort to discover the truth. Those who did were shocked at what they found. What began for many as a quest to validate Adventism turned instead into a lurid discovery of the plagiarism, false prophecies, and heretical teachings of Ellen G. White."—Narrator.

#223: Adventist leaders deceptively espoused the view of salvation by grace alone in the 1950's.

Actually, they espoused this view long before. Mrs. White, who died in 1915, wrote:

[The mother] is to exemplify Biblical religion, showing how its influence is to control us in its everyday duties and pleasures, teaching her children that by grace alone can they be saved, through faith, which is the gift of God.—*Adventist Home*, p. 235.

He who grudges the reward to another forgets that he himself is saved by grace alone.—*Christ's Object Lessons*, p. 402.

The Jewish leaders discerned the truth that Christ presented, but they also realized that it meant the greatest humiliation to them to accept of the rich salvation brought to them through this humble teacher. To be saved through grace alone, to confess that in and of themselves they deserved no favors, was to acknowledge that which was contrary to their cherished ideas, and to lay in the dust their pride, vanity, and ambition.—*Sabbath-School Worker*, Aug. 1, 1895.

But our own efforts are of no avail to atone for sin or to renew the heart. Only the blood of Christ can atone for us; his grace alone can create in us a clean heart, and enable us to obey God's law. In him is our only hope.—*Signs of the Times*, Feb. 9, 1891.

We are to surrender ourselves unreservedly to Him; for His grace alone has sufficient power to save the soul of the repenting, believing sinner.—*Signs of the Times*, Sept. 7, 1904.

There is need to cultivate every grace that Jesus, through his sufferings and death, has brought within our reach; for that grace alone can remedy our defects; Christ alone can transform the character. —*Youth's Instructor*, Jan. 28, 1897.

So Adventist leaders in the 1950's weren't being deceptive.

In the *documentation package*, this is supposedly dealt with under "Point 100," "Point 100a," and "Point 100b," the last of the points it covers. However, there is no substantiation given for this charge at all. The photocopies shown concerning Walter Martin, who was the one supposedly deceived by Adventist leaders in the 1950's, concern the role of Mrs. White within the Adventist Church, not salvation by grace alone. And that's the end of the *documentation package*.

#224: Many followers felt betrayed by such an espousal. No, they felt betrayed because of what M.

L. Andreason said. A prominent Adventist theologian, he said that the book *Questions on Doctrine*, produced as a result of this dialogue, contained capitulations on some finer points of Adventist theology. Andreason was correct in some of his assessments, and incorrect in others.

#225: The ones who felt betrayed began to search, and they were shocked to find plagiarism, false prophecies, and heretical teachings. The narrator is confusing two distinct groups of people. The conservative element in the church felt betrayed, but they didn't make the "discoveries" referred to. It was the liberal element that did that, but they weren't the ones who felt betrayed.

Pastor Leroy Moore lived through that time period and has been writing a book about the subject. According to him, the "quest" on the part of the liberal element was not to "validate Adventism," but rather "to retain cultural Adventism while casting off all inspired theological and life style constraints." By "all inspired" he means the Bible too.

This writer asked Pastor Moore, "If you can think of some who felt betrayed and made such discoveries after searching for themselves, I would be interested in getting your opinion of how many or what percentage fall in this category." Pastor Moore responded:

I know of none. But it is true that there were "conservatives" along the way who fell into the liberal camp because they had not an adequate gospel. They were too spiritually emaciated to stem the infidel flood that spoke with such authority as to paralyze those who had not learned to search for themselves.—Feb. 15, 2000, personal email.

Thus, conservatives who felt betrayed, who were well read and knew how to search, weren't affected that much by all the "discoveries." On the other hand, the ones who did not feel betrayed, the ones who made the "discoveries," now compose the influential minority referred to under #204 and #196. This is the camp that does not take the Bible as an authority, and that believes in evolution. This is the group that rejects the substitutionary death of Christ, the blood atonement, and other essential pillars of the Christian faith.

Testimonials, Documentation, and the Video Jacket

#226: "I was educated in the SDA elementary system, was baptized at a young age and truly committed to what I believed was the only true church. The turning point was when I got invited by several different people to come to a church that had a pastor that was a former SDA pastor. And I agreed to meet with him, and didn't think he'd have anything to show me, but he did, and I realized that the Adventist church had deceived me."—Kim Marshall.

#226: "The Adventist Church deceived me." If the one who talked with you was on this video, it is highly likely that it was he who deceived you, not the Adventist Church. At least, it's highly likely that he didn't know what he was talking about.

#227 & #228: "When I found out what the church actually knows about what Ellen G. has written, how she obtained her material. I was never presented with that in the school system. I never, never heard anything about all these writings that she had copied, plagiarized, and when I saw that, that just about, that hurt me a lot. I felt like I had been lied to."—Kim Marshall.

#227: I was never presented with that in the school system. Under the previous number, Ms. Marshall said that she attended Adventist elementary schools, but she does not say she attended their high schools or colleges. So when she says she was never presented with this in the school system, we are left to conclude that she means that she wasn't presented with this in *elementary school.*

These are obviously not the kind of issues for first graders or fifth graders to grapple with. Is elementary school the place to discuss how either Peter or Jude copied from the other, and how some out there feel that that makes one or the other of these Bible writers not inspired? Let the children wait until high school or college before grappling with such issues, or at least till seventh or eighth grade.

#228: Mrs. White plagiarized; I felt lied to. Does Ms. Marshall feel lied to because 14 of the 25 verses of Jude are similar to verses in 2 Peter, indicating that one of these authors copied from the other (#101)?

Does the fact that the Bible writers borrowed words from others, even from uninspired authors, make them less than inspired and authoritative? Should we adopt Walter Rea's stance, that we cannot take the Bible literally (#100)?

When John put together the book of Revelation, borrowing language and concepts from the entire Bible, was he plagiarizing? Is that even the correct term? Can Ms. Marshall prove that Mrs. White, Jude or Peter, Matthew or Mark or Luke, ever plagiarized? Is not the calling of John or Jude, or Matthew or Mark a plagiarist an example of unwarranted disrespect?

When Mrs. White predicted the civil war (#38), predicted two world wars separated by a little time of peace (#39), said that cancer was caused by an infectious agent (#121), said that "cancerous humors" could lie "dormant" in the body (#118), and said that there was a substance in the brain that nourished the system (#118), from whom was she plagiarizing?

#229, #230, & #231: "I began to see the church was inconsistent theologically and politically. When expedient they contradicted the Bible, contradicted Ellen G. White, and contradicted their own church manual."—Sydney Cleveland.

#229: The Adventist Church is inconsistent. Can't disagree here. Such things are indeed troublesome, yet the point is essentially irrelevant. From the very beginning of the Christian church, inconsistencies and heresies have existed. And Jesus said that this is the way it would be. The wheat and the tares, the true and the false, the sincere and the insincere, will be together until the end:

> Let both grow together until the harvest: and in the time of harvest I will say to the reapers, Gather ye together first the tares, and bind them in bundles to burn them: but gather the wheat into my barn. (Mat. 13:30)

Since Jesus said it would be this way, this argument means nothing.

#230: That's why you shouldn't be an Adventist. Bible-believing Christians out there, have you ever had someone tell you that the reason they're not a Christian is because of all the hypocrites in the church? Is not this argument of Mr. Cleveland's used by unbelievers to justify their not coming to Christ?

Does this argument not attack the Bible as well, since God's followers in the Bible were inconsistent too? From the Old Testament:

1. Noah got drunk.
2. Abraham lied about his wife and was a bigamist.
3. Isaac and Rebekah played favorites with their kids, and Rebekah told Jacob to lie to Isaac.
4. Jacob did lie to Isaac, married four wives, and played favorites with his son Joseph.
5. His twelve sons committed murder, deception, incest, and fornication, and sold one of their number into slavery.
6. Moses murdered.
7. The Israelites worshipped a golden calf and rebelled repeatedly.
8. Once they got into Canaan, they didn't wipe out the Canaanites like God told them to.
9. Gideon started a different priesthood.
10. Jepthah apparently offered up his daughter as a human sacrifice.
11. Samson had a liking for wine and women.
12. Eli didn't discipline his sons.
13. Saul attempted to murder his own son, as well as David.
14. David murdered Uriah, a convert from heathenism, after getting Uriah's wife pregnant.
15. Solomon built temples to false gods on the Mount of Olives.
16. etc., etc.

Let's look at the disciples of Christ:

1. Peter denied Jesus three times.
2. Judas, the embezzling treasurer, betrayed Jesus.
3. James and John, sons of thunder, wanted to burn a town down because they wouldn't let Jesus come home for dinner.
4. Thomas doubted.
5. Philip was a bit dense.

That's half the disciples. Were the other six any better? Not likely, yet these were the leaders of the church Jesus was starting. Would you want to join a church like that?

And after Christ's ascension:

1. Ananias and Sapphira lied to the Holy Spirit.
2. Simon Magus tried to buy the gift of the Holy Spirit with money.
3. John Mark deserted Paul and Barnabas.
4. Paul and Barnabas split up because of an argument.
5. The Galatians were apostatizing.
6. The Corinthians had a host of problems.
7. James believed unfounded rumors about Paul.
8. Paul caused an uproar in court.
9. Diotrephes kicked people out of the church for no reason.

The church is a hospital for sinners, not a haven for saints. God's church since Eden has been filled with people that God wasn't finished with yet.

The Bible spends more time talking about the faults of God's followers than about their good points. This actually is evidence for its divine origin. A mere human book would glorify the people rather than tell us of their struggles.

Because the Bible characters struggled and overcame, we are given encouragement that, by God's grace, we may overcome as well.

Let not Mr. Cleveland's argument lead you to look down on the Bible because of its stories of "inconsistent" believers and church members who "contradicted" the Bible.

#231: When expedient they contradicted Mrs. White. Thank you so much, Mr. Cleveland, for this acknowledgement.

A good bit of the video relies on the assumption that Adventists "revere" Mrs. White, their "absolute authority figure." If this were in fact true, and if it could be proven that she is a false prophet, then the entire Adventist denomination could be discredited.

However, as Mr. Cleveland just pointed out, and as the quote from Walter Rea under #196 indicates by way of exaggeration, her counsel is frequently ignored and sometimes opposed.

Though Mrs. White must never be the "last word on doctrine," it's too bad her sensible, Bible-based counsel isn't followed more often.

#232: "The last three years have been the most spiritually rewarding of my thirty-one years as a Christian."—Dan Snyder.

#232: I spent twenty-eight years as an Adventist *Christian*. Thank you, Mr. Snyder, for being so candid. Did you get in any trouble for making this statement? After all, this video tries to make a case that Adventism is a cult or cult-like, and less than Christian. With all the time, effort, and money that went into making this video, for you to admit in its closing minutes that Adventists are definitely *Christians* must have raised some controversy. Thanks again.

#233: "I am part of the family of God that truly upholds the Bible as the sole authority of both faith and practice."—Dan Snyder.

#233: I'm part of the family that upholds the Bible as the sole authority of faith and practice. In actuality, Mr. Snyder's statement is a paraphrase of the very oath he took when he became a Seventh-day Adventist. The Adventist denomination requires all those who wish to become its members to vow that they "believe that the Bible is the inspired Word of God, and that it constitutes the only rule of faith and practice for the Christian."

This writer took that vow as well. Hence, he too is part of the family of God that truly upholds the Bible as the final authority of both faith and practice.

#234: "Jesus saves us not by our deeds, even if they may appear to be a really good deed. We're not saved by what we do. Not by lifestyle, not by diet, but by what Jesus has done for us."—Leslie Martin.

#234: We're not saved by our good deeds. Of course not. And Adventists wholeheartedly agree, despite Mrs. Martin's strong implication to the contrary.

You might find some Adventists who are uncomfortable with such statements as Mrs. Martin's, and understandably so. Where is the speaker going in her line of thought? Does she mean that we can murder and fornicate and steal and lie and covet and still go to heaven? Does she mean that Jesus saves us "in" our sins instead of "from" our sins (Mat. 1:21)?

If you find an Adventist like that, just reassure him that you believe what Mrs. Martin's husband said, that true Christians will "keep God's commandments out of a love for Him" (#153). He'll then enthusiastically agree that "Jesus saves us not by our deeds."

There is a world of difference between alleged good deeds and what Paul called the "obedience of faith" (Rom. 16:26). Good deeds will not buy us an entrance into heaven, but the absence of the obedience of faith will exclude us from entering those pearly gates.

A lack of obedience reveals a lack of love for Jesus. As the apostle John put it:

Whosoever committeth sin transgresseth also the law: for sin is the transgression of the law. And ye know that he was manifested to take away our sins; and in him is no sin. Whosoever abideth in him sinneth not: whosoever sinneth hath not seen him, neither known him. Little children, let no man deceive you: he that doeth righteousness is righteous, even as he is righteous. He that committeth sin is of the devil; for the devil sinneth from the beginning. For this purpose the Son of God was manifested, that he might destroy the works of the devil. Whosoever is born of God doth not commit sin; for his seed remaineth in him: and he cannot sin, because he is born of God. (1 Jn. 3:4-10)

John acknowledges the possibility that the believer might sometime stumble (1 Jn. 2:1). But he is also crystal clear that those who are born again will not be continually, moment after moment, day after day breaking the commandments of God. One who is "of the devil" will live a life of disobedience, but the true believer will live a life of obedience to God's commandments. Yet the believer's obedience, which is the *result* of justification by faith, will in no way buy his or her salvation.

All these mental gymnastics that people do in order to avoid obeying the fourth commandment, what kind of effect does it have on our society? "The law is nailed to the cross." "Jesus abolished the law." "The law was part of the Old Covenant, but we are under the New." "The Christian is not under the law." With the people in the pews getting bombarded with all these arguments supposedly proving that the believer can disobey and still go to heaven, it's no wonder that iniquity abounds: homicides, rapes, burglaries, sodomy, fraud, adultery, embezzlement, pornography, divorce for non-biblical grounds, and disobedience to parents. The fact that we have so much of this corruption in our society is evidence that too many are believing the sermons that say, "You can keep on sinning and still go to heaven. You don't have to repent after all. God is more loving than that."

Surely the Lord will hold accountable for our moral decay those preachers who preach such sermons.

#235: "Talk to people that have come out of the church and ask them why. See if they have anything to share with you. Because you're not going to be able to get this information from your church."—Kim Marshall.

#235: You can't get this information from your church. Ms. Marshall should have used the word "misinformation" instead of "information."

Of course you can't get this from your church. It would be difficult to find a single Adventist church that could produce this much misinformation. The only exceptions would be churches filled with gullible people who had all seen and believed this video.

#236: "A documentation package substantiating the information contained in this program is also available."—Text appearing on the screen.

#236: The *documentation package* substantiates the information found on the video. In reality, the *documentation package* substantiates hardly anything. Instead, it gives misleading information about Adventist beliefs, and reveals that its compiler was unacquainted with Mrs. White's writings (see #160, #42).

In many cases it fails to substantiate the 100 points which it claims to substantiate (see #5, #13, #27, #50, #60, #70, #86, #88, #91, #98, #117, #140, #163, #185, #196, #223). In a number of instances, it or the immediate context of the quotation it provides discredits or disproves the very point it is supposed to be proving (see #7, #10, #24, #26, #45, #52, #59, #75, #76, #77, #94, #95, #96 #97, #103, #118, #119, #123, #157, #191, #197, #200, #204). Sometimes the quotes it gives prove unquestionably that the quotations that appear on the video are not genuine (see #37, #142).

At least once it provides information that destroys the credibility of the video's script writer, co-producers, and first-mentioned researcher (see #194).

Twice it exhibits either carelessness or dishonesty on the part of its compiler (see #169, #172). One of its selections exhibits either carelessness or dishonesty on the part of the author of that selection (see #78).

Twice it appears to be attacking Scripture (see #71, #156).

#237: "You will meet a number of former high-ranking Seventh-day Adventist Church leaders . . . ."—Text on back of video jacket.

#237: High-ranking leaders appear on this video. Really? Did they forget to show up on filming day? Consider what the video itself says about the participants:

1. "David Snyder spent twenty-two years as an Adventist pastor."
2. "Sydney Cleveland was an ordained Seventh-day Adventist minister who pastored thirteen churches between 1979 and 1990."
3. "Dale Ratzlaff was a fourth generation Seventh-day Adventist who served as a pastor and Bible teacher."
4. "Leslie Martin was a devoted third-generation follower of Seventh-day Adventism . . . ."
5. Wallace Slattery: "Former SDA Member"
6. "In 1982 an Adventist pastor, Walter T. Rea . . . ."
7. "Dan Snyder followed in his father's footsteps by becoming a Seventh-day Adventist pastor."
8. "Mark Martin . . . is a former Seventh-day Adventist pastor . . . ."
9. "Steve Cannon, Southwest director of Personal Freedom Outreach, a highly respected cult research ministry . . . ."
10. Kim Marshall: "I was born and raised a fourth generation Seventh-day Adventist, tracing our family roots back to the Kellogg family. I was

educated in the SDA elementary system."

11. Don and Vesta Muth: "Don and I are both third-generation Seventh-day Adventists. We were educated in the Adventist high schools and colleges. Later we were both faculty members at Pacific Union College."

Which one is a "former high-ranking Seventh-day Adventist Church leader"? Not one!

Mrs. Martin, Mr. Slattery, and Ms. Marshall were just members, and Mr. Cannon wasn't even that. Five of the remaining eight were but local church pastors, not one of whom held an elected leadership position in the denomination.

What about Mr. Ratzlaff? His being a former Bible teacher at a *high school* in California doesn't make him "high-ranking." If he had taught Bible on a college level, maybe, but high school, no way.

The Muths? If Don had been chairman of the theology department instead of teaching art while taking classes, some would call him a former high-ranking leader. And without a doubt, Vesta would be acclaimed by all to be a high-ranking leader if she had been the college president instead of an *elementary school teacher.*

But such maybes are not reality. Though it makes for good advertising, the jacket's statement has no basis in fact.

#238 & #239: "Recommended for Christians who seek answers based on the best scholarship and firm adherence to the truths of God's Word."—D. James Kennedy on back of video jacket.

#238: This video is some of the best scholarship. After examining both sides of the question, does the reader consider this video to contain answers based on the "best" scholarship?

#239: It exhibits a firm adherence to the truths of God's Word. In actuality, this video 1) appears to undermine faith in the final authority of Scripture (#32, #35, #49, #89, #101, #198), 2) appears to attempt to change the gospel and the New Covenant (#73, #150), and 3) appears to call into question some of the basic teachings of the Bible (#62, #69, #71, #149, #151, #156, #179, #203, #205, #230).

How was a man of Dr. Kennedy's stature ever persuaded to endorse this video?

Final Thoughts

Presumably, this video should contain some of the best arguments in existence today against Seventh-day Adventism. Jeremiah Films has been highly respected in the Christian community for its products. If a case can be made, surely they would have made it on this video.

The fact that the case is made so poorly suggests a question: What is being covered up? What is really behind the dense smoke screen conjured up by all these alleged authorities?

Consider a little history. The faith of the early Christians could not be refuted by the wisdom of Jew or Greek, so other arguments were found. Justin Martyr tells us that the Christians were accused of cannibalism and immorality in their religious services (*Dialogue*, ch. 10).

Such baseless accusations didn't end with the early centuries. Consider the Albigenses, a people of whom we know nothing firsthand, since all their writings were destroyed by their persecutors. It is said that they practiced immorality at their meetings, after the devil appeared in answer to their request. Then, after murdering eight-day-old infants and burning them to ashes, they used these ashes as a "heavenly food." Yet at the same time, "Their intelligence, and the spotless purity of their lives, are well attested."—Translator's note in Mosheim, *Institutes of Ecclesiastical History* (Harper and Brothers, 1841), vol. 2, pp. 202-204.

Jesus Himself faced the same kind of problem. "No man was able to answer him a word, neither durst any man from that day forth ask him any more questions" (Mat. 22:46). Since He spoke but the truth, other arguments had to be found. They accused him of being a glutton and drunkard (Mat. 11:19; Luke 7:34). He foretold that He would rise from the dead on the third day. His enemies misinterpreted His words, and endeavored to make them a crime worthy of death (John 2:19-21 Mat. 26:61; Mark 14:58).

Then we have Stephen, the first Christian martyr:

> And they were not able to resist the wisdom and the spirit by which he spake. Then they suborned men, which said, We have heard him speak blasphemous words against Moses, and against God. (Acts 6:10, 11)

The apostle Paul likewise met with the same kind of treatment.

In light of all this, is it possible that Adventism has a relevant message for today, a message of truth from the Bible, a message you should prayerfully consider? If it indeed does, then expect that message to be incontrovertible. Expect its opponents to resort to other arguments.

Perhaps Adventism does have a relevant message, a message of truth for today. Why not check into it further? See if what Adventists really believe is biblical or not. And if it is, then do the right thing and make those beliefs a part of your life.

Jesus gave His all for us. In comparison, He asks so little in return. Dear reader, if you have not already done so, won't you give your all to Him today?

God bless you in your search for truth, and in your walk with Jesus.

Appendix: An Attempt at Dialogue

Why give such a public response to the video? Would it not be better to speak privately with the parties involved and resolve the matter that way? Such was attempted, and what follows is a description of that attempt.

I first made contact with Jeremiah Films about my concerns regarding their video on October 13 and 14, 1999. The lady that took my call was pleasant. She informed me that Jeremiah Films really couldn't help me, since they had not done the research for the video, but had only done the filming. She told me to call MacGregor Ministries, since Lorri MacGregor did the research and wrote the script.

The morning of October 14, I called Lorri's Canadian Office and found her quite irate. She was kind enough, amidst her irritation, to offer to send me the *documentation package* offered at the end of the video, free of charge. For this I am grateful.

I then called Jeremiah Films back and asked if there was anyone else I could speak with. The lady there gave me the number of Mark Martin's church, which I then called that day and the next. Someone other than Mr. Martin returned my call.

This gentleman acknowledged that he was not an expert on Adventist beliefs. We discussed a number of subjects, and he assured me that he would do some research and then get back with me.

One point he kind of attacked me on was the Adventist position on Michael. I shared with him from Daniel, John, 1 Thessalonians, and Jude, after which he was a bit subdued. He said, "I wouldn't have come up with that by reading on my own," but he could see, it seemed to me, that we just might have a biblical case for our belief.

Though he said he would get back with me, I never heard from him again.

After returning in December from an evangelistic campaign in Hungary, I took a look at the *documentation package* that had arrived. Topics I had raised questions about in the phone calls thus far included the alleged threatened lawsuit over *Sketches from the Life of Paul*, and the quotations from *Solemn Appeal* seemingly attributed to Mrs. White but which were never written by her. The *documentation package* failed to address these points. Furthermore, its use of a description of Almira Pierce's depression in 1852 to prove that Mrs. White was in despair in 1844 was disturbing.

So I called MacGregor Ministries again on January 4. There was no yelling this time, so the conversation was much more pleasant. Lorri was helpful, offering me the names of a few people who might be able to answer my questions.

However, she said she didn't want any more phone calls, which was troubling. If a Christian ministry is going to put out information against someone's faith, and some of that information is incorrect, a ministry which is really Christian will want to investigate and correct the matter. However, as she explained, she really did not know a lot about Adventism. She had never been a Seventh-day Adventist, and was not an expert on Mrs. White's writings.

On January 3 and 4 I also called Mark Martin's church again. I got a return call from someone around the following Thursday, the 6th. He listened to my list of questions, and assured me that he would try to call the first part of the following week. I never heard from him again.

Lorri had said that maybe Dale Ratzlaff could help me. He would respond by email, but did not want any phone calls. I sent my first email on January 4. In reply to my question about his quotation of a non-existent statement, he said:

> Have you read my book, The Cultic Doctrine of SDA's? I am now beginning to think that you have not studied the early writings of EGW. Have you read Ford's 1844 book? This is well documented in both.

This of course did not answer my question, so I asked it again on January 6. He replied, "Just read the intro to *Early Writings*. She left out the section that shows she believed in a shut door of mercy for the whole world." This again dodged the issue of his false charge that Mrs. White had said there was no change in idea or sentiment in the 1851 reprinting of her first vision, when she actually said that she had left out a portion.

He closed his reply with: "I can tell you have not read *Cultic Doctrine*, *Sabbath in Crisis* or Ford's book on 1844. Read these and then let's talk." I took this as being another kind of run around and put off, similar to what I had already been experiencing. So on January 7 I responded:

> As far as the books you mentioned, I've been over similar material time and again. . . . I feel no burden to read these books and see no point in it. Hope you don't mind. If in dialoguing about a particular point, you asked me what I thought about the reasons given in a particular part of one of them, then I would consider looking at it.

The same day came a reply with only these words: "Sorry, but I don't have time to dialog with those who are closed to reading anything that does not agree with their paradigm of truth."

On the 10th I sent this clarification:

> You must have misunderstood what I wrote. I didn't say I was closed to reading anything that disagreed with my paradigm of truth. I don't have time to read multiple books before talking to someone, especially when I've already read and discussed similar material many times before. However, if in dialoguing you want me to look at a particular section of one of your books that makes a particular point, as I said before, I'm open to that.
>
> Sometimes I've felt that asking me to read a book before talking further is a diversion tactic. You may not have meant it that way, but that is how I have felt a number of times in the past. . . .
>
> I am in no way closed to reading just about anything, if there is a definite point to it.

To this his only reply came on the 11th: "Good answer!"

Two days later I called Jeremiah Films again. This time I talked with Brian. My wife and I were going out to California to visit her ailing grandmother, who just happened to live about 20 miles from Hemet, headquarters for Jeremiah Films. I thought maybe I could sit down with someone and show them my material questioning the points in the video.

Brian avoided the idea. After all, they didn't do the research, and they really couldn't help me. The best one to help me was Lorri MacGregor.

When he found out that I was coming from Colorado, he highly recommended that I sit down with Mark Martin in Phoenix, who was supposed to be able to help me.

Even though Phoenix is no way near the route between Loveland, Colorado, and Cherry Valley, California, I called Mr. Martin's church to set up an appointment. "May I speak to Mark Martin?" Up to this point I had never been permitted to talk to him. Would I get to now?

"He is busy. May I take a message?"

"Jeremiah Films told me that I should sit down and talk to him on my way out to California next week. I wanted to set up an appointment."

"Just a minute."

I had not suggested a day or told her anything about my itinerary. After a while she returned and said, "Pastor Martin's schedule is really busy. He cannot visit with you. But if you write a letter, he will respond in that way." Perhaps if I had said that I was thinking about leaving the Adventist Church, he would have talked to me.

So I called Jeremiah Films back. Brian said he could understand why I would feel frustrated when getting answers like that. He told me to write up what I had and fax it to them, and they would fax it to those who put the video together to get a response. I offered to drop it by when I was out in California, but he said faxing it was better.

So I wrote out twenty-nine points on ten pages, all the time thinking, Why is this so hard? Why am I getting the run around? It's not my video. Why am I having to do all this work?

I finished it at 12:30 am the morning we were to leave, the 16th or 17th. Since we left at 6:30 am, I didn't get it faxed. So Thursday, January 20, I drove down to Hemet to find Jeremiah Films. I decided I wouldn't take up their time by staying awhile, but would just drop it by.

Going into a mobile home parts store, I borrowed a phone book. To my surprise, there was only a P.O. Box listed. I asked the man there, "Do you know where Jeremiah Films is?" He didn't, so he gave them a call to ask for their street address, saying only that someone was trying to locate them. They wouldn't give it to him, for their address is a secret.

So I called. I explained that I just wanted to drop my ten pages by. The lady said that it was company policy: no visitors for any reason under any circumstances. If I wanted my material to arrive, it had to be mailed.

That was it for me. I went to the post office and mailed it, adding a handwritten note saying that I was through with this dialoging, unless they showed some interest themselves in pursuing it further. I also stated that I would not rest until every error was exposed.

To date I have received no reply whatsoever from Jeremiah Films. When this response was first published on the internet, I notified them via email, but still received no reply.

On January 28 I did receive from Lorri the *1919 Bible Conference Minutes* from the journal *Spectrum* as alleged documentation for the threatened-lawsuit myth. Attached to the minutes was a form letter from MacGregor Ministries, dated January 17 and signed by both Lorri and her husband Keith. This form letter informed me that I was not to contact them again. They must have to tell a lot of people this if they've made a form letter for it.

At the bottom was a handwritten note that included the statement, "Regarding your statements on *Solemn Appeal* — the video is correct. Sorry for you — no retractions." No proof to back this up was offered.

Having researched the inaccuracies of the *Minutes* previously, I immediately phoned MacGregor Ministries again. What else could I do? Here my faith was being slandered, and I knew it was all groundless.

Lorri was irate once more. She said she might respond if I sent her one page of email, but I could only send one page. If I remember right, she hung up on me.

Statements made to me in my three phone calls with Lorri include: "Get a life!" "You're in denial!" "You're being picky!" "No one has had a problem with the information but you." "It's all fully documented." "The Adventist Church hasn't been able to find any problems with it."

The last statement is interesting in light of the fact that the White Estate has a document dated June 1999 on their web site outlining thirty-nine problems or concerns about points raised in the video. Their document predates my first phone call by about four months.

I got the impression from Lorri that she felt that since Adventism really is a cult, it doesn't matter if the evidence used to prove it is bogus.

Maybe one day someone else will have better success at persuading these parties to right the wrongs that have been done. And if not, the Lord will take care of it all in His own good time.

There was one additional series of communications with MacGregor Ministries, this time with Keith. On March 20, 2000, I sent an email to Lorri, since she said I could send her one page of email. In that message I referred her to my critique that had just been posted on the internet. Keith was the one to reply on the 25th, ending it with the following:

By the way, can you find me ONE person anywhere at any time who ever became a JW, Mormon, WWCG, Moonie, SDA, by reading the Bible only and none of their prophets' other writings?

You don't have to respond to this, I haven't time to get into endless email debates. Will be praying for you in the meantime.

To this I replied:

A brief reply you don't have to reply to.

Many, many people have become Seventh-day Adventists from studying the Bible alone.

Out of a sense of Christian integrity, I respectfully request that you admit publicly that the video does in fact present factual errors, like the idea that William Miller predicted or even accepted the date of October 22, which he never did (unless it was after October 22).

I would definitely admit my error if I had made inaccurate statements about anyone I disagreed with. I couldn't sleep at night if I had publicly falsely accused Bill Clinton of something until I had tried to make it right in some way.

Will be praying for you in the meantime.

Keith couldn't help but respond, but only to the first part of the message:

How about names and addresses of these people. Where and who are they? How can they come up with "doctrines" that are not in the Bible like the investigative judgment, soul sleep etc. and the like? How come only SDA's can see these things and no other Bible scholars will give them any credibility?

I replied, showing how various scholars who were not Adventists have come up with soul sleep and much of the investigative judgment doctrine just from the Bible. After referring him to a paper I had written on the investigative judgment, I also stated:

If you feel my reasoning is weak in an area in my investigative judgment paper, I don't mind at all your correcting me. You are my senior in age, and I will respect whatever points you raise regarding an incorrect understanding of what the Bible is saying. I appreciate the position of Luther and try to follow it: "Convince me from the Holy Scriptures and I will retract."

He chose not to reply until I sent names and addresses on April 6. My message included the following, as well as other similar data:

I just talked with my good friend Judy Aitken in Berrien Springs, Michigan. She runs a ministry to reach Laos, Cambodia, and Viet Nam for Jesus.

She tells me that from 1986 to 1993, between 2000 and 3000 Cambodians were baptized into the Seventh-day Adventist Church without having read Ellen White's writings. They just didn't have any to read, so all they studied was the Bible. Judy was personally involved in this.

Keith's reply said: "Bob, these people were all influenced and led by your Adventist friend. I want people with NO contact with any SDA person or publications. The Bible only."

Such a position is not reasonable. It's like saying, "I will not believe until you show me ONE person that became a Christian just from reading the Old Testament. I want people with NO contact with any Christian person or publication." How dare we put such constraints on the way God chooses to work?

God told Cornelius to go get Peter and have him explain to him Bible truths that he couldn't find on his own (Acts 10). That being so, certainly it is possible for God to do the same today. Perhaps He just might even use an Adventist in the process.

Bibliography

CD Databases

Britannica® CD. 1999 Standard Ed. Encyclopædia Britannica, Inc., 1994-1999.

Master Christian Library CD, ver. 5. Albany, OR: Ages Software, 1997. Contains works cited in this book by Anderson, Etheridge, Clarke, Finney, Henry, Justin Martyr, Lactantius, and Spurgeon.

Online Bible CD. Winterbourne, Ontario: Timnathserah, Inc., 1994. Contains works cited in this book by Barnes; Gill; Jamieson, Faussett, and Brown; and Johnson. Also contains the *1599 Geneva Bible Footnotes.*

The Published Ellen G. White Writings. Silver Spring, MD: Ellen G. White Estate, Inc., 1994. Contains all works cited in this book by Ellen White, as well as the biography set by Arthur White.

Words of the Pioneers CD. Loma Linda, CA: Adventist Pioneer Library, 1995. Contains material cited in this book by Andrews, Bates, Bliss, Bush, Everts, Jones, Loughborough, Miller, Alvarez Pierce, Smith, E. J. Waggoner, J. H. Waggoner, and James White. Also contains *Review and Herald* articles through 1863, and the citations from *The Daily Argus, General Conference Daily Bulletin,* and *Lest We Forget.*

World Book. 1999 ed. World Book, Inc., 1998.

Books and Encyclopedias Not in the Above Resources

Bacchiocchi, Samuele. *From Sabbath to Sunday.* Rome: Pontifical Gregorian University Press, 1977.

Ball, Bryan. *The English Connection: The Puritan Roots of Seventh-day Adventist Belief.* Cambridge: James Clarke & Co., 1981.

Blanco, Jack. *The Clear Word: an expanded paraphrase of the Bible to nurture faith and growth.* Hagerstown, MD: Printed and distributed by Review and Herald Pub. Assn., 1994.

Charles, R. H. *The Apocrypha and Pseudepigrapha of the Old Testament.* Oxford: The Clarendon Press, 1913.

Dail, Clarence, and Charles Thomas. *Hydrotherapy, Simple Treatments for Common Ailments.* Brushton, NY: Teach Services, 1995.

Damsteegt, P. Gerard. *Foundations of the Seventh-day Adventist Message and Mission.* Grand Rapids, MI: William B. Eerdmans Pub. Co., 1977.

De Cesare, R. *The Last Days of Papal Rome.* New York: Houghton Mifflin Company, 1909.

De Groot, J. F. *Catholic Teaching.* Trans. James H. Gense, S.J. Bombay: 1933.

Documentation for the Video, Seventh-day Adventism: The Spirit Behind the Church. Nelson, B.C.: MacGregor Ministries, 1999.

Durand, Eugene F. *Yours in the Blessed Hope, Uriah Smith.* Washington, D.C.: Review and Herald Pub. Assn., 1980.

Froom, Leroy E. *The Conditionalist Faith of Our Fathers: The Conflict of the Ages over the Nature and Destiny of Man.* 2 vols. Washington, D.C.: Review and Herald Pub. Assn., 1965-66.

————. *The Prophetic Faith of Our Fathers: The Historical Development of Prophetic Interpretation.* 4 vols. Washington, D.C.: Review and Herald Pub. Assn., 1946-54.

Hogan, Richard M., and John. M. Levoir. *Faith for Today: John Paul II's Catechetical Teaching.* New York: Doubleday, 1988.

Horn, Siegfried H., and Lynn H. Wood. *The Chronology of Ezra 7.* 2nd ed. Washington, DC: Review and Herald Pub. Assn., 1970.

John Paul II, Pope. *Apostolic Letter Dies Domini.* Chicago, IL: Liturgy Training Publications, 1998.

————. *Crossing the Threshold of Hope.* New York, Knopf, 1994.

Koranteng-Pipim, Samuel. *Receiving the Word.* Berrien Springs, MI: Berean Books, 1996.

Lesher, W. Richard, and Arnold V. Wallenkampf. *The Sanctuary and the Atonement: Biblical, Historical, and Theological Studies.* General Conference of Seventh-day Adventists, 1981.

Martin, Malachi. *The Decline and Fall of the Roman Church*. New York: G. P. Putnam's Sons, 1981.

Martin, Walter R. *The Kingdom of the Cults*. 1985 ed. Minneapolis: Bethany House Publishers, 1985.

New Catholic Encyclopedia. New York: McGraw-Hill, 1967.

Neufeld, Don F., ed. *Seventh-day Adventist Encyclopedia*. Rev. ed. Washington, D.C.: Review and Herald Pub. Assn., 1976.

————, and Julia Neuffer, eds. *Seventh-day Adventist Bible Students' Source Book*. Washington, D.C.: Review and Herald Pub. Assn., 1962. Contains copies of many of the citations used in this book regarding Sunday observance.

Nichol, Francis D. *Ellen G. White and Her Critics*. Washington, D.C.: Review and Herald Pub. Assn., 1951.

Odom, Robert Leo. *Israel's Angel Extraordinary*. Bronx, NY: Israelite Heritage Institute, 1985.

Pierce, R. V. *The People's Common Sense Medical Adviser*. 66th ed. Buffalo, NY: World's Dispensary Printing Office and Bindery, 1895.

Price, E. B. *Our Friends the Jehovah's Witnesses*. 1992 ed. Sydney, Australia: 1992.

Rea, Walter T. *The White Lie*. Turlock, CA: M & R Publications, 1982.

Robertson, John J. *The White Truth*. Mountain View, CA: Pacific Press Pub. Assn., 1981.

Robertson, Pat. *The New World Order*. Dallas: Word Publishing, 1991.

Russell, Charles Taze. *The Finished Mystery*. Brooklyn, NY: International Bible Students Association, 1917.

Ryan, Kenneth. *What more would you like to know about the Church?* St. Paul: Carillon Books, 1978.

Seventh-day Adventists Believe. . . A Biblical Exposition of 27 Fundamental Doctrines. Silver Spring, MD: Ministerial Assn., General Conference of Seventh-day Adventists, 1988.

Seventh-day Adventist Church Manual. Hagerstown, MD: Review and Herald Pub. Assn., 2000.

The Spirit of Prophecy Treasure Chest. Ellen G. White Estate, Inc., 1960.

Whitehead, John W. *The Second American Revolution*. Wheaton, IL: Crossway Books, 1982.

Articles Not in the Above Resources

Calman, E. S. "Present State of the Jewish Religion." *American Biblical Repository*, Apr. 1840, pp. 411, 412.

Editorial. "Chronology." *Signs of the Times*, June 21, 1843, p. 123.

Miller, William. "Bro. Miller's Letter on the Seventh Month." *Midnight Cry* Oct. 12, 1844, pp. 121, 122.

Videos

Seventh-day Adventism: The Spirit Behind the Church. Hemet, CA.: Jeremiah Films, 1999.

Unpublished Materials

"Did *The Great Controversy* Contain Stolen Illustrations?" Ellen G. White Estate, 1982.

Miller, William. Letter to J. O. Orr, Dec. 13, 1844.

Internet Materials

Ellen G. White Estate. "Comments Regarding Unusual Statements Found In Ellen G. White's Writings." <http://www.whiteestate.org/issues/faq-unus.html>. This site contains helpful material on a number of subjects, besides the material cited about wigs.

Gordon, Nehemia. "[Karaite Korner Newsletter] #6: Biblical Holidays 1999." Aug. 31, 1999. Email newsletter. Those wishing to subscribe to Mr. Gordon's newsletter may visit his web site at <http://www.karaite-korner.org>.

Pickle, Bob. <http://www.pickle-publishing.com/papers>. Contains papers dealing with conditional immortality, Michael and the divinity of Christ, Anderson's theory regarding the 70 weeks, the Sabbatical years, and other topics. This site is dedicated to building faith.

Index